SOUNDS LIKE LONDON

100 Years of Black Music in the Capital

SOUNDS LIKE LONDON

100 Years of
Black Music
in the Capital

Lloyd Bradley

SOUNDS LIKE LONDON

First published in the UK in August 2013 by

SERPENT'S TAIL

3A Exmouth House
Pine Street
London EC1R 0JH

www.serpentstail.com

10 9 8 7 6 5 4 3 2 1

Printed and bound in Great Britain by Clays Ltd, St Ives plc

A CIP catalogue record for this book is available from the
British Library.

ISBN 978–1846687617

Contents

‖‖

3. Maybe it's because I'm a Londoner

Thanks, photo credits, index

Why *Sounds Like London* needed writing

|||||||||||||||||||||||||||||||||||||||||||||||||||||||||||||||||||||||||||||||||||||||||||

by Jazzie B

I was born and brought up in Hornsey, north London, and I remember music from a really early age because I was always interested in the Blue Spot gram we had sitting in the front room. It wasn't just the glowing lights; one of the things that attracted me to it as a young kid was the smell. The gram would go on at maybe seven o'clock in the morning, and wouldn't go off until midnight or one the next morning, so those valves used to get very, very warm, almost part of the central heating system, then they'd give off a certain smell!

So you could say I grew up fully immersed in the music. I was about seven or eight then, but subconsciously I was becoming aware of how important music was to the lives of the immigrant communities – not just from the Caribbean, but also the Irish and the Greek communities that were all around us. We were all working-class people, out all day, and the ultimate prize once you owned your own house or your own room was to get some entertainment in there. For black people in London in the fifties and sixties, the Blue Spot gram came a long way before the telly. It became the central piece of furniture, and a showing of your wealth.

Critical to all this, though, was the music – the software, if you like – which was the link back to the Caribbean, as it became a story of what was going on back home, and kept people in touch with who they were. Then, moving on a few years, for us that was born here, a lot of the reggae music we listened to in the seventies, we lived our life by it, listening to people like Big Youth or Brigadier Jerry articulating about life. The difference between what my parents listened to – there was calypso and ska, but country & western was massive, and then there was Engelbert Humperdinck – and what my generation listened to, was that my parents were trying to adapt, but we were trying to make our own way. All of this was reflected in the music we were listening to before we were making any of our own, and as we took the lyrics of this story-telling music seriously the messages were coming through.

Not that our relationship with our music was always so serious. One of the greatest things about having our own music was that it could be like our own private world in the middle of London. Take the calypsonians. Everyone was so coy and conservative in their attitudes *outside*, but these records were very explicit and that was our own world. It was particularly fun for us young people, because we knew they were covering things we shouldn't know about, so we'd make up our own lyrics. It was only years later we discovered *that* was what they were singing about.

I got into sound systems early. All my older brothers owned sound systems, so I was born into it and it was synonymous with us as young black men coming up at the time – we didn't go to the pub and we had our own style and culture. I must stress that this wasn't so much a black and white thing among my generation, it was a working-class thing, and so many white kids were genuinely interested in experiencing our culture. I lived the sound-system life through my brothers, and the white and the Greek kids in our area all knew all about the sound systems and the music.

The importance of the sound systems was far more than just playing music, it was your connection with people in the Caribbean, with each other here. It was a refuge from

At the Soul II Soul clothing launch, Jazzie B and Lloyd Bradley show Frank and Dino how it should be done.

everything that went on during your week at work, where you could be around like-minded people or where you could meet people, and it was how you expressed yourself. For the operator too, it was a business opportunity, and there were others that made money from around the sound systems, so it was a fusion of music, business and life, and something we were in control of for ourselves – in our Sunday football league there were a load of sound systems that put out football teams.

The music was absolutely key to how we lived in London. It helped to relax us, it helped to educate us, it helped us to enjoy ourselves, and the sound systems were always central to that music's success. They provided the platform for the music we were making to get heard, and they also kept it under the radar, meaning this story of London's black music is something that hasn't been talked about much in the regular media. Mostly that's been a good thing, because it's allowed the various genres to thrive, away from influences that might have turned them around a bit. It's a story that shouldn't remain hidden, though, for future generations and people now who want to know about what went on before you saw the Dizzee Rascals and the Tinie Tempahs. It's a story that needed to be told by somebody who really cares about it, and the most important thing about this book is Lloyd Bradley. The reason this story of London's black music hasn't been told before is because we haven't had a Lloyd Bradley before, and up until now he wasn't ready to write it.

I first met Lloyd when he wrote a press release for us about twenty years ago. As I got to know him, I realised that during my years in the music business I'd never really met anybody who had his level of knowledge or experience of this music, and had such a passion for it – he's as much a part of it as anybody else. Lloyd's one of the few people out there who have dug as deep as he has to build up a real genuine knowledge, and then been dedicated enough and smart enough to take on this role as historian. You've only got to look back to some of the things he's done in the past, like his book about reggae, *Bass Culture*, or his writings in *Mojo* or the newspapers, to see the depth of his interest in those arts, how he understands the power and the passion of all of this black music, and, most importantly, how he looks into the truth of it all.

Lloydie loves London too. He went to school just up the road there in Hornsey, he's a lifelong Gooner, and knows exactly how this music is such an essential part of London and why it couldn't happen anywhere else. Which all comes through in the book, as it puts London as probably the most important city in black music history worldwide, because it wasn't just one style that started here, it's been years of different movements. Lloyd is aware of all of that, and he's seen so much of it happen around him.

Personally, I've been inspired and been informed by a lot of the stuff he's written over the last few years, and now I'm proud to say I'm a friend of his, meaning I'm one of the select bunch of people who knows just how good the lemon meringue pie he makes is.

Introduction

STAND FOR LONG ENOUGH on any street corner in London, and you'll hear music. Chances are, these days, it'll be black music of some description – dubstep, hip hop, grime, reggae, R&B … It's been like that for a while, at least since cars had cassette players and 'portable' stereos evolved to the size of suitcases. The difference between then and now, though, is that the black music you'll be hearing will probably have been written and recorded within a few miles of wherever it's disturbing the peace.

British black music has never been so prominent. Indeed, it's at the point now where artists such as Labrinth, Tinie Tempah and Dizzee Rascal are bona fide pop stars, with a young mainstream audience that accepts them in the same way as they would anybody else. Just as hip-hop stars like Jay-Z or Beyoncé have across-the-board acceptance in the US and beyond.

The brilliant thing – sorry, the *most* brilliant thing – about the current state of British black music is not so much that it has come so far in a mere fifty years (less than three generations), but that it has done so almost entirely by itself. Unlike the Americans cited above, who for the most part benefited from the full might of a global entertainment industry, our guys have very often succeeded *in spite* of the UK music business rather than because of it. In almost every case, enduring stylistic advances have been the result of intuitive and inspired individuals nurturing their ideas away from the lure of the mainstream. In fact, as the story unfolds, it's when black music has opted to put itself in the hands of the regular music business that progress has fallen apart. Mostly, though, and in true immigrant style, it's been shrewd self-sufficiency and a work ethic that's never scared to learn or look for opportunity that have powered this astonishing trajectory. 'Doing a t'ing' as it used to be called, is now all over the British charts.

Sounds Like London is a tribute to the many single-minded characters who have trusted judgements honed by years of servicing black audiences that were never slow to let them know if something wasn't up to scratch. A Saturday-night crowd in a Harlesden dancehall will be far more informative than any amount of focus groups. Furthermore, when the mainstream punters are presented with the genuine article, it's usually far better received than anything specially tailored for them.

Sounds Like London also documents how the city's black music has made a steady transition from being viewed as something that came from abroad, and therefore didn't need to be taken seriously, to a music that so completely *has* to be that the BBC have devoted a digital channel to it. Attitudes towards the musicians themselves have similarly shifted. As the music has evolved from calypso and jazz to dubstep and grime, so the people making it have gone from being clearly identifiable as immigrants to being second-generation Londoners, blurring geographical backgrounds to the point that British is all they could possibly be. Despite what certain aspects of the media continue to think.

It's an arc that leads from Lord Kitchener coming down the gangplank of the *Windrush* singing 'London is the place for me ...' to Tinie Tempah sitting on the Breakfast TV sofa giving advice about what tea is best to use with London's hard water (Yorkshire Gold, he reckons). And in between those two points, large numbers of black people have arrived in London, mixed it up with their new neighbours, done pretty well regardless of establishment attitudes, and now, for better and for worse, are part and parcel of life here. Most importantly, they are doing so on their own terms.

AS MY PREVIOUS BOOK, *Bass Culture: When Reggae Was King*, also made clear, it's impossible to separate this social transition from the development of the music. Throughout the entire story, we see the former reflected in the latter. At first, black music held back, seeking to accommodate a broader audience. When that didn't work, it tried too hard to identify with other established black music forms. Next, after trusting the mainstream perhaps a little too much led to its being patronised, it responded by retreating into itself in a conscious attempt to find an identity. That in turn provided the confidence to bring the mainstream to the music, rather than the other way around. Finally, black music displayed the intelligence to set itself up in such a way that it didn't need the mainstream, but if the mainstream wanted to join the party ... *Sounds Like London* is about the triumph of spirit as much as the triumph of music, which along the way enriched the host nation as much as it did the arrivals.

Coming to grips with a saga that begins in 1919, just after the First World War, was a mountain of a task. (OK, so it falls a little short of the advertised *100 Years of Black Music in the Capital*, but that made a much snappier sub-heading than *94 Years of ...* or *Not Quite a Century of ...*). Some selection process therefore had to be employed. *Sounds Like London* is not a chronicle of every form of black music that has touched down in the capital during that period; that alone would take a hundred years, and require four or five volumes. Instead it discusses the impact several of those forms have made on mainstream music and culture.

That means the city itself is as important as the music, and the styles and scenes that this book examines could only have happened here – lovers' rock reggae was a *London* music; Osibisa's sound was the result of sessions in a Finsbury Park rehearsal room; Brotherhood Of Breath were a product of a particular Soho jazz club. Among the most pleasing aspects of many of these London developments was that they also found success abroad. In several instances – calypso, African rock and lovers' rock in particular – they influenced the styles from which they emerged, after being taken on board because they came from London. It's also worth mentioning, incidentally, that although for reasons of space and continuity this book is devoted to London, several other British cities – including Manchester, Liverpool, Bristol and Birmingham, to name but four – had their own unique and pulsating black music scenes.

SO THE BOOK IS ALL ABOUT STYLES that evolved because of life in London, and either left a footprint on the mainstream music or culture, as with calypso, or were invented to service a community that could only have been found here – jungle, f'rinstance. The key is for the music to interact with its London environment, rather than exist as a hermetically sealed subculture, or simply develop as a duplicate of some overseas style. Therefore, even if the vast range of black music to be found in the capital can offer all sorts of exciting nights out, this is a book about London music, first and foremost. Not, say, Zimbabwean music *in* London, or Londoners trying their best to sound like they're from the Bronx. Which is not to denigrate such scenes; there simply wasn't room to include them here alongside their more interactive counterparts.

Sounds Like London begins even before the great wave of Commonwealth immigration, with the moment in 1919 when the Southern Syncopated Orchestra made its debut as the first black band to play in London. Although the music in its earliest incarnation did little to affect its environment, the story of the pre-war era provides a solid basis for what is to come. It also gave me a few surprises, with regard to the cultural contributions made by black people in Britain over the last hundred – sorry, *ninety-four* – years. Did you know there was a very successful black ballet company in London during the 1930s, run by two Jamaican immigrants?

14

Apart from that, the book does its best to beat a chronological path from calypso to black pop in ten stylistically self-contained chapters. Sometimes the timeline crosses over itself within chapters as well as from one to another, and in a couple of instances different chapters run in parallel. Please bear with me; it's all part of showing how British black music has evolved and diversified. It's been astonishing to see the shared connections and characters that carried the story forward in a single evolutionary sweep. You don't need six degrees to connect Lord Explainer to Light Of The World, or Maxi Priest to Matata.

Ultimately, the whole story is a tribute to individuals, most of whom refused to play by the rules of what had gone before, and used whatever was available to make their music and to get it across to the widest possible audience.

1

'They come over 'ere ...'

'It was hard to leave my home country. I made the decision with tears in my eyes, but I don't regret it. It turned out very good for me.'

Sterling Betancourt, *steel pan maestro*

CHAPTER ONE

Mash Up in the Mother Country

Calypso, cold winters and a black ballet company

WHEN CALYPSONIAN LORD KITCHENER stepped from the gangplank of the SS *Empire Windrush* at Tilbury, on 22 June 1948, he barely had a chance to feel Mother England beneath his feet before a microphone was shoved into his face. The coterie of English reporters waiting for the five hundred new arrivals from the Caribbean knew to look out for this imposing, snappily-dressed figure, whom they'd been told was a bit of singer. Never one to pass up an opportunity, Kitch, unaccompanied and apparently ad-libbing, broke into song:

'London, is the place for me

London, this lovely city

You can go to France or America, India, Asia or Australia

But you must come back to London city …'

Captured by Pathé News, against the rusting hull of the former troopship, this cheerful, assured performance of "London Is The Place For Me" is still dusted off as an easy-fit encapsulation of the start of mass immigration from the Caribbean into the UK. And, indeed, of the immigrants themselves – happy-go-lucky souls, never too far from spontaneous song. Neither assumption is particularly accurate. Not entirely the carefree, spur-of-the-moment songster he might seem, Kitch was already a big star all across the Caribbean, and had written the song during the four-week voyage for exactly this moment. For that matter, West Indians had been present in London in significant numbers since the First World War, while the *Windrush* itself had brought over a considerable number of Jamaican settlers the previous year. Kitch and fellow Trinidadian calypsonian Lord Beginner made the decision to pay the £28.10s passage on the *Windrush* precisely because they knew there was a healthy African-Caribbean music scene in London, and they could find a relatively wealthy black audience.

As a symbol of specifically *musical* immigration into the UK, however, Kitch's quayside concert is priceless. For a calypso so vividly to reference the capital was a defining moment. This wasn't simply music performed and consumed in Britain, on a strictly insular level, by immigrants and reverent aficionados; it was music that while remaining faithful to the Caribbean was adapted to fit its new setting, and found itself in a creative environment that was prepared to make efforts to accommodate it. Much like the passengers on the *Windrush*, who came in, got their feet under the table, got to know the neighbours, and mixed it up a bit with them. One reason the ship has assumed such significance is that 1948 marked the start of the process whereby Caribbean immigration made a cultural impression on the UK, as arrivals began to see the country as a long-term home. While staying true to who they were, they were changing how they did things, and the world in which they found themselves would never be the same again.

WHEN DISCUSSION TURNS to West Indian musicians who were active in London before the dawn of ska, the story usually begins with the beboppers of the 1950s: the likes of Joe Harriott, Wilton Gaynair, Harry Beckett and Dizzy Reece. Caribbeans had, however, been at the forefront of British jazz for almost as long as British jazz itself. Their influence

In 1948, passage on the *Windrush* from Jamaica to the UK cost £28.10s; the voyage has come to symbolize the start of mass immigration from the Caribbean. From the left, passengers John Hazel (21), Harold Wilmot (32) and John Richards (22) lead a style offensive on the capital.

is one of the great untold stories of the London scene of the 1930s and 1940s. By adding elements of their own countries' music, players from the colonies were responsible for much of the originality in early British jazz, which otherwise, essentially, imitated jazz from the US.

The very first black band to make its mark in the UK, the Southern Syncopated Orchestra, brought West Indians into the British jazz world in 1919. Put together by composer Will Marion Cook in New York the previous year, the 27-piece African-American band arrived in London to fulfil long-term contracts first at the Philharmonic Hall in Great Portland Street, and then at Kingsway Hall in Holborn. Along with the all-white Original Dixieland Jazz Band, who came from the US for an extended stay at around the same time, the SSO can be credited with introducing jazz to the UK. Such was its quality that it included operatic soprano Abbie Mitchell, pianist/conductor Will Tyers, and clarinet legend Sidney Bechet – who first encountered the soprano saxophone in London, seeing one in the window of a Shaftesbury Avenue music store and buying a specially modified version.

This versatile black band made an immediate impression on straight-laced Edwardian London, then recovering from the First World War. The Prince of Wales, later Edward VIII, invited the SSO first to play at Buckingham Palace, and subsequently to headline a grand ball at the Albert Hall to mark the first anniversary of Armistice Day. With demand high, the band stayed on beyond 1920. Over the ensuing years, its original American members drifted away, to be replaced by London-based musicians who hailed from Barbados, Guyana, Trinidad, Jamaica, Antigua, Haiti, Sierra Leone and Ghana.

During the 1930s and 1940s, London's better swing and rhumba bands were either entirely or largely West Indian – even if these British colonials frequently pretended to be Cuban, because the most fashionable dance rhythms came from the island. More than one musician of the day has maintained that Caribbean players were sought after for their trademark combination of exuberance and discipline, vital for the very swinging-est swing – a trait that later manifested itself in ska. Above all, though, as citizens of the British colonies these black players had the right to work in the UK, whereas from 1935 onwards the Ministry of Labour made it difficult for US musicians to get permits. UK bandleaders could thus pass them off as Americans, thereby greatly increasing a band's glamour factor at a fraction of the cost of the real thing and with minimal bother.

A veritable flood of Caribbean musicians were therefore flowing into London long before the *Windrush* hove into view. Big bands like Ken 'Snakehips' Johnson and his West Indian Dance Band, Frank Deniz and his Spirits of Rhythm, and Leslie 'Jiver' Hutchinson's All-Coloured Orchestra were in huge demand for ballrooms and wireless broadcasts. As both musician and socialite, the smooth, well-spoken Hutchinson was a particular favourite of the aristocracy. It was not unusual for him to accompany the hard-drinking Prince of Wales back to York House in the early hours to continue carousing. Recordings by the higher-profile early British black bands can be found on Topic Records' anthology, *Black British Swing*.

At the same time, any number of small groups, pick-up bands and informal, shifting house bands were appearing in nightclubs of all sizes, all over London. Besides such well-known venues as the *Café de Paris* in Coventry Street, the *Florida Club* in Bruton Mews, the *Embassy Club* in Mayfair and the *Hammersmith Palais de Danse*, the West End also held a remarkable number of black-owned establishments, even before the Second World War. Soho was home to the *Caribbean* in Denman Street; the *Nest* in Kingly Street; and the *Fullardo*, and later the *Abalabi* and the *Sunset*, in Carnaby Street. Just outside, and somewhat tonier, were Edmundo Ros's high-society haunt the *Coconut Grove* on Regent Street, and the *Paramount Ballroom* in Tottenham Court Road, under the apartment block Paramount Court. The latter is now an upmarket strip joint, but back then it was a big plush ballroom, owned by a Jamaican immigrant.

At the Royal Albert Hall, in 1942, Guyanese conductor, composer and clarinettist Rudolph Dunbar became the first black man to conduct the London Philharmonic Orchestra.

ARGUABLY THE MOST NOTEWORTHY of the pre-war West Indian influx was Guyanese clarinettist Rudolph Dunbar, who arrived in 1931. Dunbar had studied his instrument at Columbia University's Institute of Musical Arts (later renamed the Juilliard) in New York; was involved in the Harlem jazz world of the 1920s; learned conducting and composing from Phillipe Gaubert and Paul Vidal, respectively, in Paris; and had been taught classical clarinet by Louis Cahuzac, considered the world's leading soloist of his time. Once settled in London he fronted his own dance orchestras – the All-British Coloured Band and the Rumba Coloured Orchestra – and played alongside fellow Caribbeans including Cyril Blake, Joe Appleton and Leslie Thompson. As a sideline, he became the first black man to conduct the

London Philharmonic when he led them in front of seven thousand people at the Royal Albert Hall in 1942. Dunbar also conducted the Berlin Philharmonic in 1945, and conducted in Russia, the US and Poland. Whenever he could, he'd perform works by black composers.

Being Guyanese, however, Dunbar was in the minority among London's overwhelmingly Trinidadian musical contingent. Because Trinidad had its own unique music scene, centred on calypso, its players tended to be more evolved. Double-bassist Al Jennings came over in the 1920s, and led his own bands through the 1930s and 1940s, most notably at the *Kit Kat Club* in the Haymarket – in the basement of the building that until recently housed the Odeon cinema – and at the *Hammersmith Palais*. He returned to Trinidad after the war, where he formed the All-Star Caribbean Orchestra, only to bring them back for a long-term residency in London in 1947.

Clarinettist Carl Barriteau moved to London from Trinidad in 1937, and played with bandleader Ken Johnson. After Johnson was killed when a German bomb scored a direct hit on the *Café de Paris* in March 1941, Barriteau, who suffered a broken arm in the incident, formed his own West Indian Dance Orchestra. As well as entertaining British troops on ENSA tours, he performed nightclub and variety-hall gigs, and broadcast extensively on BBC radio.

Sax man Freddy Grant, who also arrived in 1937, made quite an impact on London. He was Guyanese, but might as well have been Trinidadian, having spent a long time in jazz and calypso orchestras on the island. After playing jazz with Appleton, Dunbar, Blake and Hutchinson through the 1940s, he prospered with his own bands, including Freddy Grant and his Caribbean Rhythm, Freddy Grant and his West Indian Calypsonians, Frederico and the Calypsonians, and Freddy's Calypso Serenaders, many of which employed the same personnel. During the 1950s, while working the calypso angle in dancehalls, the supremely talented Grant hooked up as a sideline with Kenny Graham's Afro-Cubists. He also formed a partnership with Humphrey Lyttelton as the Grant/Lyttelton Paseo Jazz Band, recording calypso-ish takes on jazz and blues favourites.

Acclaimed Nigerian composer Fela Sowande provides a vivid example of wartime London's cultural melange. The acknowledged founding father of Nigerian classical music, a Fellow of the Royal College of Organists and choirmaster at Kingsway Hall, he could be found duetting with Fats Waller on the piano in London clubs, and was a regular in Grant's bands, playing calypso to audiences who assumed he was West Indian.

BETWEEN THE LATE 1920s and the mid-1940s, a black intelligentsia started to find traction in London. The city became a gathering point for African and West Indian students, professionals and political dissidents. Organisations like the League of Coloured Peoples, the West African Student Union and the Union of Students of African Descent all set up shop, exchanging ideas and experiences from around the world. Much of what was discussed in London was to influence the break-up of the British Empire. Groups in the capital maintained strong links with nascent trade unions in the colonies, and many who studied in London attained political office on returning home. There was also a considerable degree of interplay between the black students and the English intellectual hipster-types who were to become the beat generation. Soho became one of the very few genuinely multi-racial, multicultural areas in Britain, where black lawyers, waiters, students, dancers, seamen, doctors and actors rubbed shoulders with cockney market traders, jazz fans in from the suburbs, pimps, prostitutes, debutantes and landed gentry.

Trinidadian singer Sam Manning arrived in London in 1934 as calypso's first international star. His influence was much more than strictly musical. Manning had spent the 1920s in New York, recording his trademark jazz/calypso hybrids and featuring alongside Fats Waller in the original performances of the jazz musical *Brown Sugar*. That was where he met his partner, the show's producer Amy Ashwood Garvey, who had formerly been married to Marcus Garvey. The couple founded the *Florence Mills Social Club*, a jazz nightclub and restaurant in Carnaby Street. Named after the legendary black American cabaret star, it became a gathering place for London's Caribbean and African intellectuals, and students of the growing Pan-Africanism movement.

Given Sam Manning's prominence as a singer, he's often, understandably, credited with introducing calypso to London. Both in Trinidad, however, and when it first reached Britain, calypso was regarded as being as much about the playing as the singing. Indeed, the very first example of recorded calypso has no vocals: in New York in 1912, Lovey's String Band, a ten-piece Trinidadian fiddle, guitar, banjo and upright bass outfit, cut a danceable instrumental called "Mango Vert", which was taken to be a different style of jazz. By the time the music crossed the Atlantic in the 1930s, calypso was mingling with Latin and big-band swing as an integral part of dance-orchestra repertoires all across the West Indies, with singers seen as more or less optional extras.

Things were much the same in the UK, where players integrated quickly and relatively painlessly into the established ballroom scene. Two main factors were at work. Calypso being a deceptively complex music to play well, the musicians were of a very high calibre. In addition, dance orchestras were smoothing themselves out closer to Glenn Miller than Count Basie, with barely enough South American flourishes to justify the maracas, so this injection of Caribbean flavour spiced things up in an easy-to-follow, appropriately exotic way.

Meanwhile, London's serious jazz clubs too were taking on Caribbean influences. With one branch of jazz busily repositioning itself from swing to bebop – complete with asymmetric phrasing, walking basslines and pork pie hats – the music's broader fanbase welcomed the coming of calypso, thanks to the influx of Trinidadian players, as a blessing. As played by the new wave of jazzmen, calypso's far more straightforward rhythms helped to keep bebop's feet on the ground, while still having enough to keep things exciting.

Trinidadians Lauderic Caton and Cyril Blake, respectively a guitarist and a trumpeter, were particularly significant in both these worlds. Caton, an electronics enthusiast, built some of the first electric guitars seen in London, and is credited with introducing the instrument to British jazz, while Blake had been a member of the Southern Syncopated Orchestra. Together they formed the backbone of the house band at *Jig's Club* in St Anne's Court, between Wardour Street and Dean Street. As Cyril Blake and his Jig's Club Band, their artful calypso-infused jazz turned *Jig's* into one of London's hottest clubs. Despite its insalubrious reputation, it wasn't unheard of to come across the elegant likes of Fats Waller and Duke Ellington, each of whom employed Caton at some point, down at *Jig's*. The pair also played alongside the likes of Coleridge Goode and Dick Katz, and in the dance bands of Bertie King, Ray Ellington and Leslie Thompson, and the ever-popular West Indian All-Stars.

Away from the mainstream, in the black dancehall world of the late 1930s, these various trends came together as hot jazz, which absorbed Latin and swing to osmose into jump jive and that newfangled rhythm & blues, all served with a generous side order of musical calypso. On this scene, the bebop revolution was far less evident – the emphasis at this point was on dancing and straightforward entertainment.

In the upmarket venue, the *Paramount Ballroom*, the crowd was ordinary working black London, supplemented by visiting servicemen (West Indian and American), merchant seamen on leave, a smattering of African students and musicians looking to hang out. Apart from a scattering of English women, there were virtually no white people; this ballroom scene didn't draw the bohemian or slumming aristos found in the Soho or Notting Hill clubs, where inter-racial fraternisation seemed to be the latest rage.

The *Paramount* was much more straightforward: everyday black folks who had probably had enough of white people for that week, and wanted nothing more on Friday or Saturday night than to relax with people who looked like them. White women could get away with it, even if they risked the wrath of the disproportionately few black women there, but these dancehall crowds were liable to be openly hostile to unfamiliar white men.

With its entertainment policy, too, following West Indian rather than West End traditions, the *Paramount* became a totally swinging place to be. Like working people everywhere, the audience wanted a wild night out – but it had to be worth the price of admission. The *Paramount*'s owner, himself a Jamaican immigrant, understood that if his clientele had paid two shillings to get in, he'd better give them a half-a-crown show, and recreated the excitement of dancehalls back home with a dash of London luxury. The musicians reciprocated, too. The stage at the *Paramount* gained a reputation as somewhere they could really cut loose, in front of a noisily appreciative crowd – something that often came as a relief after 'day jobs' in more sedate mainstream situations. While the *Paramount* never enjoyed the profile of some of the later, more cerebral Soho clubs – because this was jazz for dancing – it was always a fertile arena for exchanging ideas. With big-name visiting players frequently turning up after hours, it hosted all manner of sitting in, showing off and experimentation.

Situations like that, all over London – albeit smaller – served to keep many of the West Indian players below the radar. Working in the 'corn-fed' dance bands, they were never considered jazz enough, while by doing their serious playing at less glamorous venues they missed out on the attention they might have otherwise have attracted.

Because it was both big, and open until five or six in the morning, the *Paramount* was ideal for the many men who had jobs but nowhere to live – 'No Blacks, No Irish, No Dogs' – and could be arrested for vagrancy if caught dossing on a park bench or in a doorway. With staff turning a sympathetic blind eye, they could snatch some shut-eye on a banquette, then have a wash in the gents.

Calypso singers were always part of this London scene, especially in the ballrooms. The first to make a real mark were George Browne and Edric Connor, who arrived from

Trinidad as early as 1943 and 1944, respectively. Browne was a bass player who regularly gigged with Caton. During his first year in London, he had a huge hit with the tropically festive number "Christmas Calypso". As calypso grew ever

more popular, he turned to singing full time, and changed his name to Young Tiger.

Connor, a singer, actor and music-business mover and shaker, brought over the first Trinidadian steel band to play in Britain in 1951; set up London's first black talent agency in 1956; was the first black actor to perform with the Royal Shakespeare Company, in 1958; founded the Negro Theatre Workshop, one of Britain's first all-black drama groups, in 1963; appeared in numerous films and TV dramas; and still found time to cut several albums. His discography includes one of the first-ever official football records, 1956's "Manchester United Calypso":

'… Manchester, Manchester United
A bunch of bouncing Busby Babes
They deserve to be knighted …'

In recent seasons, Connor's original recording has been spun before home games at Old Trafford, and taken up by the crowd as a chant.

'CALYPSO' COMES FROM THE WORD 'KAISO', an exclamation of encouragement in the Hausa language, widely spoken in West Africa. Pronounced *kye-ee-soh*, it meant 'Go on! Continue!' Plantation slaves, who were forbidden to speak to each other in the fields and thus communicated by singing, would shout it to each other as mutual support. The rhythms of many African songs are comparable with basic calypso, and were homogenised into a single form in the seventeenth and eighteenth centuries, adopting a few Europeanisms and instruments along the way. Jamaican mento, which retains the most original instrumentation, remains the closest to what originally came over. Kaiso-based music was prevalent throughout the West Indies, but became known as calypso in Trinidad because, so legend has it, Europeans on that island wouldn't make the effort to pronounce the word properly.

Developing a strong narrative bent among the slaves, who used it to mock slave masters, comment on everyday life, tell tall tales and have some bawdy fun, kaiso evolved into the combination of satire, protest, innuendo, social commentary and observational comedy we know today. The sharpest calypsonians were contemporary griots, as influential as they were informative. Champions of the underclass, they frequently took the colonial government to task, and criticised the social invasion that accompanied the setting up of American bases on Trinidad during the war. Inevitably the authorities responded: songs were banned, and singers prevented from performing. Despite being exclusively based in New York, the calypso recording industry found itself officially censored – producers at the American record companies had to submit their recordings of Trinidadian singers to British government officials on the island who would – or, as was mostly the case, would not – sanction their release. Contentious titles included "The Censoring Of Calypso Makes Us Glad" – a hilarious piece of sarcasm by Lord Executor that was, of course, banned. In the face of such harassment, many singers opted for life in the UK.

BY THE TIME THE *WINDRUSH* DOCKED, calypso was pop-ular enough in London to offer all sorts of opportunities. For Kitch and Beginner, it was more a case of how soon would a gig find them than how soon would they find a gig. They were celebrated artists all over the Caribbean, who were happy to front an orchestra playing big-band arrangements, but could also hold their own interacting with boisterous audiences in small clubs, backed by local players, or accompany themselves on guitar on a variety bill in music halls or between orchestra sets in a ballroom. It was not unusual for a star of Kitch's calibre to dash around the West End playing sets in three or four clubs in a signle night.

One much-told story tells that, days after landing in England and in search of a gig, Kitch began to perform solo in a London pub, where the customers were so outraged that their noisy protests almost reduced him to tears. Supposedly, the disgruntled drinkers' problem lay in the fact that they 'couldn't understand a fucking word' of the songs. The story continues that Kitch had to risk similar humiliation in several other pubs before anybody would take any notice. While this may or may not be an urban myth, it sounds highly unlikely. Kitch arrived as a big star and didn't need to scratch around looking for work; it's unlikely any pub landlord without a reasonably sized West Indian clientele would have let him through the door, let alone put him on stage; and what makes a good calypsonian great is his diction and very correct use of English.

The real problem with this tale is that it crops up time and time again, and is taken to represent the truth. As such it has come to define the relationship between London and the *Windrush* generation of West Indian arrivals. It depicts Lord Kitchener as some exotic alien, plaintively trying to impress a host who was going to bully him for a while before reluctantly accepting that he might have something of some small value. It epitomises the idea that West Indian immigrants were in London under sufferance, had precious little sense of self worth, and existed only in relation to white English people. That might explain why it gets repeated so often, yet questioned so rarely.

The reality was that, to a large degree, Londoners didn't know what to expect from the new arrivals or what to do with them. West Indians who endured that period speak of attitudes that varied between openly welcome, outright hostile and completely indifferent in pretty much equal measure. In the years during and immediately after the war, native Londoners made very little attempt to engage with the new arrivals. That wasn't simply a matter of racism, although there was no shortage of that. It was more the case that the city, being naturally insular, was still recovering from the Luftwaffe onslaught and the wider implications of being at war. West Indians contributed to this lack of engagement, too. Few believed that they needed to instigate any kind of relationship with the host country, as they didn't think they'd be here very long – maybe five years, certainly no more than ten. The worker recruitment drives across the Caribbean – London Transport in Barbados, British Rail in Jamaica, and the newly formed NHS everywhere – sold the adventure on the notion of rebuilding the Mother Country after the war, and then, job done, going home with pockets bulging with

Lord Kitchener, seen here with a double bass, was an accomplished musician as well as a singer.

cash. Although it was rare for anybody to go home quickly, the dream was so cherished that among this generation the notion of a black British identity didn't even begin to form. Their emotions buoyed by the Independence Fever that washed through the Caribbean from the late 1950s onwards, Jamaicans saw themselves as *Jamaicans*, Kitticians as *Kitticians*, and so forth. That said, it's important to remember that while such nationalism promoted a certain amount of inter-island antagonism, and different nationalities tended to live and primarily socialise among their fellow countrymen, everyone was aware that they all had much more in common than they did keeping them apart. After all, it wasn't as though most Londoners cared whether you were a Grenadian, a St Lucian or a Dominican; generally all that registered was a black face and an unfamiliar accent.

In such an environment, calypso was massively important to the new arrivals, who felt an understandable sense of disconnect with the West Indies they'd left behind. Hearing a new song was like getting a letter from home. It didn't even matter that 'home' would always be Trinidad, the fact that it was *Caribbean* tended to override inter-island rivalries. Calypso's traditions of wordplay and story-telling were embedded all over the West Indies, so a house party that spun calypso records, or a pub featuring a lyrically clever singer, would put you back in touch with who you were.

Almost exclusively experienced live – what records were available were imported from Trinidad, which had an established music industry – calypso functioned much like kaiso, secretly mocking those in power. The sharper wordsmiths would comment on London life and London people with in-jokes and slang that kept things pretty much closed off from anyone apart from themselves and their own crowds. The music owed its popularity to more than just its amusement value; it played a vital role in retaining a keen sense of self in difficult times. Immigrants performing for immigrants, the original London calypso singers would appear as support acts in venues like the *Paramount*, while also headlining in smaller West Indian clubs and turning up during popular Friday night and Sunday lunchtime sessions in such pubs as the *Queens* in Brixton or the *Colherne* in Earls Court. While every bit as exciting and ad hoc as you might find in Port of Spain, however, this was pretty much the original Caribbean form frozen in aspic with very little evolution. Ironically, that lack of reinvention became increasingly significant, as more and more West Indians came to accept that they weren't going home for anything longer than a visit, and such snapshots from the islands meant so much more.

AS THE 1950s ROLLED AROUND, the big-time London music business began to take calypso seriously. Recording calypso in London was nothing particularly new; as far back as the 1930s, Decca and Regal Zonophone had cut sides by the likes of Sam Manning, Lionel Belasco and Rudolph Dunbar. These were for export only, however, and treated as novelties by the domestic operations. From 1935 onwards, Decca UK tried to release calypso recorded in New York by its American division, but even stars like Attila the Hun, Roaring Lion and Growling Tiger failed to ignite sales. Releases were discontinued in 1937, and all titles deleted in 1940.

By the time the *Windrush* arrived, most calypso recording was happening on a below-the-radar scene, which put Kitch and Beginner in the studio almost as soon as they arrived. Both cut tunes for London's most successful calypso label, Hummingbird Records, run by expat Trinidadian businessman Renco Simmons (Trinidad is also known as 'the Land of the Hummingbird'). Simmons would hire RG Jones' studio in south London and record well-known calypsonians who were either living in London or passing through. He'd then get records pressed in London primarily for export to Trinidad, with supplementary sales in the capital. Back home, he retailed his records through *Hylton Rhyner's*, a chain of tailor's shops that also sold calypso records (there's still a *Rhyner's Records* in Port of Spain). In London he'd place them in the network of black-owned grocers, cafes and barbers, which had been beyond Decca's distribution arm.

While this enhanced reputations in Trinidad, and catered to West Indian London, it had no wider impact. That all changed when Denis Preston, a suave, charismatic hipster who had been on the London jazz scene since the early 1940s, discovered calypso. Preston, who briefly dubbed himself Saint Denis, was a contributor to *Jazz Music* magazine and an announcer on the BBC's *Radio Rhythm Club*. He was also a groundbreaking independent music producer and a savvy record businessman. It was Preston who pioneered the model of recording artists at his own expense and then leasing the results to record companies. He also hired the fledgling Joe Meek as his engineer, and built Lansdowne Studios in Ladbroke Grove in 1957.

Preston happened on calypso in 1946, when, as jazz editor of *Musical Express* – today's *NME*, just after it dropped the words '*Accordion Times &*' and before it added '*New*' – he was promoting a ragtime concert in London at which Freddie Grant & His West Indian Calypsonians were halfway down the bill. Three years later, when working for Decca in New York, he came across the music again as a favourite of the dance bands in Harlem clubs. Seriously impressed, he convinced EMI's Parlophone Records on his return to Blighty to get into the calypso business, and took Kitch and Beginner into the company's prestigious Abbey Road studios early in 1950.

As an independent recording supervisor – the term 'producer' was not yet in use – Preston was not obliged to use the in-house musicians, so he backed each singer with a Cyril Blake group. Astute enough to realise that these artists understood the genre better than he did, and enough of a jazz fan to respect musicianship, he simply let them get on with it, and sat back digging the crazy sounds. Preston's calypso sessions during the next few years faithfully reproduced the sounds of the capital's nightclubs and black ballrooms – big- and small-band arrangements; usually percussion-heavy and Latin-jazz-based; mostly liltingly sophisticated, sometimes disarmingly rustic, yet always beautifully sung. His intelligent and deferential approach succeeded on several levels.

Requirements in the Caribbean were little different from those of expats in London, so these high-quality recordings – featuring stars like Bill Rogers and Roaring Lion as well as Kitch and Beginner, often performing songs that had been previously recorded elsewhere, and spared modification by mainstream record companies, went down very well in the West Indies. The subject matter, too, remained traditional with such bawdy lyrics as Roaring Lion's "Ugly Woman":

'If you want to be happy and live a king's life
Never make a pretty woman your wife …
From a logical point of view
Always have a woman uglier than you …'

or "Tick! Tick! (The Story of the Lost Watch)" – a hilariously ludicrous story of a woman who steals a watch and hides it in her vagina:

'What a confusion
A fellow lost his watch in the railway station
A girl named Imelda was suspected of being the burglar
She had no purse, no pockets in her clothes
Where she had this watch hidden, goodness knows …'

While satisfying EMI's primary objective, to compete with US companies selling calypso records in the Caribbean, these recordings simultaneously had the edge over the imports in the London market, as the singers referenced their new home. On "The Underground Train", Lord Kitchener sang of the perils of getting distracted on the Tube:

'Never me again, to get back on the underground train
I jump in the train, sit down on a seat relaxing mi brain
I started to admire a young lady's face
Through the admiration I passed the place
To tell you the truth I was in a mush
When I find myself at Shepherds Bush …'

Meanwhile Beginner's commentary on the 1950 election result, "General Election", came complete with a stylistic explanation as an introduction:

'Me, Lord Beginner, make this calypso in the style of the old minor calypso which we sing in Trinidad since many years.'

At much the same time, EMI chanced upon another lucrative sales opportunity for calypso: the UK mainstream pop market. An audience with no previous interest in calypso – Johnnie Ray, Tony Bennett or Rosemary Clooney was where it was at – had been introduced to it by the dance orchestras, and was now buying it on EMI's readily accessible gramophone records. Other British record companies raced to add calypso to their release schedules. Not the London version, though, or even the original imported direct from Trinidad; the major labels opted for American calypso, made in America by Americans.

ASTONISHING AS IT MAY SOUND, calypso – or at least, a strictly white-bread version thereof – was a major force in US popular music of the 1950s. As a mainstream-friendly fad, calypso had been kicked off when Trinidad-stationed US servicemen brought it home after the war. The biggest US pop hit of 1945, the Andrews Sisters' "Rum & Coca-Cola", was a plagiarised version of a Trinidadian hit by Lord Invader and Lionel Belasco, from two years earlier. Despite being banned by some radio networks – because it mentioned an alcoholic beverage, not because it's actually a song about prostitution – the record sold 2.5 million copies.

In the US, as in the UK, calypso rhythms were taken up by orchestras in ballrooms and on the radio, as part of the trend for South American experimentation. Things consolidated in 1947, when the calypso-powered, big-budget musical *Caribbean Carnival* became a long-running Broadway success. Into the 1950s, and boosted by the emerging American/ Caribbean tourist industry, calypso became a big part of US pop music. Amid widespread disapproval of the new 'degenerate' teenage soundtrack of rock'n'roll, many in the music industry wishfully imagined that calypso might prove a serious rival.

Dozens of calypso records came out in the US during the first half of the decade. High-profile artists – black and white alike, and including Rosemary Clooney, Louis Jordan and Ella Fitzgerald – covered Trinidadian favourites. Nightclubs

opted for tropical decor and names like the *Calypso Hut* or the *Island Rooms*, while all manner of crooners invested in flowered shirts and frayed straw hats. TV variety shows incorporated calypso-themed numbers as a matter of course, while sitcoms wrote bursts of calypso into scripts. Hollywood too got in on the act, creating low-budget, teen-oriented movies like *Bop Girl Goes Calypso*, *Calypso Joe* (starring a young Angie Dickinson) and *Calypso Heatwave*. The latter featured Maya Angelou – yes, *that* Maya Angelou – who, prior to her literary calling and social activism, had a career as a calypso singer and dancer. Indeed, she took her stage name because Marguerite Johnson was deemed insufficiently exotic.

Another improbable pop-calypsonian was the man who would later be addressed as Louis Farrakhan, National Representative of the Nation of Islam. Back in the 1950s, while still Louis Eugene Walcott, the Brooklyn-born former child-prodigy violinist turned his musical talent to singing, and recorded six well-received calypso albums under the soubriquet The Charmer. He was no stranger to controversy then, either. His 1953 hit "Is She Is Or Is She Ain't?" – also released in the UK – told of George Jorgensen Jr, the first sex-change celebrity, who hit the US talk-show circuit after having the surgery in Denmark:

'With this modern surgery
They changed him from a he to a she
But behind that lipstick, rouge and paint
I got to know is she is or is she ain't? ...'

Almost as remarkable was screen tough-guy Robert Mitchum's 1957 album *Calypso – Is Like So*. It's not noteworthy simply because he made it – *everybody* was making calypso albums by then – but because Mitchum, an accomplished singer and songwriter, insisted on making genuine, as opposed to watered-down, calypso. He recorded the album in Tobago, where he had discovered the music while filming 1957's *Fire Down Below*, co-starring Edric Connor. Mitchum used local musicians, and studied the island's inflections and colloquialisms to incorporate them into his vocals. Although his album didn't sell nearly as well as Jamaican American Harry Belafonte's 1956 *Calypso*, it remains one of the few US offerings that Caribbean calypsonians respect. Belafonte's album, incidentally, which included "The Banana Boat Song (Day-O)", was the world's first-ever million-selling LP, and represented the peak of American calypso. Hardly surprisingly it began to wane when, later that year, a 21-year-old Elvis Presley appeared on the *Milton Berle Show* in front of forty million viewers. Suddenly, lilting Caribbean rhythms were no longer quite cutting it with the kids.

During calypso's American ascendancy, US companies shipped records in large quantities to their UK labels. In 1957, for example, "The Banana Boat Song" was a UK hit for three different acts – Harry Belafonte, Shirley Bassey, and future actor Alan Arkin's pop/folk group, the Tarriers. Although British audiences had previously seemed to prefer their calypso with an earthier tone, British record companies were dazzled into believing that the US music business was showing how things should be done. However, spectacularly missing the point of calypso, they pulled out as soon as sales palled – if these glamorous Americans couldn't find traction, how could a bunch of unknown West Indians?

Even EMI came to think their calypsonians would never pay back any more than their export sales, so it fell to London's thriving independent record labels to take up where they let off. Emil Shallit, an immigrant of indeterminate Eastern

European origin, seized this moment to move to the forefront of the calypso market.

A CHARACTER SO COLOURFUL he deserves his own paintbox, Shallit had arrived in London just after the war. He claimed to have been an Allied spy, and that the start-up capital with which he founded Melodisc Records in 1947 was a pay-off for his clandestine services. He had originally based his office in the US, licensing American jazz and blues for British release. That allowed him to do what he did best – schmooze New York hipsters. After falling out with his business partner, he decamped to London where he looked to record rather than simply licence in. The music he knew most about was black music.

Sure of his ability to go anywhere and get on with anybody – apparently, that's what made him such a good spy – Shallit moved among the subcultures of London, and seemed innately to understand what they wanted. Time and time again, his small company was agile enough to shift from style to style on no more than his say-so. Not tied in to any particular distribution channel, he could put Melodisc records anywhere he thought they'd sell. If that meant using a cosmetics wholesaler to put the records in hairdressing salons, or a food importer to get them into African-owned grocery stores, he didn't need a series of management meetings and a risk-assessment strategy. During the 1950s, Emil Shallit built Melodisc into one of the largest independent labels in London, while himself becoming a radical and important figure in the development of British black music.

Shallit was aware how important it was for music to be genuinely of a genre, while shrewd enough to realise that any transplanted music also needed to represent its new home. He understood that the core market had new influences and experiences to reflect, and, vitally, that any cultural crossover to a larger audience could only happen if it acknowledged those surroundings. During the 1950s, Melodisc was the first label to record West African Londoners playing highlife with contributions by West Indians. It also brought in Jamaican artists like Miss Lou to cut mento in London, backed by Jamaican players who'd been steeped in the capital's music scene for years, and was one of the first labels to recognise the value of Caribbean jazz, promoting the likes of Joe Harriott and Russell Henderson to be bandleaders.

The backbone of the Melodisc catalogue, however, was calypso. Shallit had employed Denis Preston to produce some of Melodisc's earliest releases at the start of the 1950s, but he proved to be more of a facilitator than proactively creative. Seeking to move the music forward, Shallit soon replaced him with Rupert Nurse, a Port-of-Spain-born multi-instrumentalist and childhood friend of Lord Kitchener, who became Melodisc's musical director, A&R man and in-house producer. Shallit knew Nurse from the clubs, where he had played jazz, calypso and swing since arriving in the UK in 1945.

As a working musician and orchestrator, Nurse had the theoretic and practical understanding to feel confident about taking chances. Long determined to modernise calypso by applying big-band jazz and swing arrangements to a traditional framework, he'd left Trinidad after incurring the displeasure of the local musical establishment for doing exactly that. It was thanks to this musician-friendly approach, on the other hand, that Melodisc had no problem hoovering up Parlophone's calypso roster when that company abandoned the genre towards the end of the 1950s.

Melodisc sessions took place in Esquire Records' make-shift studio, in the basement of Bedford Court Mansions in Covent Garden. Nurse used a core of Trinidadian and Guyanese musicians – saxophonist Al Timothy was the effective bandleader, with pianist Russ Henderson, guitarist Fitzroy Coleman, trumpeter Rannie Hart and clarinettist Freddie Grant as regulars. He then brought in players like Joe Harriott, Latin-style trumpeter Peter Joachim and John Maynard on trombone to make up a bigger band sound – essentially the same unit that backed Kitch and the other singers on their bigger club dates. Nurse also introduced the steel pan into the recording sessions. That was an unusual move, as despite the instrument's Trinidadian roots it was seldom used in calypso backing bands. Nurse simply loved its sound, and felt that its semitone capabilities added an extra harmonic layer within his jazz arrangements, giving the music instant appeal.

As Nurse's method was entirely opposite to the standard ballroom method of sprinkling calypso-ish rhythms and accents atop standard dance-orchestra arrangements, his results were always going to be *genuinely* calypso. He also wrote out formal charts rather than depending on improvised arrangements. Far from restricting the players, this gave them more freedom, as it built a reliable framework within which they could operate. Suddenly, a new level of sophistication gave the melodies a whole extra dimension and depth of structure. While the rhythm section drove the momentum, supplemented with brass riffs, the melodies were so securely anchored that players could weave their own patterns. Innovative yet still making complete sense, the new approach brought calypso up to date, and made it a much more powerful means of communication. It also allowed continuity within a band if the musicians changed.

The bebop sensibilities that were always around dovetailed perfectly, giving things a London jazz flavour, and Nurse's innate sense of swing kept the music easily accessible. Top singers like Kitch or Roaring Lion could now sing with all

43

their energy, instead of the semi-crooning style that better suited ballroom calypso. In giving the singers free rein, Nurse knew that they would carry the calypso swing, and leave the band free to play jazz. Obvious examples of this include "Calypso Be" by Young Tiger, which ironically decries bebop and beboppers against a background that embraces it:

'This modern music got me confuse

Tell you, friends, I'm quite unenthused

I like Pee Wee Hunt and the great Count Basie

But can't make head nor tail of this Dizzy Gillespie ...'

Similarly, Kitch's "Bebop Calypso", which eulogises bebop with list of recommended artists and records. A talented melody writer, Kitch loved working with his old friend Nurse. He'd sing his calypso tunes to the musician, sometimes down the phone, and the arranger would write them down and come up with the orchestration.

THE MELODISC STYLE BROUGHT CALYPSO right into the modern era, giving it an edge that impressed jazz fans while making the Caribbean music sound familiar enough for broad appeal. Musicians loved it because it gave them a chance to show off on record as well as on the bandstand. One of those players was Russ Henderson, a jazz pianist and steel-pan player who came to London from Trinidad to study piano tuning in 1951, but quickly opted for life as a full-time musician. Still active and perpetually cheerful at 87, Russ remembers backing jazz players, highlife musicians and calypsonians at Melodisc, as well recording there under his own name. He still marvels at how those sessions turned out:

'Although there was a good live music scene in London back then, there wasn't much recording. At the time Melodisc was really the main company doing West Indian recording, and they recorded African highlife as well, like Ambrose Campbell, so there was always a lot of African influence. They recorded jazz, too. But this was very good, it was like a big melting pot in there. Rupert Nurse had his key players – I was one of them – who were Trinidadian and West Indian musicians, mostly from a jazz background, but knew all about calypso. Then there would be other players who might be West Indian or might be African, or even English like Cab Kaye [*Finley Quaye's father, a singer and pianist born in London to a Ghanaian father and English mother in 1922*]. Because we all played in the clubs together, you know how musicians are, they say to each other "Can you play this gig?" or "Can you play that gig?" So if Rupert Nurse would say he needed a trumpeter for tomorrow, you'd see somebody that evening in a club that you'd bring with you. We didn't care where we was actually from, because we were all of us black in London.

'It was important for the music, because at Melodisc it had a feel it didn't get anywhere else. There was jazz and calypso mixed elsewhere, but this was calypso but played with a real jazz swing, we could solo … everything … and some of these guys were the best jazzmen in London. Also, what made it so much like jazz was that we all brought bits of our own musical backgrounds and musical tastes to the studio, and everything counted, because Rupert Nurse could organise it. We [*the musicians*] all understood what he was doing because that was the kind of thing we'd been trying, so it was a joint effort really. He wrote the charts, but it was down to us to interpret them in our playing.

'It was very good for us as people too, because it brought different people together. Before I came to England I hadn't a personal African friend. We knew of a few Africans, and we could say, "Oh he's from Ghana". But once I came here, I went on tour with African drummers when I travelled in 1952 to Belgium, and I recorded with Jamaicans … everybody. When you got over here, there would be the question of, "Where are you from?", but it didn't matter, you were Caribbean! Or you were African! We all became friends and we all learned a lot from each other – not just music, but about life. As a Trinidadian, I used to think that coming into contact with other people like that was the greatest thing that happened in my life. Making us get to know the other islands, because when I was at home you didn't really get to know anybody else from elsewhere.

'Really it wasn't just for us musicians that happened, it was happening in life too. So many of the people that came to England at that time were getting to know people that they would never have met if they'd stayed at home [*in the West Indies*]. People socialised and worked together, and realised how they had to support each other. That everybody had something to offer the others.'

THE CROSSOVER WAS COMMERCIALLY useful too. With a great deal of to-ing and fro-ing between London and Nigeria, Ghana and Sierra Leone by musicians for studio and live work, the London recordings had a considerable influence on the development of local highlife music. West Africa, and Ghana (then the Gold Coast) in particular, had been a huge market for Parlophone's calypso, and Melodisc followed suit. Such Lord Beginner tunes as "Gold Coast Victory" and "Gold Coast Champion" went down a storm, and he toured the region extensively. The biggest London hits were Kitch's "Birth Of Ghana", celebrating the new nation's 1956 independence, and Young Tiger's "Freedom For Ghana"; twenty thousand copies of each were exported to Africa. Young Tiger was such a star in Nigeria that when the country became independent from Britain in 1960, its new government asked him to write a national anthem – he declined. The other Caribbean islands were not forgotten either. Both Kitch and Beginner cut Jamaican-friendly songs – "Jamaican Woman", "Sweet Jamaica" and "Jamaica Hurricane" among them – but the most striking example was Young Tiger's "Jamaica Farewell", in which the singer's broad

Trinidadian accent can be heard rueing the day he left his lovely Jamaica.

Russ believes that those calypsos did much to break down barriers between the immigrants and native Londoners:

'What we were doing at Melodisc helped English people to get to know us a bit more, because they didn't have a clue about calypso before those records Kitch started making. When we played in the big ballrooms in the West End, most of the time it was rhumbas, sambas and show tunes, because they wanted music for dancing. All they knew about calypso was songs like "Mary Ann" or "Rum & Coca Cola" that was left over from the war. We played calypso at the West Indian ballrooms or the late-night jazz clubs or a place like the *Sunset*, which was owned by a Jamaican, and used to have a cabaret on.

'When Rupert Nurse added jazz to the basic calypso, it moved it to where it began to appeal to English people because they knew how to dance to it. Up until then, unless it was some dance band playing Latin or something with a bit of a calypso beat, they didn't know what to do. After this, they figured out how to dance to it. Which was the best thing that could have happened, because it introduced the Caribbean culture to the English.'

There was no record-label exclusivity within the capital's calypso community; under various, often hastily conceived group names, the same players would crop up recording for anyone who would pay them. For example, the singer Marie Bryant recorded the same song, "Tomato", for two labels using pretty much the same backing band. This led to something of a boom in London calypso recording; although Melodisc dominated the market, they didn't have it all to themselves.

With London recordings as well as tracks licensed in from the US, Decca had a considerable roster. So too did Lyragon, an independent founded by Jack Chilkes, Emil Shallit's original partner in Melodisc. Pye Nixa built up a sizeable made-in-London catalogue, while the jazz label Savoy imported tunes it had already put out in America. Even Parlophone dipped a toe back in the waters, but with strictly comedy, pop chart-chasing fare, as they revived the comedy line they'd started in the 1950s with Peter Sellers' "Dipso Calypso" (1955) and Ivor & Basil Kirchin Band's "Calypso!!" (1957) – so shouty and boisterous a dance track that it needed two exclamation marks – with Bernard Cribbins' "Gossip Calypso" (1962).

ONE OF THE MOST SIGNIFICANT developments as the music migrated from Parlophone to Melodisc was a shift in lyrical approach. While Parlophone's output had been witty, articulate, verbally dexterous and undoubtedly of Caribbean descent, the songs tended to come at things from as all-embracing a perspective as possible. Thus Lord Beginner's "Housewives" focussed on the problems of rationing and stretching a housekeeping budget; Kitch's "My Landlady" bemoaned interfering proprietors; Young Tiger's "I Was There (At The Coronation)" rhapsodised Queen Elizabeth's Coronation parade:

'Her Majesty looked really divine
In her crimson robe trimmed with ermine ...'

Now, however, independents like Melodisc and Lyragon, which saw themselves as catering to the core audience, felt less constrained. Increasingly, therefore, the next wave of calypsos supplemented the sophisticated arrangements with more raucous and colloquial vocals. And, of course, the bawdiness factor was ratcheted up.

As the origins of calypso singing – chatting about the slave master in a way that he couldn't understand – had required so much to be said without actually saying it, innuendo was something of an art form. Caribbean dancehall crowds loved a lewd lyric. Melodisc put out such risqué gems as "My Wife's Nightie", "Short Skirts" and "The Big Instrument", but pride

If you wanted innuendo, calypso was always happy to give you one. Singer, jazz dancer and all-round sex bomb Marie Bryant's recording of "Don't Touch Me Nylon" was so suggestive it prompted questions in Parliament. Meantime, her record company put a stripper on the sleeve.

of place went to Kitch's double entendre-laden "Saxophone Number 2":

'From the time the woman wake
She wouldn't leave me sax for heaven's sake
She say she like to play the tune
That remind her of the honeymoon ...'

While this kind of 'Ooh err, Missus!' humour might seem somewhat puerile from a twenty-first-century perspective, in London in 1956, two years before the first *Carry On ...* film, it caused quite a stir. The BBC was moved to sticker a selection of discs in their library with the stark warning 'Do not play this record!', while Marie Bryant's 1954 Melodisc hit "Don't Touch Me Nylon" – a song about statically charged underwear – prompted questions in the House. Brixton's Labour MP Lt Colonel Marcus Lipton, was so enraged that he stood up and spluttered about 'gramophone records of an indecent character', saying that it couldn't possibly be 'in the public interest that the wretched things should continue to be publicly sold.'

Incidentally, Marie Bryant was one of Melodisc's more interesting London-based recording artists. Born in Meridian, Mississippi, in 1919, she was dancing with Louis Armstrong's band at age 15, had a residency at the *Cotton Club*, toured with Duke Ellington's orchestra for three years. and worked in films and stage shows. By the time she moved to London in the early 1950s, she had become a black superstar and one of the world's most sought-after jazz and exotic dancers – her YouTube clips are a joy.

ANOTHER ASPECT OF THE GREATER freedom of the independent labels was demonstrated when the cheerful optimism of "London Is The Place For Me" gave way to a starker view. When the police seemed incapable of stopping racist attacks perpetrated by Teddy Boys, Lord Invader's "Teddy Boy Calypso (Cat-O-Nine)" proposed a straightforward solution. Kitch summed up how many new arrivals felt about their treatment in the capital in "If You're Brown":

'It's a shame it's unfair but what can you do
The colour of your skin makes it hard for you…
If you're brown they say you can stick around
If you're white well everything's all right
If your skin is dark, no use, you try
You got to suffer until you die …'

He also issued a clear warning to fellow immigrants that, in London, there was none of the shadism that might have made life easier for light-skinned black people back home:

'If you think that the complexion of your face
Can hide you from the negro race
No! You can never get away from the fact
If you not white you considered black …'

Later, on an album entitled *Curfew Time*, he would include the track "Black Power".

Not surprisingly, with nosey landladies, troublesome mothers-in-law and bedroom transgressions being the same for everyone, the saucier strand of London calypsos captured a sizeable domestic audience. Such innuendo-laced numbers were not so different from the lewd music-hall comedy that lived on in theatre variety shows, which indeed often featured calypsonians. Calypso had no less enthusiastic a following among the educated elements of Britain's post-war generation, determined not to make the mistakes of their parents. Evolving out of London's jazz-loving, anti-establishment bohemians, and latching on to aspects of America's folk revivalism, a UK protest movement was gathering momentum. As they preached peace and revolution from coffee bars in Soho, Fitzrovia and Notting Hill, it was an easy leap for them to ally with victims of institutionalised racial prejudice, whose singing mocked the establishment and spoke of how hard life was for black folk in the capital. In addition, the apparent spontaneity of small-scale live performances of a singer, his guitar and a witty narrative-led song precisely fit the folk-music criteria – Soho's very underground, beat generation *Club du Faubourg* frequently featured calypso singers.

After the war, this influential boho crowd contributed greatly to the cultural reshaping of Britain. Forerunners of the hippies, they thought internationally, concerned themselves with philosophy as much as action, and were fundamentally anti-racist. They were responsible for CND (the Campaign for Nuclear Disarmament), devising the symbol that's now known as the peace sign (it's the letters C, N & D in semaphore). On the anti-nuclear Aldermaston marches, from 1958 onwards, it was more or less obligatory to have a pan-round-the-neck steel band. The movement connected with the wave of Caribbean thinkers, writers and trade unionists who settled in London during the 1950s, a disproportionate number of whom were Trinidadian. Cultural heavyweights and social activists such as CLR James, Sam Selvon, Claudia Jones, John La Rose and VS Naipaul all made strong links with London's modern intellectuals.

West End aristocrats had long since adopted calypso. too. At toney establishments like the *Café Royal*, the *Embassy Club*, and the *Hurlingham Club* in Chelsea, calypso performers became regulars, and they were also in demand for deb balls and Oxbridge bashes. The music had first made its mark on the royal family, with an incident involving the Duke of Edinburgh and Young Tiger at Mayfair's *Orchid Room*. When the singer spotted the future Prince Philip, who was engaged to then-Princess Elizabeth, he substituted the lyrics of "Rum & Coca Cola" with some that discussed upcoming nuptials in a less-than-totally-reverent manner. The horrified club manager apologised from the stage and gave Tiger a thorough dressing-down. The next night, however, a much larger royal party turned up, with one request: 'Sing it again, man!' This upper-class audience received another fillip in 1955, when Princess Margaret, the Queen's nightclubbing younger sister, took a Caribbean cruise. With the princess seeking local entertainment at every port of call, the holiday came to be known as her "Calypso Tour", while the lagoon at Pigeon Point in Tobago was renamed the Nylon Pool after the stockings she removed to dance barefoot on the sand.

Incidentally, the two ends of London's calypso audience presented something of a sartorial irony. Players at a West Indian club or suburban ballroom wouldn't have dreamed of taking the stage in anything less than a suit or a dinner jacket – even in the studio, it would be unusual to even loosen the tie. Yet when they played to high society, they were expected to kit themselves out like beachcombers: flowered shirts, cut-off stripey or white trousers, and straw hats that had clearly been chewed by a donkey.

WITH ALL THIS INTELLECTUAL, Oxbridge-educated and patrician support, calypso soon staked a serious claim on the television side of the BBC. There, as the colonies' most fully formed musical expression, it was a shoe-in when exotic music and dance was called for. Calypso's earliest regular showing was on the hour-long, Friday-night variety show, *Kaleidoscope*, transmitted from London's Alexandra Palace, from 1946 until 1953. Calypsonians would feature amid the antiques experts on Collectors' Corner, the Amazing Memory Man and the whodunit drama segment. Set against today's tightly-formatted TV, such a line-up seems astonishing, but in the 1940s and 1950s Britain still had a flourishing music-hall circuit where practically anything went, and on TV, 'variety' meant exactly that.

In 1950, Trinidadian dancer and choreographer Boscoe Holder had his calypso music and dance extravaganza, *Bal Creole*, screened not once but twice, in June and August. All TV was live back then, so it couldn't be repeated, and was performed again. Similarly, the *Caribbean Cabaret* series featured Holder and his wife Sheila Clarke; lords Kitchener and Beginner; Edric Connor; steel bands; and all manner of London's West Indian musicians. There were also specials, loaded with Britain's black talent, like *It's Fun To Dance*, *We Got Rhythm* and *Bongo*, in 1951, 1955 and 1958 respectively, the last of which was produced by former Sadler's Wells ballerina Margaret Dale.

In 1957, the Beeb screened the second series of *The Winifred Atwell Show* after outbidding ITV who had broadcast the first ten episodes of the variety series. Trinidadian Atwell had arrived in London in 1946 to study classical piano at the Royal Academy of Music, where she became the first woman to gain that establishment's highest grading. At the same time, she became one of the brightest stars of the capital's concert hall circuit as she supported herself by playing ragtime jazz and boogie-woogie. Such was the success of what began as a sideline, she became the first black artist to have a number one hit and sell a million records in the UK; and she remains the only female instrumentalist to have topped the UK singles charts (with "Let's Have A Party" in 1954). Atwell's playing will be familiar to British snooker fans of a certain age, as it's her recording of "Black and White Rag" that was the theme tune for BBC TV's long-running snooker show *Pot Black*. She made a follow-up series for the BBC, then took the show to Australia where it was broadcast during 1960 and 1961.

Another early instance of the Beeb's commitment to multiculturalism came when Young Tiger was broadcast singing his celebratory calypso "I Was There (At The Coronation)", on the very evening of the event. The speed with which the song went on air saw it lauded by the broadcasters as the perfect example of the calypsonian's art of improvisation. It didn't seem to occur to anybody that, as with Kitch's Tilbury performance, the song had been written in advance – three weeks previously, when Tiger read newspaper reports of the coach's route, and what Her Majesty what be wearing. How else could Parlophone have had copies in the shops the next day?

WHEN CALYPSO MADE ITS MOST significant impact in the UK, the man responsible was Cy Grant. He had come to England from British Guyana when he joined the RAF in 1941, and served in a bomber crew during the war. After his plane was shot down, he spent two years in a POW camp, classified by the Nazis as 'of indeterminate race'. He qualified as a barrister on demob, but found employment opportunities limited in London's institutionally racist legal system. Driven by a fierce sense of social justice, he took acting and singing lessons, and set out to use the performing arts to promote attitude change.

In the wake of immediate success on the folk-singing circuit and regular acting work on TV and stage, Grant was given a television chat show on ATV in 1956. Hosting *For Members Only*, he'd intersperse his interviews of newsworthy figures with singing and playing the guitar. Grant's quick intelligence, drama-school diction and rich baritone got him noticed by *Tonight*, a daily, early-evening BBC show that covered current affairs in an ultra-relaxed fashion – the first flowerings of television satire. Grant was signed up to sing the day's news highlights as a calypso composed that afternoon, with lyrics co-written by the incisively witty political journalist Bernard

Cy Grant provided the voice for Captain Scarlet's Lieutenant Green. Yes, Green was black all along.

Levin. These clever, cutting, frequently hilarious songs returned calypso to its slave master-mocking kaiso roots, and it became the accepted language of musical satire.

A huge hit, this was also the first time a black person had appeared regularly on national television (*For Members Only* was only shown in a couple of ITV regions). Grant stayed for two years, before quitting in case people thought it was all he could do. In the 1960s Grant scored another first for a black actor, as the voice of Lieutenant Green in the puppet drama *Captain Scarlet And The Mysterons*.

As satire grew better established, and comedy ever more biting, it became almost unthinkable not to include a humorously scathing calypso in the mix. The most vividly remembered example formed part of the BBC's *That Was The Week That Was* in 1964, which was groundbreaking in its merciless lampooning of political and establishment figures. No one on the programme cared if technicians or studio equipment came into shot, and as the night's final broadcast it was open-ended, continuing until the team decided to stop. Keith Waterhouse, John Bird, Peter Cook, Dennis Potter, Bill Oddie, Kenneth Tynan, John Betjeman and several future Pythons were on the *TW3* team – and so too was Lance Percival. A middle-class white lad from Kent, Percival had spent the mid-1950s in Canada, where he'd achieved fame singing calypsos as Lord Lance – laid-back calypso-style (flowered shirt and stuff) from the neck down, monocle and top hat above. His actual performance was far more conventional, his singing was top class, and Trinidadian calypsonians still talk with reverence about his lyrical talents. Percival's role on *TW3* was to take suggestions shouted from the audience, usually concerning current events, and make up and sing a calypso.

The segment was a major success, and he continued to supplement his career as a comedy actor by singing calypso in cabaret and on TV. In 1965 he notched up the biggest hit by a British calypsonian, when his version of "Shame And

Calypso Time No. 2

The Peanut Vendor · Matilda, Matilda
Trinidad · Calypso Boogie

GEORGE BROWNE

(Young Tiger)

PARLOPHONE
EXTENDED PLAY 45 r.p.m. RECORD

Scandal In The Family" reached number 37 in the charts. When *Tonight* and *TW3* were giving calypso its largest British audience, however, the music had for around half a decade ceased to count as a pop style. That wasn't anything to do with calypso itself, more the environment in which it found itself. By the end of the 1950s, rock'n'roll had pretty much swept away everything in its path, with the likes of Cliff, Adam Faith and Johnny Kidd leading the homegrown wave. When Lance Percival was doing his thing, the Beatles had released three albums, and the Supremes were spearheading the arrival of Motown on British shores.

Calypso's new popular context even served to work against it, as the public were seeing the genre purely as comedy, not a pop style to be taken seriously. Anywhere outside the satirical environment, that gave it novelty status, a perception heightened by an obviously Caribbean art being delivered by a pasty white boy. To be fair, though, calypso had done itself no favours, as there had been little musical advancement since Rupert Nurse's sessions at the start of the 1950s.

WHEN, CRUCIALLY, THE JAMAICAN recording industry got underway at the end of the 1950s, JA boogie (the island's take on R&B) and ska took over London's West Indian scene. This happened almost overnight, thanks to the Jamaican-owned sound systems that had previously played American R&B, jazz and calypso, and the large Jamaican audience that was poised, waiting for something of its own to dance to. By now, half of all Caribbean immigrants in London were from Jamaica.

A steady stream of Jamaican recordings was already being informally imported into London when Emil Shallit got involved in 1960. Never slow to spot a developing trend in an ethnic market, he launched the Melodisc subsidiary label Blue Beat, dedicated to Jamaican music. Shallit travelled to the island to make deals with the biggest producers for UK rights to their material. He transferred the resources that would otherwise have gone into calypso into ska instead, and marketed it to exactly the same audience. He also hoovered up many of the same players for his London ska sessions. Suddenly ska became the official soundtrack of black London; and entirely understandably, many Trinidadian calypsonians, Kitch included, went home for good when their island gained its independence in 1962.

EVEN THOUGH IT CEASED TO HAVE MUCH SWAY beyond specialist circles, London calypso did not die out. When soca – a modern, danceable fusion of soul and calypso – emerged during the 1970s, the music got a considerable boost in the capital. The London Calypso Tent at the Notting Hill Carnival, and the junior calypso competitions held during Black History Month, remain lively affairs. The Association of British Calypsonians, formed in 1991, maintains links and exchange programmes with the Caribbean. Calypso in twenty-first-century London has evolved into a far more world-embracing scene, with performers likely to have roots from anywhere in the Caribbean or even Africa, and its subject matter tends to deal with global rather than parochial concerns.

While calypso may not have made as deep an impression as reggae or funk, the very fact that it established itself as part of mainstream British entertainment marked a historic cultural moment. It represented the first time in the United Kingdom that an immigrant group had expressed its relationship with its new home in song, and developed a style that had absorbed that environment. For the first time too, an imported musical style made a significant impact on the domestic music industry. Calypso had not merely existed in immigrant or left-field environments, speaking more about 'back home' than 'new home'. In a two-way process, both host and arrival musical cultures had borrowed from each other with a healthy degree of respect.

A mere fifteen years after the *Windrush* docked, this truly marked the beginnings of Britain as a *culturally* multicultural society. It indicated an acceptance for new arrivals on a social level, and a genuine curiosity as to what they had to offer. That didn't end with calypso. The fact that the more genuine side of the music had shown itself to have domestic appeal set something of a precedent. Ever since then, the British, and Londoners above all, have shown a consistent appetite for imported music, provided it has some meaning and substance.

The success of calypso served as a blueprint for the musical integrations that were to occur over the next fifty or so years. And that in turn says a great deal about attitudes towards 'newcomers' in the capital. As one of those two celebrated *Windrush* passengers predicted in his 1952 recording, "Mix Up Matrimony":

'With racial segregation I can see universally
Fading gradually ...'

CHAPTER TWO

'Are They Going to Play Music on *Dustbins*?'

||||||||||||||||||||||||||||||||||||||||||||||||||||||||||||||||||||||||||||||||||||||

How London learned to love the steel pan

TUCKED AWAY BENEATH THE WESTWAY, just up from Latimer Road tube, the *Maxilla Social Club* is everything you'd expect, early evening in an old-school working men's club. The television, nestled among the darts trophies above wood panelling straight from the 1970s, is showing a football match with the sound off, while the two or three old geezers sitting on bar stools contemplate their competitively priced pints and don't say very much. The other end of this medium-sized hall, though, is a riot of sound and activity. *Maxilla* doubles as the rehearsal space for Nostalgia Steel Orchestra, and with a week to go until the Notting Hill Carnival, this is a crucial time in their calendar. As the musicians warm up, and settle into their groove, you realise that, at quarters this close, there's little as thrilling as a big, inspired steel band in full flow.

The second thing that strikes you is Nostalgia's demography: more or less equally male and female; just over fifty percent white, about forty percent black, with a smattering of other ethnic types; and an age range that extends from teen to pensionable. In other words, a remarkably accurate cross-section of the immediate area, between the Westway and Holland Park, with White City to the west and Ladbroke Grove to the east. It's a vivid example of London's capacity to absorb foreign culture with the minimum of fuss. An instrument that wouldn't be everyone's immediate choice, is Caribbean to the point of cliché, and is relatively young – among the mere handful invented as late as the twentieth century – has quietly seeped into London's soundtrack. Not merely as some sort of island-invoking soundbed for calypsonians, either, but as an art form in its own right.

Calypso and steel band have been kept apart in this book because despite their shared Trinidadian origins, their histories are almost entirely distinct. In classic uptown/downtown style, the two coexisted for years in mutual musical animosity. Steel pan was seen as trifling, a DIY ghetto extension of Port of Spain's violent street gangs, while calypso's associations with jazz and nightclubs were judged the height of sophistication. Not until 1946, with steel pan fan Lord Kitchener's calypso "Yes, I Heard The Beat Of A Steel Pan", did calypso even acknowledge the existence of steel bands.

Having come together out of the Russ Henderson Steel Band in 1964, Nostalgia are the longest-standing steel band in the capital, and they're the only big band that still performs in the traditional 'pan round the neck' manner. In their initial manifestation, they had the idea, one August bank holiday, to take a children's street festival on walkabout around the roads of Notting Hill. Over the years, they've become so London that they played a prominent part in the Opening Ceremony for the 2012 Olympics.

Nostalgia apart, though, the fact that the steel pan has established itself so deeply as part of life in Britain actually says as much about the British themselves as it does about the players who put it there. Of course, it hasn't always been such a mutual admiration society.

The Trinidad All Steel Percussion Orchestra making their debut at
the Festival of Britain in 1951. The bemused-looking audience needed
convincing that music could be made on what looked like scrap iron.

'WHEN WE CAME OUT AND PUT OUR PANS around our
necks, people started to laugh at us, pointing and shouting
"What are you going to do with those dustbins?"'

Sterling Betancourt, a sprightly septuagenarian who needs
little encouragement to demonstrate his steel pan virtuosity,

is thinking back to 29 July 1951. He was a member of the Trinidad All Steel Percussion Orchestra (T.A.S.P.O.), who had been brought over to open the inaugural concert of the Royal Festival Hall. Set proudly on the south bank of the Thames, the new hall was the centrepiece of the Festival of Britain, a national morale-booster designed to show that Britain was bouncing back after the Luftwaffe had done its worst. Focussed especially on architecture and new buildings, the Festival featured arts, crafts, exhibitions and cultural events from all around the country and the Commonwealth.

Initial audience scepticism was encouraged by the fact that the band's instruments had rusted badly on the three-week Atlantic crossing. As the musicians emerged from the gleaming new building, the pans looked like so much scrap iron. That was, Sterling laughingly explains, all part of the plan:

'Of course we'd tuned them, but we didn't clean them because we decided to really give the audience a good surprise – they would never have seen a steel band before, and then they would be amazed when the beautiful music started coming out of these rusty-looking objects.

'It worked too, because they were looking at us as we set up and we're doing run-throughs, then when the captain calls us to order and we start to play the first tune, a mambo called "Mambo Jambo", these people watching are astonished. They just staring at us. Then when we play Brahm's "Lullaby", the "Blue Danube Waltz", and Toscelli's "Serenade", they definitely can't believe what they are hearing!'

Newspaper reports the next day ran out of superlatives, hailing the performance with such praise as 'virtuoso jazz', 'wonderfully skilled' and 'first-class playing'. Next, Edric Connor, the Trinidadian singer, actor and radio presenter who had been instrumental in persuading the Festival organisers to bring over a steel band, used his influence at the BBC to get them on the radio, and Britain's affection for steel bands began. That said, it might have fizzled out just as quickly, had the 21-year-old Sterling not made a life-changing decision and opted to stay in London. With his steel drum:

'We toured Britain for three weeks, it was great, and I made my mind up to stay here. I was the only one who remained in London, because things happen that just make me see it all a certain way. When we were in Paris and we were waiting to go back home, we have some time off, and we're young guys, been away from home for a long time all cooped up together, and a lot of frustration was happening between the boys. There was a bit of a misunderstanding with two guys, they had a fight and all of that, and one of the chaps got stabbed in his hand. I decided to myself "Listen, I'm not going back to that sort of thing in Trinidad again."

'I know in those days they used to have a lot of riots and things between the different bands, because they take the rivalry so seriously, and I was thinking to go back home with this sort of thing happening … it just wasn't on. I said I'd rather take my chances back in England. I figured that after that tour I could continue the steel band form in England, so I took my steel drum and my passport and returned to England from Paris. The next day the band took the train to Bordeaux and the boat to Trinidad without me.

'Although I was told by the rest of the boys that I would suffer if I go back to London, I said "No". Before I had left I remember talking to my brother and telling him I would be a fool to come back to Trinidad, so I think I knew what I was going to do even back then. The incident in Paris just showed me that it was the right thing to do. Yes, it was hard to leave my home country, and I made the decision with tears in my eyes, but I don't regret it. It turned out very good for me.'

When Sterling talks about riots in the steel band world, he's not exaggerating. The whole purpose of T.A.S.P.O. was to cool inter-band rivalry. Like the sound systems in Jamaica, steel bands were born in the ghetto, and many of the first pan men were gang members who carried those affiliations into the bands. With some seventy orchestras in and around Port of Spain, each attracting its own passionate supporters, bloody armed conflict and the breaking up of each other's dances was commonplace. T.A.S.P.O. was an initiative sponsored by the government of Trinidad & Tobago, drawing one member from each of the island's top twelve bands in the hope that bringing them together would stop the violence. They travelled under the watchful eye of Nathaniel Griffiths, a no-nonsense police lieutenant who ruled the volatile young men with a rod of iron. Being invited to London was a timely bonus, as the government saw it as a way to elevate steel pan music into what it saw as a bona fide art form. At the time, it was more or less standard for the middle and upper classes in Britain's Caribbean colonies to sneer at ghetto culture until it was successful abroad – witness ska and reggae.

SINCE STEEL PAN BEGAN IN THE 1930s, the Trinidad-ian establishment had not considered it proper music, while pannists themselves were known as 'badjohns', local slang for hooligans or ne'er-do-wells. The change in attitude came about when calypso achieved international acclaim, and the government saw immediate benefits in promoting another exportable, tourist-friendly and identifiably Trinidadian form. Steel pan, however, had to travel a long way to get uptown, as it progressively expanded beyond the island's poorest com-munities after bamboo orchestras were banned during World War II as part of the official suspension of Carnival.

The bamboo orchestras, or 'tamboo bamboo' – adapted from 'tambour', the French for drum – originated in the slums of Laventville, on the eastern side of Trinidad's capital Port of Spain. Money for instruments was non-existent there, but invention and innovation were in abundance: these entirely percussive but surprisingly melodic ensembles consisted solely of bamboo poles. For tuning purposes, the bamboos ranged from roughly 1.5m long and 12cm across for the lowest bass to 63cm by 3cm for the sopranos, with differing numbers of holes bored in the sides to further vary the pitch. The smaller poles were supported on the player's shoulder and struck with a piece of hard wood, while the larger ones were banged on the ground; the angle at which the pole hit the floor would also affect the note, just as the force could alter the volume. With the bamboos concentrating on melodies, rhythms were supplemented by bottle-and-spoon players.

Sterling was in a bamboo orchestra as a kid, and remembers going out at night to select and cut poles – bamboo cut in sunlight is said to be more susceptible to fungus.

'We used to go way up to Trou Macaque [*a rural area to the east of Trinidad's capital*] and look for what we needed. It could take a week to properly dry out a good bamboo.'

When the tamboo bamboos were banned, the musicians simply explored the percussion possibilities of the scrap metal that could be found on any rubbish tip – paint cans, food tins and automobile brake hubs were favourites – supplemented with everyday domestic items like pots, pans, dustbins and buckets. Players swiftly realised that stretching surfaces, and forming different indentations through persistent beating, produced varying notes, and thus a formal tuning process could be instigated.

The switch to adapting oil drums into the steel pans we know today came about because so many such drums were discarded on the island by the US military during World War II, and they offered the perfect raw material. It is, claims Sterling, impossible to pin down the time or the individual responsible for the steel pan:

'Everybody was innovating, there wasn't just one man who did it. Everybody see what was happening and start trying themselves, all at the same time, to produce better sounds and a greater range of notes.'

Which they certainly did, very quickly too, as during the 1940s steel pans evolved into around a dozen different instruments, from soprano to bass, enabling orchestras to play anything from folk songs to jazz, dance music, calypso or the classics.

Amazingly enough, such musicianship failed to impress the island's calypsonians, who shared the stance that because it came from the ghetto, it must be of no value. With the notable exception of Lord Kitchener, who loved melody and saw the steel drum as an important Trinidadian cultural statement, the calypsonians all but ignored these new orchestras. As a result, steel band music rarely made it onto the radio or into the recording studios; much like Jamaican sound systems, it remained in the ghetto, for the ghetto, and completely of the ghetto. Again like the early sound systems, the violence that went on around steel bands, and the ferocity with which supporters and players protected their outfits, had a great deal to do with the fact that this was pretty much all many people had to get excited about. It was totally theirs, and they were going to guard it.

Young Sterling Betancourt poses with his instrument.

To a great extent, the government strategy worked. T.A.S.P.O.'s success in Britain resonated back in Trinidad in the form of radio interest and acknowledgement by the tourist trade. In London, however, the music was having a much more immediate effect on the upper classes.

WHEN STERLING BETANCOURT RETURNED to London in 1951, he wasn't the city's first-ever steel pan player. That distinction went to Boscoe Holder, a Caribbean renaissance man who reached the capital from Trinidad, via New York, in 1950. As musician, dancer, choreographer and producer of large-scale folk-based shows, Holder made it his mission to take his island's culture around the globe. Later, as a renowned painter, he's also credited with introducing African Caribbean art to the world.

Along with his wife, dancer/singer Sheila Clarke, Holder set up a dance troupe, Boscoe Holder and his Caribbean Dancers, which was an immediate hit in London theatres. In 1950, the couple had a radio series on the BBC Home Service – the predecessor of Radio Four – built around his piano playing and her singing, and called *Caribbean Carnival*. He also showed off limbo dancing and the steel drum to the viewing public with the televised music and dance extravaganza *Bal Creole*, broadcast live from Alexandra Palace in June and August. The show was such a success that the troupe was recalled for a repeat performance in August. As the 1950s progressed, Holder's company became BBC favourites. Besides appearances on shows ranging from *Tonight* to *Six-Five Special* and *Kaleidoscope*, they were regulars on the black variety series *Caribbean Cabaret*. They also found support at Buckingham Palace: Boscoe Holder and his Caribbean Dancers performed on a barge on the Thames as part of the flotilla marking Queen Elizabeth's coronation in 1953; Holder and his wife took part in a Royal Command Performance in 1955, and the following year they were among a select party of eighteen invited to dinner with the Queen and the Duke of Edinburgh at *Claridges*.

Although Holder's pan playing never reached Sterling Betancourt's standard, he was the first to give the instrument a wide audience, and his high-class connections through the art and dance worlds gave it a profile in London society. Holder also became a part-owner of a swish nightclub in Mayfair's Hay Hill, where he made sure the Caribbean quota in the entertainment remained high.

Meanwhile Sterling, the city's only specialist pan player, could only do so much by himself. He played solo in mainly West Indian-patronised venues, like Sunday or Saturday lunchtimes or Friday evenings at such pubs as the *Colherne* and the *Colville Hotel* in Ladbroke Grove. He also performed spots during the orchestra breaks at dancehalls like the *Paramount*, and cabaret sets at a few Soho clubs. It was in one of these that he met fellow-countryman Russell Henderson, who quickly realised they could help each other. Russ still enjoys talking about those early days in the West End:

'I got to know Sterling at the *Sunset Club* in Carnaby Street, where he would do steel drum at the late cabaret. I used to go there after the job I had at the nearby *La Ronde* finished. I wanted to incorporate more steel drum into the conventional jazz thing I was doing here, both to reference Trinidad and because not many others were doing it. This was in 1952, when there might have been a couple of other steel drum players in London, but Sterling was the most prominent.

'We got together to record a couple of tunes I had written – "Ping Pong Samba" was one of them. This was for Melodisc, and we had a bassist and a guitar, with Sterling on tenor pan and me playing piano. It sounded good and we looked to develop the sound. But mostly for club gigs it would be more conventional jazz or show tunes. Me on the piano, Sterling on drums, a bass player and a guitarist, and sometimes a chap on the accordion or a trumpeter. We had a few residencies at clubs, the *Sunset* was one of them, and we played music for dancing with a bit of our own calypsos stirred in. Sterling was playing the drums, because as a steel pan player back then you had to do something else or you couldn't earn enough money. He'd had a few lessons, and somebody had given him some drums.'

Sterling remembers how, after those recordings with Russ, they developed the notion of steel pan in London, but with music tailored to that environment:

'What we did on those recordings sounded good, and we knew there was an audience for steel band in London not

Half a century later, and Sterling has hardly changed.

only among the West Indian community who knew it, but the English people who usually liked it when they heard it. So we thought we'd go for it and go further in that direction. We wanted to create a small steel band out of the music [*jazz*] band, so we could do both styles to the same audience. Because the steel band would have elements of the jazz in it, we figured it would go down easier.

'We needed more than one pan, so I sent to Trinidad for two drums, steel drums. One was for Russell Henderson to play, so I taught him what to do on the drum so he could play second pan. Of course it wasn't hard for him to catch on, because he's a musician, and we add a guitar and we could start to do a three-piece thing. But by now there's other guys who can play pan in London, so we could use three pans together. The band became a quartet, with three steel drums and a guitar, or a music band with piano, guitar, bass and me playing drums. I had booked ten drum lessons in London, but stopped after five because I was doing OK! Then we would go into clubs and cabarets playing music then changing over to steel drum – our first gig was the *Sunset Club*. We were the only band that could do this, and we did quite a few recordings too, up until about 1955.

'Why the steel band was called the Russell Henderson Steel Band, even though I was the lead pan player and the original pan player in it, is because it was with the music band and that was Russell Henderson's band. He was well known, so had the reputation to get the gigs. I was happy for him to call it the Russell Henderson Steel Band because he was the elder one and he was the boss of the band. I learned an awful lot from him, musically, and he learned the steel drum from me, so it was like a marriage. It was very, very good.'

The most immediate effect of this uniquely London-styled steel band was on English high society. Whether it was a result of the royal patronage, or perhaps thanks to the prestigious gig T.A.S.P.O. played at the *Savoy Hotel* in 1951, the aristocracy couldn't get enough of the sound. While the Russell Henderson Steel Band played pub gigs, West Indian social club dances and even house parties, there were just as many hunt balls, Oxbridge events and debutante parties. Russ describes their apparently polarised popularity:

'We used to play West Indian gigs all the time. Sometimes they were in town halls – St Pancras Town Hall was always popular – but really it was anywhere that would hire out to West Indians. There was a guy called Hugh Scotland, who I think was Jamaican and had been in the RAF, and he used to put on West Indian functions somewhere every holiday, like on Boxing Day or at Easter. Then they might just be West Indian parties like a wedding or a christening or somebody's birthday. And of course there were the pubs we'd play in, usually on a Sunday lunchtime, that's where you'd hear about the other gigs because people that wanted to book you knew where to find you.

'Then there were the society balls. How that started was somebody from Cambridge University had come to the *Sunset Club* and seen us playing steel band, and asked us to come up and do a Cambridge ball. We did that and they asked us back, then *Oxford* wanted a steel band too, so then we did that, and now Oxford or Cambridge can't have a ball without getting us up there to play. Of course, that spread to other universities and the students would take the idea home, so we were playing all sorts of society balls and parties in big houses and hotels all over the country.

'Most of the time at those society parties, they'd have three or four bands. Although you might think that, just after the war, this was a very austere time, they were rich people and they wanted to enjoy themselves, so a party would have plenty of bands. There would be a West Indian band, you could dress up in a costume and play Latin American music and Caribbean music like we played steel pan. What they really liked about it was, when we weren't on stage playing dance music, we could put the pans around our necks and be there to greet the people arriving, or we could walk through the crowds playing. If it was an outdoor event that could be wonderful.

'I think what appealed to them about our music was, here they were with their stiff upper lips, and here they saw people ready to smile and jump up and shout and say what we want – uninhibited. And I think that made the difference. They saw West Indians and they thought "Well here's somebody who can speak, at least, when there's the Englishman who is quiet and wouldn't say anything at all!" [*Russ chuckles greatly at this idea*] I think that is the difference – we're more open. That's the only way I can think to put it, the openness of the Caribbean people was appealing to the English people, and that was coming through the steel band music, because it's a very appealing, infectious sound.'

However, Sterling remembers the guests at those society balls having one particular problem with steel band music. He laughs as hard as Russell as he recalls it:

'We used to play for royalty and at the deb parties and the universities and so on, and it caught on so quickly. They took to it immediately, they loved it. At first it was the novelty of the steel band, then they started to really enjoy it. But the one trouble was when we play steel band at first, English people didn't know how to dance to it. They used to foxtrot! I remember in the very early days when our steel band was playing in the *Lyceum*, we were playing a kind of jazz calypso thing, and they were moving so stiffly around the floor, holding on to each other and *foxtrotting around the floor*! Eventually they saw how the West Indians would dance to it and were shaking, and they soon follow. Then they really get to enjoy the steel band because it loosened them up a bit. They fall into the groove of the calypso rhythm, and they start dancing a bit more carefree. I think it helped many of them understand we West Indians a bit better.'

The only major concern for the band was the supply of steel pans. Getting them shipped over was not something just anyone could do, as Sterling describes:

'You had to send to Trinidad for steel drums, because in those days you couldn't find no place that would make them in London. Although I could have made the drums – I knew how to because I'd learned that skill at home – I would have had to find a place to do that. And that was impossible because it makes a lot of noise, you have to get the oil drum, cut it down, and then bong and bang on it to make the notes. It's too much noise to do in most places in London. In Trinidad the pan

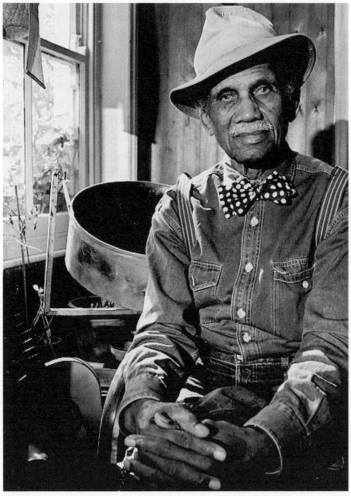

The legendary Russ Henderson still performs on piano and pan.

yards are where they do nothing but that, and it is like their business premises. The easiest thing was for me to send for the drums. I send to somebody name of Anthony Williams, in Port of Spain, he made the drums and another chap brought them over for us himself. That was the best way to do it, so they wouldn't get damaged, and I knew enough about pan tuning to check them over when they arrived.

'Back then, this was the only way you were going to get drums in London – you had to know steel band men to send to, so it was only steel band men in London that was going to get them. It keep the traditions amongst us. Russell couldn't have got his own drum because he didn't know the right people. You needed the connection. I knew the chap who was bringing it up [to England] because we were in Trinidad together. I knew he was coming up to England and my brother organised to get the drums made. That's the only way we could have that steel band.'

While the Russell Henderson Steel Band was getting English aristos shakin' their blue-blood booties, the group was also redefining the role of the steel pan and the steel band. The image of the two- or three-piece pan-round-the-neck group may now be something of a cliché in tourist hotels and on cruise-ship docks, but back then it was virtually unheard of, and meant the music itself had to change. Steel bands had always been orchestras of at least twenty players, possibly as many as a hundred. To make a small band viable, Russell had to compose specifically for the pan, and for the group's jazz manifestation as it incorporated the pan. This represented a massive advance for steel pan, as previously almost no original music had been written for the instrument. The Port of Spain orchestras played their interpretations of jazz and big-band standards, plus indigenous folk songs and the classics. By writing regular jazz tunes with the pan in mind, Russell expanded how it performed within a piece of music – the term 'pan-jazz' was first applied to his 1950s London tunes.

Russell's jazz sensibilities enabled him to reposition the three steel drums within any piece of music, bringing

The Russell Henderson Steel Band at work in the 1950s.

out the absolute melodic best the instrument had to offer, while still sounding as exotic as ever. To accommodate these developments, the band retuned their pans to a chromatic scale that incorporated more semitones, making the three instruments more harmonically responsive and, very subtly, more familiar to European ears.

Naturally, it didn't take long for such London-based experiments to cross back to Trinidad. News that Sterling was doing well convinced other T.A.S.P.O. members to come over, and pan players regularly came and went between London and Port of Spain. At first the Trinidadians scoffed that such a shallow sound couldn't possibly make sense. Once the practicality of a small band became obvious, the new format caught on quickly. No longer confined to bigger nightclubs, hotel ballrooms and carnival road marches, the music could go just about anywhere. The new London-based musical templates were embraced with similar gusto, triggering an explosion of composition and creativity that hugely boosted the instrument's potential. Thanks largely to the Russell Henderson Steel Band, steel pan players could show off exactly what they were capable of under practically any conditions.

Oh yes, and as well as all that, the Russell Henderson Steel Band invented the Notting Hill Carnival as we now know it.

IN THE 1950s, CARIBBEAN PROMOTERS would commonly hire whatever halls would let them, book in a couple of bands, and put on dances. Porchester Hall in Bayswater was a favourite, as were Lambeth Town Hall, Battersea Town Hall, Archway Central Hall and so on. School halls too would be unofficially opened up on a Saturday by their West Indian caretakers. Putting on a function with a dance band, a steel band and, in later years, a sound system was the best way to celebrate a holiday back home, or just to dress up and get away from the tribulations of the working week – spiritually and culturally, to get back to the West Indies for an evening. Musically speaking, these affairs would be a mixture of Trinidadian and Jamaican, but pretty much everybody would fetch up. Occasionally they had a purpose beyond feast-day celebrations or commercial gain. One such dance was organised by the Trinidadian-born Claudia Jones at St Pancras Town Hall in January 1959.

Then 45 years old, Jones was not a dance promoter but a seasoned political activist, black nationalist and multicultural advocate. Having moved to Harlem with her parents as a child, she grew up so incensed by the treatment of black people and poor white people by the US establishment that she joined the American Communist Party, and swiftly rose to become National Director of the Young Communist League. Following four jail terms resulting from politically motivated charges, Jones was deported to London in 1955, where she settled in Notting Hill. There she continued to fight what she saw as essentially the same system, and joined the British Communist Party to become active in its struggle for justice and fight against racism. A distinguished writer and journalist throughout her adult life, Jones co-founded the West Indian Students Association in 1958, and also launched and became editor of the country's first black newspaper, *The West Indian Gazette*. As well as London West Indian news and stories from back home, the paper campaigned for an end to colonialism, a united West Indies, world peace and, above all, fair treatment for Britain's black communities.

At the end of that year, after intensifying racist attacks in the Notting Hill area had culminated in a summer of street violence, Jones called a meeting of local people to ask what could be done to raise spirits, demonstrate resilience and celebrate Caribbean culture. The answer came, 'a carnival, just like back home'. Timing-wise that raised a few eyebrows; winter in London offered far-from-ideal carnival conditions. That didn't worry the indefatigable Jones. She booked St Pancras Town Hall for 30 January, and took on Edric Connor as overall director and Trinidadian dancer Stanley Jack as choreographer. After eight hours spent transforming the chilly North London civic building into a West Indian paradise, the event featured Boscoe Holder, Fitzroy Coleman, Mighty Terror and Edric Connor, as well as a black beauty contest – another London first – and the crowning of the Carnival Queen. The BBC televised part of the proceedings to an enthusiastic, across-the-board audience.

Around a thousand people jammed themselves into the venue; almost as many were shut outside, but still grooving on the clearly audible music. It speaks volumes as to how much London's West Indians wanted to be part of an event like this that they stayed outside in sub-zero temperatures, with a bemused contingent of police looking on. (Incidentally, while it's often stated that this first Carnival took place in response to the racist murder of the young black man Kelso Cochrane, that's not the case. That tragedy didn't happen until a few months later.)

The success of the Carnival, which was sponsored by the *West Indian Gazette* under the slogan 'A people's art is the genesis of their freedom', dictated that it become an annual affair. Clearly bigger premises were required. The following year's Carnival took place at the 2,000-capacity Seymour Hall, just behind Marble Arch, but once again vast crowds were unable to get in. The 1961 event transferred to the even larger *Lyceum Ballroom* just off the Strand, and within three years

Claudia Jones' Carnival had become engraved on black London's calendar.

It would probably have continued to be so, but in December 1964 Claudia Jones passed away, due to a heart condition and tuberculosis brought on by a lung condition that dated back to her impoverished childhood and American jail terms. Paul Robeson read the eulogy at her massively attended funeral, and she was buried in Highgate Cemetery, next to Karl Marx, one of her heroes. She was later commemorated on a Royal Mail postage stamp. Without Jones' energy and direction, there was no Carnival the following year, and the *West Indian Gazette* folded.

THE RUSSELL HENDERSON STEEL BAND had been part of Jones' Carnivals since 1960. While acknowledging the events as a vital contribution to Caribbean culture in London, the band were involved in an equally significant occasion during the year Jones passed away.

On the August bank holiday in 1964 – then at the start, not the end, of the month – a Ladbroke Grove social worker and community activist named Rhaune Laslett organised a street party for local children whose parents couldn't afford to take them on holiday. Although Laslett and Claudia Jones knew each other, Jones had nothing to do with this event. Far from being any sort of Caribbean celebration, it was simply about the area itself. Laslett was of mixed Native American and Russian descent, and the children who attended were a junior United Nations of English, Polish, Irish, African, Russian, Portuguese and West Indian. The entertainment laid on for them was equally varied, including a donkey cart donated by traders from Portobello Market, an African drummer with an elephant's-foot drum – he might well have been Ginger Johnson, but nobody seems able to confirm that for sure – a clown, a box of false moustaches, and the Russell Henderson Steel Band. The group took part at the suggestion of Laslett's partner Jim O'Brien, who knew them from Sunday lunchtimes at the *Colherne* pub, where they played and he enjoyed a pint. He figured they'd be a good representative of the local Caribbean community, and would make proceedings go with a swing. They went along as a strolling pan-round-the-neck trio of Russ, Sterling and a third player named Ralph Cherrie.

The local council had given Laslett permission to cordon off a section near the top end of Portobello Road. Tables for food and drink were set up, the steel band wandered around playing music, and the children enjoyed themselves. Pretty much all anybody could have asked for, until Russ and the boys had a better idea. As Russ recalls:

'We never had stands for our instruments, so we are completely mobile. Although this is really only a children's fete, it still had quite a carnival flavour, so I'm thinking that, like when we have carnival in Trinidad, we should go on a bit of a road march. Give the children a little taste of it – I knew they would follow. So I told the organisers "Let's move the barriers from the street and make a block of it." They agreed, I moved the barrier, got the children and everybody else to follow. This block was the biggest block that ever happened!

'When we got to the corner of Ladbroke Grove, instead of turning back we turned left, and from there we went straight down to Holland Park. Then we turned left and continued to Notting Hill Gate. We made it up as we went along – if we saw a bus coming then we'd take another street. The police didn't know what to do, so they just let us get on with it and I kept telling them "Oh it's all right, we're just going to the next corner then we'll go back." After a while, we'd attracted such a big crowd they started clearing traffic for us!

'It was real exciting and people were swept up with it, so we just kept on going. We went along the Bayswater Road and turned up Queensway, from there we could go along Westbourne Grove and back up Ladbroke Grove. That was actually the biggest carnival route ever, because when it became organised they cut it down to make a little short route. But the one we went on was impromptu, we was walking, walking, walking. People followed for a bit then dropped out, but I remember the ones that had been with it all the way asking us "How do we get home from here? We're lost!"'

Sterling remembers how the parade grew as it went on its way, but not everybody was one hundred percent supportive.

'The West Indians knew what was going on and they join in immediately, some really participate just like at home. At first it was just the three of us with the drums round our neck, but people were joining in with all sort of percussion instruments, even if they were just banging a bottle with a spoon. It was like we were the Pied Pipers; the police did nothing because they thought if they stopped us there might be trouble.

Steel band floats were the basis of the first Notting Hill carnivals.

'A lot of English people joined in too, most of them were happy to see it, but some didn't know what it was – they saw so many West Indians on a parade like this and they thought it was a demonstration. They were shouting at us 'What have you got to demonstrate about? If you want to complain go back to your own country!' The thing was, in those days we did go on demonstrations, we used to go on the Ban The Bomb marches, and when they come up from Aldermaston we used to join in at Kensington and go up to Hyde Park with them. So some people thought this was the steel band doing a demonstration again. But they did not know this was the carnival thing, that we were just going along the street enjoying ourselves.'

In spite of all that, the procession was such an overwhelming success that it was repeated the following year, and then became an annual event. The Russell Henderson Steel Band were, of course, invited back to lead the road march, and Russ remembers how it grew:

'That is the one that started it, then after that they wanted to do it again and I started to get friends to come along. West Indians from all over London started to hear about it and turned up, and it just started to develop, getting bigger and bigger. It really did *evolve*, because that's how these things need to be – you can't just sit down and say "I'm going to start a carnival", it has to develop naturally because it's a people's thing.'

Within three or four years, it was being called the Notting Hill Carnival. Over that time, the Caribbean content started to dominate, as entertainers and organisers who had been part of Claudia Jones's events got involved. It was fast becoming *the* London West Indian event, and by the 1970s had swelled into something recognisable as what it is today. Claudia Jones is quite rightly remembered as the Mother of the Carnival, as she recreated a Trinidadian carnival in London, but the *Notting Hill Carnival* probably wouldn't have happened if it hadn't been for Rhaune Laslett and the Russell Henderson Steel Band.

THE FASHION FOR STEEL BANDS at posh English functions proved not to be hugely enduring. By the 1970s it had fallen victim to the changing styles in clubland, as establishments moved away from live bands and cabaret towards recorded music instead. By the end of that decade, the Russell Henderson Steel Band had all but broken up, with Russ going back to piano and Sterling taking on other pan players to start the steel orchestra that became Nostalgia. Steel band itself was far from finished, though; it spearheaded a revolution in the way English kids were taught music at school. Not surprisingly, Sterling Betancourt and Russell Henderson were somewhere near the front of that development too.

It all began on an ad hoc level at the end of the 1960s. Aware that interest in steel pan was waning, Russ and Sterling wanted to keep the form alive in Great Britain. Figuring the best way would be to get kids into it – as 'they would carry it through to adulthood, and even if they didn't play they'd still be appreciative of the steel band' – Russell hatched a scheme to introduce it to the London schools' music curriculum. He devised a course and lesson plans, but found it difficult to gain acceptance within the very traditional education authorities. An expat Trinidadian friend of his came up with a plan:

'I'd been trying to break steel drums into schools for some time, but been unsuccessful. Then I met up with a friend of mine, a social worker in south London, and he said "What about bringing a steel band up into schools?" As well as the music aspect, he thought it would be a good idea to let the Caribbean kids see a bit of their culture in action. We tried several schools, until there was one willing to take it on, Elmwood Junior School in Croydon. The headmistress there, Mrs Ethel France, said she'd give it a go, and that was the first one ever to have a steel band in their music department.

'We went down there and the kids loved it – not just the black kids, all of them – and it was such a success we got a regular job up there. It wasn't all completely straightforward though, as some of the music teachers were jealous of what we were doing. Largely because we had so many kids genuinely interested in the music, because it was exciting and different, and because what we were teaching them was getting through. Learning music on the steel drum gave them a sense of rhythm and an understanding of the scales and notes, and for some of the unruly kids it gave them a sense of discipline that they could get into easily.'

Although this was all pretty unofficial, a direct arrangement between Russ and the school, it didn't take long before the Inner London Education Authority (ILEA) found out about it and wanted to know what was going on:

'When ILEA heard about us, they got onto my head teacher and wanted us to come and give a talk on it and a demonstration of how to start it. So the ILEA people came and we told them what it was all about, and I brought my kids out and they played. They were all juniors, no older than eleven, and they showed what kids that young could get out of a steel band. After that, ILEA said they wanted a steel band in every school, and that was the start of the steel band programme they brought in. But mine was going already.'

Russ's protégés at Elmwood once reached the finals of the National Schools Music Festival at the Royal Albert Hall, and within a few years ILEA had installed dozens of steel bands in schools around the capital. Their motives went beyond music, and fell in line with the well-meaning but horribly patronising thinking that too often informed the official approach to multiculturalism forty years ago. For a number of relatively complex reasons, a disproportionate number of black kids were getting into trouble, and to 'give them a bit of their culture' was seen as the best way to fill some sort of hole.

Dr Lionel McCalman, Nostalgia Steel Band's current captain, is a senior lecturer in Education and Community Development at the University of East London, and the UK's most knowledgeable steel pan archivist. Every year he runs the well-attended, never-less-than-lively International Conference on Steel Pan, which discusses and holds seminars on steel pan, calypso and mas, the three elements of the Caribbean carnival. Born in Guyana, Lionel came to

Dr Lionel McCalman, pan maestro, Nostalgia captain and music historian.

London as a child in 1965, and takes a rather cynical view of the ILEA programme of which he was a beneficiary:

'Steel bands became very attractive to the ILEA at the time – the late sixties to early seventies – because schools found, in the beginning, that this was a very, very simple instrument to teach, and it covered them as regards doing something for the Caribbean pupils. After three or four lessons they'll play a simple tune, like "La Bamba" or whatever, and they'll play for the assembly and everyone will clap. But try to teach "La Bamba" on the trombone or something, and you know where you're heading for – you're heading for nothing. So, yes, it was perceived as an easy instrument, and head teachers liked it because they could look at the Caribbean kids and say "If they're not achieving in that then they can surely achieve in this".

'It looked to the world like they were signing up to the equal opportunities agenda. I think it probably did give the kids the sense of achieving something, never mind they were all leaving school with no GCSEs at the same time.

'But while the story is a catalogue of what they [ILEA] did wrong and all of that, the schools programme is what kept steel band going in this country, because there's no evidence to show that ordinary Caribbean people are keeping it alive. Not to the scale that, say, Irish families might keep their traditional music going. The actual teaching and the setting up of the bands was done with all good intentions, and because it's so easy for the kids to master, it mushroomed. Today there are over a thousand steel bands in schools in London, and another three thousand in schools up and down the country.'

Once the ILEA had decided steel bands were the way forward, practical involvement started with Gerald Forsythe. A steel pan player and maker who came to London from Trinidad in 1960, he was always very keen to promote his island's culture, and was tasked with setting up a steel band at Islington Green School in north London in 1970. The attendant media coverage and the more or less instant enthusiasm from the kids led to requests from other schools, and Forsythe was appointed the country's first peripatetic steel band teacher. By the end of the decade he had been appointed Steel Band Organiser for the ILEA, and was in charge of hiring teachers and organising the curriculum in the capital. He continued to teach first hand at numerous schools and youth groups, set up festivals and workshops, and was captain of the National School Steel Pan Orchestra. Lionel remembers Forsyth's greatest contribution as being that 'through the steel pan he uncovered and nurtured musical talent that might otherwise not have been noticed, and very often he took it to great heights.'

Russell, who continued to teach and give demonstrations after ILEA got involved, still believes that the steel drum is the perfect instrument for introducing children to music, as it's such a user-friendly item:

'Kids grow up with the formal instruments and that can be intimidating, they look at the piano and think they are going to have to be Mozart or something. But they look at a steel drum with no notes on it or anything, and think "Well I could get in there too." They think anybody could have a bash. Because there are no formalities in it they look at it and think they could have a bit of fun. They feel they could do it and *bash*! Then before they know it, they're playing something that sounds like music, and I think that's a liberating feeling. If you give a kid a violin, then they've got to be really into music and couldn't just jump into it and have a bash.

'Yes, it has some rules, because every instrument needs them, but at the same time it will always have that carefree way about it. It shouldn't end up like the conventional instruments when you are told "Oh, it has to held that particular way". There are a few rules to steel bands, but you don't need to get so bogged down in the rights and wrongs that people get scared of it. Everybody can enjoy it, and I think that's why it appeals to English people in general, because it seems so carefree.'

THESE DAYS IT'S BECAUSE OF THE SCHOOLS programme that the steel pan has most resonance among young people in London. Diana Hancox is a steel pan teacher and Director of the Steel Pan Academy, a Warwickshire-based organisation that's committed to giving access and opportunity to steel pan teaching and learning for all ages, with a focus on schools. Diana backs up Russ's notion that the instrument is especially child-friendly. Steel pan is so popular in primary schools that some schools in which the Academy teaches have as many as a dozen different steel bands. The number of young pan players continues to grow steadily, although the recession is starting to affect things:

'Sadly, the children on free school meals that used to get free music lessons are no longer funded to do so. The

Ever since Aldermaston in the 1960s, protest marches have involved steel bands. Here, Nostalgia continue the tradition at the TUC's 2012 anti-spending cuts protest.

Academy tries to allow a few students to have free lessons but as we get no government funding, this is limited.

'We often do class workshops in schools that don't even have pans, because it greatly increases their musical understanding which makes it easier for them to learn. Because the pans play different parts, and playing pan involves playing in a group, their understanding of timing, how music fits together, and so on, increases. And because early pan is taught without standard notation, we also access those pupils that might struggle with other instruments.

'I would, of course, like to see steel bands in every school, with increased access for all pupils. The Academy has managed to get a number of pupils onto music scholarships with their pans, but I would like to see more development on grades for pan in this country – not for all pupils, but for those that wish to take pan to university level. But the standard of teaching has to be there – not all pan players are teachers, and I have had to take over some pretty poor teaching at times. And not all music teachers understand pan, and again I have gone into schools where pan is so wrongly taught by music teachers who use them as xylophones. A respect for the instrument and its value is needed, but also an understanding that teaching itself is a skill, and just being able to play an instrument at a high level is not enough to teach and motivate our pupils.'

TOGETHER WITH INVITED PLAYERS including Diana, Nostalgia marched in the opening ceremony of the London Olympics, in a section representing Commonwealth immigration. Lionel sums up the current state of play:

'As an orchestra we play a lot of festivals around Europe, particularly in Switzerland where they love the steel pan. Over here there seems to be a revival lately for single or two- or three-piece pan-round-the-neck players at weddings or garden parties or corporate functions. That goes up quite a bit in summer. Recruitment for the band, and others like us, usually comes about through people who see us at gigs, remember playing a bit of pan at school, and would like to start again.

'That's why taking part in the London Olympics Opening Ceremony was so important to us. Of course the atmosphere was electric, and for the fifty steel pan musicians who took part in this historic event, the memories will remain with them for decades to come, but it was great to have the steel pan taken seriously in the UK, and being projected on a world stage like that as coming from the UK as well as the Caribbean. That's the sort of thing that will attract people to the instrument when they see it as a part of something that historic, and we'll always sort anybody out with a drum if they want to come down and have a try.'

Most noticeable, though, is the effect London steel pan playing is having in Trinidad, home of the art form. Dudley Dickson, acknowledged to be the best pan tuner in the world, is a Grenadian who developed his craft and learned all he knows in London, then took it to Trinidad and the US where the demand is greatest. Because the London pan world is every bit as multi-culti as Nostalgia's band members, it brings in all sorts of outside influences, and the music created in this city is far more eclectic. Nowadays, of course, this gets carried across the Atlantic instantly, as Lionel explains:

'You've just go to look on YouTube and you can look at all the top pan players and study their style or learn their new tunes. So really, everybody's influencing everybody else, and there is no best country in the world any more. But it means others are copying us, and we more than hold our own in London.'

CHAPTER THREE

Sounds of Freedom and Free Jazz

||||||||||||||||||||||||||||||||||||||||||||||||||||||||||||||||||||||||||||||||||||||||||||||||||||

South Africans in exile move modern jazz to progressive rock

SOUTH AFRICAN JAZZ DRUMMER Louis Moholo-Moholo is telling the story of how, in the early 1960s, Blue Notes' pianist Chris McGregor – the white South African son of the headmaster of a Church of Scotland mission school – would blacken his face and venture into the Cape Town townships. Not that McGregor thought such latter-day minstrelsy would fool local residents – it was simply the best way to avoid police attention when getting to his gigs in the black areas.

'When Chris, the only white member of the Blue Notes, would come to the townships to play, he had to wear a hat pulled down low and dark glasses, and put some [*shoe*] polish on his face. South Africa was under heavy manners back then, and bands with black and white players weren't permitted. When I used to play with some white guys in town, I was playing from behind a curtain because we couldn't be on the same stage. I wasn't allowed to play in front of a white audience – even my mother wouldn't be allowed to come in the hall where I was playing.'

Life is far less fraught for Louis these days. The cheerful, laid-back 73-year-old lives comfortably in Cape Town, tours

The Blue Notes circa 1963. Left to right: Nick Moyake, Mongezi Feza, Dudu Pukwana, Chris McGregor, Johnny Dyani and Louis Moholo-Moholo.

internationally, and gigs locally when he fancies it – 'I played the week before last in a small club, with just a duo, I do things like that, otherwise I don't bother, man, just keeping it cool!' He tells me he was listening to a Blue Notes live in Amsterdam album in his car, just before I called him, and as my call was completely out of the blue, we marvel at the sheer spookiness of it all for a good few minutes. He laughs a great deal, and with language peppered with hipster-ism, it's sometimes hard to grasp the brutality of the era he's describing.

After the Afrikaner-rooted National Party was elected to power in 1948, new legislation introduced apartheid as official government policy. Racial segregation was nothing new in South Africa, but for it to be enshrined in law for the first time introduced new levels of oppression. Over a decade later, it would affect how Louis was able to ply his trade, as the inclusion of McGregor as the sole Caucasian alongside Louis Moholo-Moholo, Dudu Pukwana (alto sax), Nikele Moyake (tenor sax), Johnny Dyani (bass) and Mongezi Feza (trumpet), meant that the Blue Notes were a multi-racial sextet, and therefore illegal on several counts. In a particularly vindictive piece of harassment that outlawed quartets or bigger groups, no more than three black musicians were allowed to play together, on the pretext of precluding anti-government conspiracies. Further legislation made it illegal for black people to be anywhere liquor was being served, so the police targeted township shebeens and weekend-long yard parties, and dancehalls were shut down or, in many cases, burned to the ground.

Arbitrary police violence against musicians was commonplace, on the catch-all grounds of sedition. This increased massively during the State of Emergency that followed 1960's Sharpeville Massacre, when the authorities cracked down on black African culture as a means of spiritual repression. The government bracketed jazz alongside South African music as having a political aspect, assuming – mostly correctly – that jazz musicians were supporting and fundraising for such resistance groups as the African National Congress, or its armed wing Umkhonto we Sizwe, founded in 1961 by Nelson Mandela.

In spite of all this, South African jazz thrived and the 1950s were a particularly fertile time, thanks in part, somewhat ironically, to the Group Areas Act of 1950. By designating which ethnic groups could live in which districts of South Africa's cities, the Act triggered a massive upheaval of the population, and created vast slum conurbations where urban and rural black South Africans, and people of widely differing backgrounds, were forced to live close together. The resulting cultural crossflows produced modern yet traditional-sounding South African musics including kwela, marabi and mbaqanga, which combined with the hugely popular influences of Art Blakey, Monk, Miles and John Coltrane. The result was a uniquely African bebop style, epitomised by the Jazz Maniacs, a large band with a mission to orchestrate marabi along the lines of Duke Ellington. Although they didn't last long, they inspired a younger generation of township jazzers that included Abdullah Ibrahim – then still answering to the name of Dollar Brand – and Hugh Masekela, both of whom were in the seminal Jazz Epistles group.

THE BLUE NOTES BEGAN LIFE during the late 1950s, as a bebop outfit with a sideline in danceable township jazz. Later, as these two aspects came together and the group's personal playlists shifted towards the likes of Ornette Coleman, Sun Ra and Cecil Taylor, they started to throw off restrictions. Their style evolved into a pulsating free jazz that acknowledged its township environment with celebratory, dance-oriented modern South African accents. Characterised by an improvisers' lack of restraint, an immediate, infectious joyousness, and a very African singularity, they won a huge following in their homeland. Their music, Louis believes, was so popular because of its inherent political statement:

'It was modern, and it was international and it was African; it was important for people to be able to have that sort of expression.'

South Africa in the 1960s, however, was hardly the most accommodating environment for innovative, culturally aware black jazz players. To grow as artists they were going to have to go abroad. Not surprisingly musicians formed a large part of the South African cultural exodus of the 1950s and 1960s. Which suited the authorities. Artists seldom had problems getting out; then their passports would be cancelled, leaving them unable to return. In 1964, the Blue Notes followed Miriam Makeba and Hugh Masekela and got out. Louis remembers the decision:

'It was impossible for us to work. We had to go away from South Africa to preserve the music – they [*the authorities*] were arresting every development of black people developing something of their own, and we were too restricted. So we left to save the thing, but also to show the world that we are not all really racist ourselves, because there we go playing with a white cat.'

The group accepted an invitation to perform at the Antibes Jazz Festival on the French Riviera in July 1964. They made such an impact on the European jazz scene they spent nine months gigging in France, Switzerland and Scandinavia, before fetching up in London in the spring of 1965 as a quintet, Nikele Moyake having returned to South Africa. Starting on 26 April, they played five nights to great acclaim at Ronnie Scott's club, before opting to make the capital their home. Incidentally, the positive statement that Louis believes was made by their multi-racial line-up was spectacularly misinterpreted in Denmark.

'White people sometimes didn't understand us. When we were in Copenhagen when we played with Chris McGregor, they thought we were some of those people who were like pimps, that we were selling out! They'd say to us "You're not supposed to play with a white cat on the bandstand – you're supposed to be fighting every white person in South Africa!" And it wasn't like that.

'The thing was, Scandinavia was very straight, it was one of the countries that really helped liberate South Africa, and I don't blame them for that reaction. They had heard that every white person in South Africa is evil, so they were not really wrong in how they reacted. The good thing was we were in this position to be asked "Why are you playing with this white man – are you one of the pimps?" So we were able to explain, and in the end it was cool, man.'

IRONICALLY FOR THE BLUE NOTES, it was not unusual for white men to black up before going on stage in London. While many would agree in retrospect that it should have been breaking some sort of law, back then the *Black And White Minstrel Show* was one of the most popular programmes on TV, while the stage version was setting attendance records.

This thoughtless offensiveness from the BBC was a vivid example of how Britain's approach to race relations had shifted in almost two decades since Lord Kitchener's quayside calypso. By the time the Blue Notes arrived, race had become entrenched in London politics as well as London life, and doors that had been thrown open were slamming shut. The Commonwealth Immigration Act of 1962 required prospective immigrants to be in possession of government-issued employment vouchers before they could enter the UK. These vouchers were linked to declining job opportunities with the likes of the NHS or London Transport; the idea was that the closer Britain came to being rebuilt, the fewer vouchers would be issued. Because South Africa quit the Commonwealth in 1961, pre-empting their being kicked out for the National Party's refusal to comply with a ruling that prohibited slavery or segregation, the Blue Notes were not subject to the Act.

Seen as a sop by the Conservative government to the party's recently formed far-right pressure group, the Monday Club, the Act failed to address the 'problem' as it was perceived by sections of London's population. Their worries had less to do with the numbers arriving than with their predecessors not going home. Although it was never explicitly stated, when Clement Attlee's more benevolent Labour government sold the notion of mass immigration to the British public at the end of World War II, the implication was that once these sons and daughters of the Commonwealth had helped to set the Mother Country back on its feet, they'd have the good manners to go home. A kind of lengthy working holiday. When those same arrivals started putting down roots, suddenly Albion was seen as being 'swamped'.

This was the line energetically played out in some parts of the press, which resulted in disturbances like the so-called Notting Hill riots of 1958 assuming a far greater significance than they deserved. Such events were always less a matter of wide-reaching political consequence than of bullying Teddy Boys getting their comeuppance – John Williams's excellent biography of Michael X, *A Life In Black And White*, nails quite how socially parochial those disturbances really were. Notting Hill's treatment of Oswald Mosley, when the former leader of the British Union of Fascists stood for parliament on an anti-immigration ticket a year later, was a more accurate barometer of London opinion. After his supporters stabbed to death a young black man, local people rounded on Mosley to such an extent that he polled fewer than 2,000 votes in Kensington North, and promptly left the country. After first demanding a recount.

ALTHOUGH 1960s LONDON WAS NOT EXACTLY a happy-clappy melting pot, for the Blue Notes it bore no comparison to the state-sponsored subjugation they had left behind. Hazel Miller, co-founder of the Ogun Records label, which is dedicated to the London improvised jazz scene of the 1970s with an emphasis on the South African contribution, describes the Blue Notes' sense of relief as they settled in London. Hazel is the widow of the white South African bassist Harry Miller, who arrived in London in 1961 and became established as part of the city's modern jazz scene:

'Back then, it was always a battle because there was still all the prejudice around and that made it difficult for them – and for Harry, because he would hang out with them and go to rehearsals. There were little enclaves of prejudice around the place that could be quite dangerous. I remember in Stockwell there was a team who would cause trouble, and there was, of course, Notting Hill... I can't remember the name of it, but there was a tailor over there with a rehearsal studio underneath it that everybody used, and sometimes that could be a problem.

'The South Africans had such a different approach, as they had come from a country that *really* knew how to push you down with apartheid. So they could cope with it! Their attitude was, they were musicians and that was it. To them it was so much freer – they didn't have to think about all being on stage together with Chris... or even sitting on the same seat together... or getting on the bus together. People

97

might not realise how much apartheid stopped them getting on with what they were born to do, so when they came here the prejudice in London didn't affect them in the same way.'

London was actually fairly welcoming to the Blue Notes, as they weren't an entirely alien concept. They might have been the first South African jazz band to set up in the capital, but African musicians had been here for a while, as had South African entertainment.

IT MIGHT NOT HAVE MADE IT ONTO Pathé News, but to anyone who was there, one of the most memorable aspects of the 1945 VE Day celebrations in Trafalgar Square was a troupe of half a dozen African musicians, kitted out in colourful traditional dress, playing drums and guitars, dancing, singing and chanting in Yoruba. Such was the spirit of the day, and the sheer infectiousness of the band's joyful noise, that pretty soon they'd gathered their own crowd and were leading an excited Cockney conga line around the square, up Haymarket and into Piccadilly Circus.

At their head was Ambrose Campbell (Yoruba name, Oladipupo Adekoya), a young Nigerian former seaman who had jumped ship in London in 1940 as he felt the wartime trans-Atlantic convoys were too dangerous. The others were a mixture of students, sailors and musicians, who would while away the blackouts making music in Campbell's St Pancras flat. They went down to the West End VE Day celebrations because, as Campbell told an interviewer years later:

'We'd lived through the Blitz, so we figured that made us as English as everybody else, so we went down to celebrate. People didn't know what was going on with us, but they joined in. I suppose it was curiosity. Everybody had been waiting for that day, so they were jumping around and dancing. We had a huge crowd following us around Piccadilly Circus. You could hardly move.'

Ironically, the one newspaper that reported their presence didn't even realise they were African, and wrote of a 'small group of West Indians' leading the dancing. It's interesting to see that assumptions that any black Londoners making music must be West Indian were in place even pre-*Windrush*. Not that this gave Ambrose Campbell any problems; after that enthusiastically received public performance, he formalised the players into the West African Rhythm Brothers, thereby creating the capital's first black group made up of resident Londoners, and one that was to have significant influence and impact.

The next year, the Rhythm Brothers provided the music for the UK's first black professional dance company, Les Ballets Nègres, and proved instrumental in its attaining international

success. The company was set up in London by two immigrant Jamaican dancers, Richie Riley and Berto Pasuka, who sought to take advantage of the enthusiasm for colonial culture among the capital's intelligentsia, and challenge conventional preconceptions of black dance. This was perfectly illustrated by the twin facts that Riley had been classically trained – at Serafina Astafieva's academy on King's Road, Chelsea, where Dame Margot Fonteyn had been a pupil – while Pasuka met Campbell when both were working on a particularly terrible British film, called *Witch Doctor*, which portrayed Africans as savages. The two Jamaicans brought a dynamism and sense of adventure to classical ballet, choreographing traditional Caribbean songs and folk tales, and building the productions around the Nigerian drumming of Ambrose's group. For years, in London and as well as on European tours, Les Ballets Nègres was hugely popular.

AT MUCH THE SAME TIME, Campbell expanded the West African Rhythm Brothers to include two Barbadian brass players. It became the house band at the *Abalabai Club*, owned and operated by the Nigerian Ola Dosunmu and his Yorkshire wife, Irene, in a basement in Maidenhead Passage just off Berwick Street Market. Thanks largely to Campbell's music, the club quickly became one of the hippest establishments in Soho. The band played a style they'd developed in London, which while distinctly African was like nothing you'd ever hear on that continent. Atop a rhythmic basis of Nigerian Yoruba juju – the group included several traditional drummers – it overlaid the melodic structures of *maringa* or

Europe's first all-black ballet company, Les Ballets Nègres, was founded in London in 1946 by two Jamaicans inspired by Marcus Garvey's self-help doctrine.

palm wine, a guitar-based urban sound from Ghana, Nigeria and Sierra Leone. Add to that jazz influences from the Caribbean and Soho, plus vocal ideas from those first cousins mento, calypso and highlife, and other jazzmen were fascinated: Ronnie Scott, Kenny Graham, Johnny Dankworth and Tubby Hayes were all fans. The club's bohemian set included *Absolute Beginners* author Colin MacInnes, who became such good friends with Campbell that a sketch of the musician, barely disguised under the name 'Cranium Cuthbertson', features in his novel *City Of Spades*. Macinnes also became godfather to one of Campbell's children. When the Dosunmus relocated to Wardour Street and the somewhat swankier *Club Afrique*, Campbell went along too. He stayed there until the late 1960s, alternating with a band called the Starlite Tempos, run by former West African Rhythm Brother Brewster Hughes.

The most remarkable thing about the Rhythm Brothers was that before the addition of the two Bajans, only one of them was a professional musician with any sort of training. The others were a teacher, students and, like their bandleader, sailors; guitarist Ambrose only took lessons on the instrument in the 1950s, when the great Trinidadian player Lauderic Caton taught him as a favour to a friend. Listening to his work on the Honest Jon's album *London Is The Place For Me Volume 3*, though, you'd never guess it.

THROUGHOUT THE 1950S AND 1960S, a large number of African musicians were operating in London. Most came for relatively short periods, like a couple of years, and never really considered themselves as living in the city. They also tended to travel to and from their home countries far more frequently than West Indians. African musicians played on London jazz, calypso and big-band sessions, indulging in all sorts of cultural intercourse, and coming together as solely African units to service the university and national association dances or to record, as detailed in the next chapter.

Although there were very few South Africans of any stripe among these musicians, the country's culture still found its way into the British mainstream. In 1961, the South African jazz musical *King Kong*, billed as 'the first all-African Opera', opened to rave reviews at the Prince's Theatre (now the Shaftesbury Theatre) on Shaftesbury Avenue. The drama told the tragic story of township-raised heavyweight boxing legend Ezekiel 'King Kong' Dlamini. When it had premiered in South Africa in 1959, it featured an all-black cast starring Miriam Makeba and a jazz orchestra that included Hugh Masekela, Kippie Moeketsie and the Manhattan Brothers vocal group. Loaded with social and political subtexts, *King Kong* played to wildly enthusiastic audiences in London's West End for the best part of a year, before departing to New York. Part of the show's legacy to the capital was the Velvlettes, a quartet of girl singers from the cast who stayed behind to work on London's R&B scene, and will be best remembered as looking fabulous as they sang "Got My Mojo Working" behind Cyril Davies on *Hullabaloo*.

Even before *King Kong*, there had been a flurry of kwela-inspired activity among London's major record labels, after the South Africa-set 1958 British TV series *The Killing Stones* took the penny-whistle kwela recording of "Tom Hark" by township favourites Elias & His Zig Zag Jive Flutes as its title song. The tune proved almost as popular as the six Wolf Mankowitz-penned plays. Released as a single by Columbia, it stayed on the UK charts for three months, peaking at number two. Thus encouraged, Columbia released more music by the group and by Black Mambazo, while Decca, HMV and Oriole sent scouts into the townships to come back with kwela to put out in the UK. None of it gained any traction, though, and the success of "Tom Hark" may have had more to do with the song than the style: it has since been covered by artists as diverse as Millie Small, Ted Heath (the bandleader, not the former prime minister), Ramsey Lewis and Georgie Fame, with ska punks the Piranhas having the biggest seller in 1980. To this day, versions of the tune can be heard at practically every English football ground.

Hugh Masekela and Abdullah Ibrahim having opted for the US, London's modern jazzers included almost no African equivalents of the Caribbeans who had made big splashes on the Soho scene, like Joe Harriott, Dizzy Reece and Harry Beckett. Hazel remembers her Harry as being 'over the moon when the Blue Notes arrived – at last here were some chums from South Africa and they linked up to become part of the family.' As well as the Millers, London's large, politically motivated, multi-racial, South-Africans-in-exile community provided a welcoming environment for the Blue Notes.

Somewhat paradoxically, although everyday London life for black people in 1965 could often be testing, white people in general displayed a strong opposition to South Africa's segregated regime. Increasing numbers of British migrants to South Africa had returned during the 1950s, in the wake of the election of the National Party. In 1959, the Boycott Movement was founded in London, urging ordinary people not to buy goods imported from South Africa and corporations not to do business in or with the country. Following the Sharpeville Massacre, Boycott renamed itself the Anti-Apartheid Movement in 1961, ramping up its activities to include political campaigning and agitation. The Labour and Liberal parties, the TUC, the National Union of Students and numerous high-profile celebrities, academics and clerics were signed up to the AAM, which also formed a partnership with the United Nations. AAM's mission was to keep South Africa on the international political agenda; they were responsible for the pressure that forced the country out of the Commonwealth, and in 1970 they successfully campaigned to have South Africa barred from the Olympics.

Such established London-based activism ensured a warm embrace for black South African arts, as a genuine expression of the country's people and to raise awareness of their struggle. The primary reasons the Blue Notes chose London was that Copenhagen and Zurich were too cold, while in Britain there would be no language issue, and, thanks to their cancelled passports, they were effectively in exile and could settle here as refugees. The group were, according to Hazel:

Mongezi Feza (left) and Dudu Pukwana in action, prior to their leaving
South Africa in 1964.

'Musicians first, but *of course* they were politicised...
they were brought up in it and they were intelligent men.
They might not have been involved once they left, but they
were very political people. They supported the ANC and did
concerts to raise money for the ANC in exile.'

Accordingly, agents of BOSS (South Africa's feared secret
police, the Bureau Of State Security) would show up at
Blue Notes gigs, because the radical black South African
intellectual Pallo Jordan was living in London and was a fan.
The future ANC minister would get up on stage at gigs, and
to huge applause point out his shadow to the crowd, with
a cheery 'Hey, there he is! Look, over there. Watch what
you say around him!' The band's performances were never
intimidated by such an ominous presence; their attitude was,

Hazel says, 'Sod them, we're in London, and they can't touch us here.'

The band's line-up and their jazz music was seen as a metaphor for a modern post-racial, multi-culti South Africa. Many of the radical South Africans in London would have been in the group's audiences back home, and almost immediately they became the house band of the AAM and South Africans in exile. All they had to do was to find a way into the London contemporary jazz scene, which had a few worries of its own.

'THE BLUE NOTES ARRIVED AT A TIME when things were at a pretty low level as far as modern jazz in London was concerned', reckons Mike Westbrook. A pianist and composer who played regularly with all the Blue Notes in various incarnations, he was a major mover in the development of beyond-bebop British jazz. Today, he is up from his home in the West Country, and happy to pour coffee for us in the Chelsea Arts Club and talk about those times.

During the 1950s, London's jazz scene was in rude health. A post-war trad-jazz revival saw players like Chris Barber and Ken Colyer exploring the music's New Orleans roots ("trad' = traditional) so successfully that the style produced its own pop stars. Barber, Kenny Ball and Acker Bilk featured in the pop charts alongside Adam Faith and Cliff. On the other side, modern jazz was establishing itself following the enthusiastic take-up for bebop after the war as an alternative to what many referred to as the 'tyranny of the dance bands'. Also known as progressive jazz, it had a big following in London, not only in the Soho clubs but in a circuit of suburban pubs that included the *Bull* in Barnes, the *Green Man* in Blackheath, the *Hop Bine* in Wembley and the *Railway Hotel* in West Hampstead. Modern jazz had become the soundtrack to the global modernisation of the time, which encompassed art, architecture, writing, product design, mass consumerism and societal thinking. However, as Mike explains, none of that lasted long into the next decade:

'When I first came up from Plymouth [*1962*] and formed a band, it was a period when there was quite a big audience in the pubs and clubs for jazz. The New Orleans revival in London was a very genuine thing, a serious art form that developed, and I had a lot of time for it. So that was going on, and the commercial thing came later when other people jumped on the bandwagon and starting playing trad. Also there were plenty of places that had modern jazz rather than trad – pubs, and clubs like the *Flamingo*.

'There was a big audience for jazz, then suddenly – it seemed like almost overnight – it stopped. I think things went wrong politically, after the modernisation of the world when consumerism, the mass-market approach and all those things took over. In the clubs that had been hosting jazz, R&B sort of took over, as venues were finding out they could get bigger audiences and generate more excitement if they started putting it on. The *Marquee* had jazz seven nights a week, and there was this guy called Alexis Korner who started a blues band – Mick Jagger, Eric Clapton and people like that came up through his band – and he started something down there on a Wednesday night, and, of course, it became far more popular than the jazz. So it gradually started increasing, and in the end the only jazz remaining was Joe Harriott on a Sunday night, then even that went. A lot of musicians changed to playing R&B – Graham Bond was a very promising young saxophone player playing in modern jazz bands, then he went on the organ and started singing rock'n'roll. It's ironic, because the New Orleans jazz revival used to include a twist of blues too, because American blues artists used to come over and perform *with* a lot of the New Orleans jazz players.

'With modern jazz, I think the playing got a bit stale, and in a way was just going through the motions. That was what I thought was happening in the English *version* of modern jazz that somehow became rather uninteresting, as there was no real communication with the audience by the musicians. There'd be the usual themes and solos all round the band and stuff like this, and it was just the same-same formula all the time. It was getting a bit dull.'

Or at least it was, until the Blue Notes set themselves up in London to blow a blast of fresh air across the scene. They played a fairly pure hard-driving bop with a verve and spontaneity that bordered on abandon, clearly enjoying themselves on stage, shouting to each other, cracking jokes – both verbal and musical – and sweeping their audience along with them. Eminent music writer Chris Welch, who then covered jazz for *Melody Maker*, was moved to describe how the quintet:

'Surprised *Ronnie Scott* club regulars with a tough, exciting hard bop. *Surprised* because excitement is not an everyday occurrence in British jazz. This scene can do with a bit of shaking up … The Blue Notes actually aroused the audience from their usual coma.'

The remarkable thing was that the Blue Notes themselves greatly appreciated the overall musical revolution that was happening in London during the second half of the 1960s, and saw the new rock groups as inspirational. Especially for a drummer:

'By the time we reached London, London was a Mecca for music, man, everybody was there, even the Rolling Stones, the pop cats were playing some drums, man! Speaking from a drummer's point of view the pop guys were playing their arses off! Ginger Baker, Keith Moon and Charlie Watts and shit, they were really kicking arse. Robert Wyatt … All around you were people who just wanted to play music.'

Powered by Louis's ferocious drumming, Johnny Dyani's agile bass created the platform for furious exchanges of ideas between Dudu Pukwana and Mongezi Feza (tenor sax and trumpet, respectively), while Chris McGregor marshalled proceedings from the piano. Unlike what they might have played back home, this was, Mike reckons, totally township-free:

'At first they were playing very internationally recognised bop – broadly, we all were at that time – very much the suits and with an impeccable American feel about it. Hard bop music. But straight away they created a theme that was on the edge of going into a freer sort of thing. My first impression of them was very modern jazz.'

But the Blue Notes had open minds, and a commitment to experimentation and free playing that had been honed by their time in Europe. Their live performances usually walked round the edge of mayhem, without ever tipping over to become impenetrable. Hazel doesn't believe they could have done it any other way:

'They were amazing people, each of them a larger-than-life character, and when they got here they just steamed in feet first. Some people said they were wild – and they were borderline wild. They were free spirits, and very intuitive as musicians, so I suppose some of what they were letting loose in London comes from being brought up in an oppressive regime, and once they had the freedom to play they just played. There was always a constructive thing in it, it was never just noise. They were too good musicians for it to be anything like that.

The Blue Notes in the late 1960s; Chris McGregor channels his inner Gandalf as Johnny Dyani keeps time.

'They joined in with the scene they found in Europe. They brought energy and a vitality to things, which brought more out of other people. Harry used to say to me there were loads of gigs where he and Louis and perhaps Chris were backing somebody else, or they had a different front line, and he'd say "We really burned their arses tonight". They were such a powerhouse they'd push people on.'

THE BLUE NOTES MADE SUCH an impact, and the music press loved them so much, that all sorts of stories keep cropping up as to their being resented by the London jazz establishment, or the group being given the cold shoulder by a combination of jealousy and racism – there weren't any black British jazz players at this time. Mike happily debunks such myths:

'A lot of stuff has come to light about the fifties and the terrible discrimination that was the case in London. *However* I don't think that extended to the jazz scene … but it becomes convenient. You can read certain accounts where people see Joe Harriott as a martyr to racism, where I'll kind of question that – the guy was a very successful musician and then there just wasn't a lot of scope for modern jazz, he had health problems and he was an unhappy guy. I don't think *racism* was the reason, but there's a lot of people who would like to say, or give the impression that all the problems were that.

'You have to remember that if you were to embrace a counter culture like modern jazz or whatever, you're joining a whole thing that is nothing to do with race. At that it's just that you're *all* a kind of underclass. And that's where we all still are, really, struggling to make the society better, but of course there are terribly entrenched forces at work here, that are probably still there.

'In the true jazz world, so much of it is to do with "Can you play, or not?", and the Blue Notes could certainly play. Jazz is largely a very honest world because you can't get away with posing and pretending, you've got to be able to back it up and deliver whatever it is you've got to do. And you've got to satisfy your peers even before the public gets to hear you. You only have to look at how those guys fitted in – there was a bit of a musical community there, and certainly they immediately became part of it.'

Hazel, who had more opportunity to stand back and observe than Mike, is more equivocal, but still adamant there weren't any major issues:

'I think some musicians might have resented them – a few people I can think of, maybe, but I wouldn't like to say that we experienced that. It wasn't a general thing, just a couple of odd people and that was their problem, not ours.

'Yes, they shook some people up, but almost everybody embraced that because jazz thinking is always changing, continually, that's the beauty of it. It's not set in little categories, that's the media and the record companies that do that. Jazz was all a sort of learning curve and a development... it's like a painter, he does a painting one day and "Ooh, that's not so good", tries again the next day and he's on a buzz and it's "*Woah*! Look at that". It's the same thing with creative music. Jazz is embryonic, it's continually developing in different directions, and the Blue Notes just pointed out another one. Most people [*on that scene*] saw that.'

Louis laughs when I suggest there might have been an element of resentment within London's jazz community:

'*We-e-e-ll*, we were likeable people sometimes and luck had something to do with it, man. We fell in love with the people in London too. We were very much accepted in England, wherever we went, not spoiled like the Beatles or anything like that, but accepted. We were just cool cats, man, likeable people, and our music spoke for us: Mongezi Feza was *amazing*, man, Dudu Pukwana *fantastic*, there you go, Johnny Dyani our baby was ridiculous, you know. We were blessed, and it wasn't easy, it was what we did, and we worked very hard to be in that position to be liked.

'Somehow we came at the right time too, and that helped. There was acceptance of whatever we did, you know, sometimes we were trying out things and they worked, sometimes they didn't but they were accepted. England was

England too, there was a buzz about it too. That helped a lot. And for the first time too we were free, away from apartheid, expressing ourselves, we were having a good time. Away from the chains! People would say to us "What? Apartheid? Jesus Christ you come from there?" And they're shocked, but we're in the United Kingdom, we're having a good time, man! We could express ourselves and we liked the people and the people like us. It was how we were.'

Louis is quite correct about their timing. Yes, the Blue Notes injected vivacity into a torpid situation, but up until then London's modern jazz was suffering, and the scene couldn't progress because it had nowhere to go. Quite literally.

'The time at which the Blue Notes arrived in London was the time that a lot of people like us, young guys, were coming up with new ideas. They fitted right into that attitude, and we might have been able to change things, but because of the change to R&B we struggled to find places to play. We'd trek around town to do half-hour spots in these clubs for five pounds for the whole band. In a sense we were all in this same boat. Fortunately, the *Old Place* opened and we could restart the scene.'

The *Old Place* was Ronnie Scott's original club, located in the basement of 39 Gerrard Street in what is now Soho's Chinatown, where the Blue Notes made their London debut. In December of 1965, Scott opened his relatively swanky (for a jazz club) and soon-to-be iconic new premises, a couple of hundred yards away in Frith Street, but as the Gerrard Street lease still had a couple of years to run, the saxophonist kept it on. He dedicated it for use by experimental and up-and-coming jazzers, and it became a place where freer-thinking souls could jam and explore ideas without the inconvenience of having to pander to an audience in order to make money. As dangerously indulgent as that might sound, it became absolutely vital to the much-needed development of modern jazz in London, and was at the core of how the South African quintet came to influence more than just that single genre.

THE OLD PLACE WOULD BE SOMETHING of a shock for anybody familiar with the second incarnation of Ronnie Scott's club. Down steep stairs, with the ticket office handily situated on a turn, the tiny cellar club was, Mike reckons:

'Like a nightclub in miniature. A very small bar, a kind of sandwich place, down the left-hand side; loads of seats and tiny little tables; and a stage that was no bigger than five or six metres across – I don't remember a grand piano on it, I think it was just an upright, but we'd still get a ten-piece band playing on it. It was very intimate, I wouldn't think the capacity was more than a hundred people, a hundred and fifty at most. There was a band room at the back that was like a cave – no windows, totally airless and, of course, thick with smoke.'

During the six years since Scott opened the club in 1959, it had as London's premiere jazz spot hosted such stars as Dexter Gordon, Sonny Rollins, Roland Kirk and Lee Konitz (both Scott and his partner in the club,

Ronnie Scott's
OLD PLACE
39 Gerrard Street. W 1   GER 0217

Nightly (except Sunday) 8-11.30
Thursday March 9th
        CHRIS PYNE SEXTET
Friday. March 10th
        FAT JOHN FIVE
Sat . March 11th, 8.30 p.m -7.30 a m
        ALL-NIGHTER
        STAN TRACEY QUARTET
        BOB STUCKEY QUARTET
        BENNY GOODMAN TRIO
        members 7/6   Guests 10
Monday, March 13th
        MIKE WESTBROOK BAND
Tuesday, March 14th
        CHRIS McGREGOR GROUP
Wednesday, March 15th
        STAN TRACEY QUARTET
        Licensed bar and snacks
        Members 5/-   Guests 7/6

Pete King, were saxophonists!). Now, as an incubator for the capital's free jazz movement, it was perfect. So exciting was the vibe, indeed, that many of the big-name Americans booked in the new *Ronnie Scott's* made sure to find the time to jam at the *Old Place*, usually unannounced.

As the other significant free jazz venue – the *Little Theatre Club*, on the top floor of a building in Garrick Yard, off St Martin's Lane – was an actual theatre, albeit a very small one, the music could only kick off after each evening's performance had finished. Sessions ran from midnight until three in the morning, and musicians frequently had to position themselves amid whatever scenery was being used.

Nobody seemed to mind; if anything, audiences appreciated free jazz coming from a living room, a forest, or even a court room. This club was set up by drummer John Stevens – one of life's organisers, according to Mike – primarily to develop group improvisation with his Spontaneous Music Ensemble, as an alternative to his day job as a bebop musician. During the 1970s and 1980s, incidentally, John's son Richie Stevens became one of London's most sought-after session drummers, particularly in the reggae world. He was a mainstay of the lovers' rock scene, detailed in chapter six.

Although Blue Notes Johnny Dyani and Mongezi Feza featured frequently in Stevens' SME, the South Africans had their greatest impact at the *Old Place*. Chris McGregor's Blue Note-ish groups were the Friday-night house band, while Mike's band did Saturdays; Louis played in both for a while. In the beginning, everybody played hard bop, with leanings toward the free. The audiences were pretty good, and everybody got paid a fiver – Scott reckoned he used to lose between £100 and £150 per week on the *Old Place*. Mike claims this generosity had a seminal effect:

'There was a real change in the jazz scene after that, because in order to get a hearing young musicians didn't have to do all that business with the dance bands that Ronnie's generation had done. You know, work your way up and hope to get a break. People were able to come in and start playing straight away, creating music.'

Louis is still excited to remember how this scene contrasted with the European jazz world of which the Blue Notes had been a part, immediately before coming to London.

'Before we came to England we came to the continent, and the Coltrane thing was happening a lot, man. It was just Coltrane Coltrane Coltrane Coltrane, and people looking to imitate people. We came to England and *bang*, there you go, even the pop guys are playing their arses off! There were some fucking good drums on the pop scene! Yeah, man! Then there were people like Keith Tippett and John Stevens, who embraced us and we embraced them, we taught each other... Kenny Wheeler, oh man, it was fantastic. England

Dudu Pukwana in the 1970s.

was kicking arse, man, cats like John Surnam and them, wow! Mike Osborne, you know what I mean? Everything was just laid out … Tubby Hayes, Phil Seamen, Jesus Christ, man!

'In a way, England was leading the way. That scene brought a lot of guys from the States, these so-called masters like Sonny Rollins and them, to play at *Ronnie Scott's*. There was a phenomenal music happening then, man. Stan Tracy, fucking hell, man! Tubby Hayes and Ronnie Scott … *Yeah*! Ronnie Scott was kicking arse, man, we even had the privilege of playing with him in the Brotherhood Of Breath, he just came in and played with us on the continent.'

Chris McGregor of the Blue Notes became fundamental in creating the music Mike describes. Although the *Old Place* offered McGregor the chance to perform new music in front of appreciative crowds, in assorted different-sized groups – 'Chris McGregor Nights' were regular occurrences – it was after hours that things really moved forward. John Jack, the venue's manager, would allow Chris or Mike to stay as long as they liked after the punters had gone home, to experiment and write, either by themselves or with other musicians. Jack would often stay and make the coffee, but if not he'd either leave the keys or lock them in until he came back about midday the next day.

As 1966 progressed, the Blue Notes were pretty much over as a bop outfit, while in demand individually to work with other groups both here and abroad. It was when they came back together at the *Old Place* as the Chris McGregor Group that they began seriously to explore a free jazz direction. Chris and Dudu Pukwana, the two who had always shown the strongest African manifestations, in composing and playing respectively, spent the most time working in London during this period. Now, with Chris leaning increasingly towards a ten- or twelve-piece sound – the Chris McGregor Big Band was an *Old Place* regular – his improvisational approach was building on obviously African influences. His work recalled the big band that he'd formed in South Africa before he left, known as the Castle Lager Big Band after the huge brewery-sponsored jazz festival in Soweto's Orlando Stadium at which it performed. That was a Blue Notes side project that featured Dudu and Mongezi Feza, and one critic described their integration of American and African music as 'a very powerful and expressive thing'. It came as no surprise to Hazel, whose husband Harry frequently gigged with Chris, that he was moving back in this direction:

'Chris was a big-band man. Always was. Even in his solo stuff that came through. I'm about to put out a solo album he did in 1977, and you can hear it's definitely a big-band man playing that piano – you can hear all the parts coming in. They were playing jazz as the rest of Europe expected it when they first got here, but as jazz musicians they were interested in improvisation – that's what jazz is, and in the sixties the improvisation scene here was *magnificent*, it was so *fertile*. You could honestly say that the guys here, Evan Parker, Derek Bailey, John Stevens, were leading the world. And the South Africans appreciated this musical freedom, and they were in there.

'They listened, they could hear it and *boom*... and they adapted it with their music. Underneath the jazz, their music was different, they had a different approach, it was almost like listening to somebody talking, because their language was very musical. If you listen to a band of South Africans who are talking Xhosa or even Zulu – the Miriam Makeba thing of the "Click Song"... the click thing, it's a rhythm, it's all in the language. It was a different area, from the idiom that was coming in from America, and the South Africans bringing a flavour of Africa was what everybody loved. That was what gave them the edge, which was why they had such a big influence.'

EVEN THOUGH CHRIS WAS THE WHITE member of the Blue Notes, his immersion in African music was as complete as any of his fellow band members, and it had long been his mission to bring together the black musics of America and his part of Africa in the same style. The same went for the others, who saw free jazz in London as a chance to explore African backgrounds that were such an intrinsic part of who they were, that they had never really thought about them before. Freed from the constraints of established styles, much of the music had a basis in South African folk songs, presented as sax-heavy big-band jazz, with plenty of scope for solo-ing and improvisation. Although always as surprising and as serrated as the best free jazz, the strong underlying lyricism from the folk music made it easy for the less committed audience members to follow – there was always a generous sprinkling of tourists and students in the crowds at the *Old Place*.

The band attracted young British players like Mike Osborne, John Surman and Malcolm Griffiths, around a South African core of Chris, Dudu and Mongezi, and frequently saxophonist Ronnie Beer and Harry Miller on bass. They exerted considerable influence on the London improvisation scene from the point of view of *how* they did things, rather than what they actually did. Their South African-isms demonstrated that America was not the only jazz touchstone, and that free jazz didn't have to suffer if it wasn't so intuitive as to exclude other players as well as the audience. John Stevens' basic rule was that there's no point playing in a group, if you're not playing as part of that group.

Mike often sat in with the South Africans, and he recalls how the band's methods impacted a modern jazz scene that was far too sure of itself to simply copy somebody else's style:

'Personally, I don't think I was particularly influenced musically. They had a different way of doing things because they were very fortunate to have that kind of folk culture to draw back on. I don't have it – there *isn't* an English folk tradition, or if there is, you'd have to work hard to find it, because any folk culture in England has been buried! The South African guys did have very strong musical traditions to draw upon, so when they thought of their homeland it was pretty obvious what they were going to do and take it in their own direction.

'I wanted to be free of copying American jazz and find my own experience, and although they showed how that didn't need to be American, it was going to be modern and *European*, that's my culture, that's what I've got. It was about acknowledging these different influences – I was acknowledging the tremendous influence of people like Ellington – but at the same time it was a different stream. Although things might have overlapped, stylistically, somewhat [*with Chris*], I was on a different path by then. It wasn't a hard and fixed thing, it was always a pretty fluid situation.'

Mike has a theory as to why it took so long for the Blue Notes' South African-ness to come out in their playing, a delay that worked out in the music's favour. By his own admission, there was a degree of disconnect between how the South Africans viewed their lot, and what sympathetic Londoners believed to be the case:

'I've always felt there was a sea change in Chris and his musicians that happened after they'd been in London for a year or so, because it may have been at that point they all began to feel very homesick. They were very, very popular, but I think, and I was never able to discuss it with anybody, they simply missed home. I remember sitting in a car with Louis one day, driving to a gig somewhere, and he started saying how they loved their country. Which was a shock to me, as I assumed, being naive or whatever, that they couldn't wait to get away from South Africa, with its ghastly, terrible regime and everything, but they absolutely loved the country... the bush, getting out in it and everything.

'When Mongezi died [*in London in 1975, of pneumonia*], the most tragic thing was he died completely alone. Nobody was there. Somebody told me that would never have happened in South Africa, everybody knew where everybody was and there was a huge community spirit, and there isn't one in English life. Really, there isn't one. It's nobody's fault, the English are just more divided somehow, I think it's a great pity. They missed that, they missed the countryside and the community thing, and in a way, I suppose, the Brotherhood was an answer to that need. Apart from Louis, who's had innumerable heart problems, they all died very young. Much too young.

'I just wonder if it was that that brought them around to the music they really wanted to play, because they came into

London very much on the hard bop sort of thing, and the sort of South African element, the township element, only asserted itself after a while in the Brotherhood. Of course combining that music with the free improvisation they'd got into was an incredibly potent thing. It was a *wild* band – twenty people or something, all kinds of characters, but the nucleus was the Blue Notes.'

Mike's disclosure that, with the very best intentions, he and others got it wrong about the musicians' feelings toward South Africa, is not unlike the Danish reaction to the Blue Notes. His making it here is testament to his earlier statement about the honesty of the jazz world, and to its generosity, inasmuch as any misconceptions didn't hold the South Africans back. Louis has a far more straightforward explanation as to why so much time passed before the Blue Notes began to explore their African roots:

'It was the time was right, because there were big bands like Osibisa and the black thing was happening, with the black sound, and you couldn't escape that. Also, we were busy at the time with different bands, where you couldn't just go back home [*musically*] because the music was so beautiful, and we wanted to voice it, but the quartet and the quintet weren't big enough. We wanted a trombone in there, to kick it off with, like that, just to play some home things and to make them proper as well. We were like perfectionists and we wanted to kick arse. So we wanted a baritone player and we wanted another alto player and in the end we wanted another one and another one ... [*laughs*] So we had Elton Dean in there and Mike Osborne and Dudu ... can you imagine? And Evan Parker and John Surman, Alan Skidmore ...

'To make the African sounds and to make them modern, we had to have a big band. We used free music players, and we would use a tuba which wasn't popular in South Africa, but because this was a modern sound we could use that. The Brotherhood was something else, man, and I'm really proud to be part of it.'

The 'Brotherhood' he and Mike are talking about is the Brotherhood Of Breath, the big band that happened when

the music for which Chris and the other Blue Notes had been
striving during those *Old Place* lock-ins hit critical mass. A
perfectly balanced blend of free jazz invention and township
swagger, it took jazz into the rock world, and made a lasting
impression on the mainstream.

BROTHERHOOD OF BREATH MADE THEIR DEBUT at the
Notre Dame Theatre in Leicester Square (now the Leicester
Square Theatre), on 27 June 1970. The core of the band was
South Africans Chris, Dudu, Louis and Mongezi, with Harry
Miller on double bass; other players included Harry Beckett,
Evan Parker and Mike Osborne. Among other South African
artists on the bill were jazz singer Peggy Phango (who also
came to London with *King Kong* and stayed) and poet Cos-
mo Pieterse. The gig was well promoted, as the Arts Council
had chipped in some cash – having studiously ignored jazz,
the organisation now acknowledged jazz composers such as
Chris and Mike – and the band played to an almost capacity
crowd, with proceeds going to help developing black musicians in South Africa. It was one of the biggest jazz events in
the capital for years and, according to those who were there,
it was 'Jazz, Jim, but not as we know it.'

Chris McGregor's all-new compositions showcased the
ideas that had been germinating, and revealed a jazz that

connected instantly to its
audience on a celebra-
tory rather than purely
contemplative level. Yet it
didn't compromise on the
Cecil Taylor-ish musical
adventures – Chris always
maintained the piano was
merely a percussion instrument that could carry a
melody. That was a neat
trick to pull off, leaving
people spiritually uplifted

and intellectually stimulated, but made a great deal easier by the South African heartbeat at the centre of it all – jazz that should be taken seriously, but that you could dance to as well. Mike explains:

'After he schooled himself in modern jazz, he was drawn towards finding something that was much more universal and simple – or superficially simple. Certainly in the material he wrote there was always a tune, catchy rhythms and things like that. He seemed to have a single unifying vision that would embrace all kinds of things, but to play it he got lots of free improvisers, so you got both this *rooted* music, but you also got this wild, anarchic improvising going on at the same time.

'I suppose that one is always looking for the grand, simple, meaningful format for your music, your art, and a lot of the time it's hard to find that. It's complicated, and means playing at different levels so it's not always possible to come out with just a simple statement. Sometimes that's not honest if you do that, it's leaving out things, but every now and then I think you find ways, as if you're rediscovering yourself and your art form [*and you come across*] a simple path. In one way, at that time jazz was developing more and more into free improvised music with no rhythm at all, but there were others who were looking for another way, and I think Chris found his with that kind of danceable pulse of Brotherhood Of Breath.'

Music with such clear communication skills meant that the group almost instantly became favourites with the *BBC Jazz Club*, TV stars in Europe, and one of the hardest-working acts both at home and abroad. With a line-up that gently shifted around the Blue Notes core, they played the jazz circuit, regularly filling Oxford Street's *100 Club*, and topping bills in festivals in France, Scandinavia and Holland.

IN BETWEEN BROTHERHOOD GIGS, the South Africans were at the core of London's contemporary jazz world as it imposed itself on Europe. As individuals they played in all manner of small groups, particularly with Elton Dean

(Louis became a member of Just Us), Keith Tippett and John Surman. Johnny recorded with Don Cherry in France, Dudu guested on a Hugh Masekela album in London, and Johnny and Mongenzi cut tracks with Abdullah Ibrahim in Copenhagen. While this maintained their jazz status, the full group's easily accessible excitement endeared them to a wider audience. The mainstream media treated them almost like a rock band – albeit an exotic one. The gig they played at London's Victoria & Albert Museum, in August 1973, at a festival organised by Hazel and Jackie Tracey, Stan's wife, is a good example:

'The weather was perfect, and it was the third day of a festival we had put on in the garden in the centre. The first concert was Steve Lacy, Steve Potts, John Stevens, Ken Carter, a real improvised thing; second was Albert Nicholas and Sandy Brown [*New Orleans style*], so this was jazz as going from one end of the music to another; and the final night was the Brotherhood. Because the V&A do concerts and they have a big mailing list – eight thousand or so – this was a big gig, one of the biggest they would have played in London, and because so many of the audience were on the V&A's list we had people turning up in evening dress. Jackie took one look and said to me 'Oh no, you've got a lot of refunds to do tonight!' I agreed, but these people stayed and came out and saying "What wonderful music, why don't we hear more of it?".'

The Brotherhood's danceable yet out-of-the-ordinary music slotted into the crossover between this generation of jazzers, determined to break with tradition and progressive rock, and the post-beat group sounds with an emphasis on musical virtuoso, improvisation and format-stretching compositions. In the US, Frank Zappa, Captain Beefheart and the Grateful Dead were among the first to bring free jazz and rock together. In 1969, Zappa promoted the *First Paris Music Festival,* which was actually in Belgium, and consisted of five days and nights of music that saw Pink Floyd, Captain Beefheart, Ten Years After, Yes and Fat Mattress share a bill with the Art Ensemble of Chicago, Don Cherry, Pharoah Sanders, Archie Shepp and the Chris McGregor Group.

Louis Moholo-Moholo at Ronnie Scott's Old Place in 1967. Now aged 73, and the sole surviving Blue Note, he still tours and records, but "only the ones I want to do".

In the UK, at that point, many rock musicians had jazz backgrounds. Direct links were provided by the likes of Soft Machine, King Crimson and Ginger Baker's Air Force, while drummers like Bill Bruford (Yes, Genesis and King Crimson) and Carl Palmer (Atomic Rooster, The Crazy World of Arthur

Brown and Emerson, Lake & Palmer) cited such influences as Joe Morello, Philly Joe Jones and Art Blakey.

The London underground scene, of clubs like *UFO* and *The Arts Lab*, and 'happenings' like the '14 Hour Technicolour Dream', welcomed the *avant-garde*. Paul McCartney famously attended an AMM concert at the Royal College of Art (his musical contribution involved tapping a coin on a radiator), and Blue Notes Johnny, Mongezi, Louis and Chris performed at the Natural Music International Avante Garde Concert Workshop in Cambridge in 1969, as did Yoko Ono with John Stevens and Trevor Watts of the SME (John Lennon was a late addition to the bill) and John McLaughlin.

Brotherhood Of Breath's entry into the rock world was all but assured, and not simply because African sounds were becoming fashionable within the new rock world (see the next chapter). The band's first album was produced by American-in-London Joe Boyd, one of the founders of the *UFO* club and producer of Pink Floyd, the Incredible String Band and Eric Clapton. (Boyd also produced the 1968 album *Very Urgent* by the Chris McGregor Group, who were the Blue Notes plus Ronnie Beer.) The Brotherhood shared a management company with assorted English folk-rockers including Nick Drake, John Martyn, Fairport Convention and Sandy Denny. Two Blue Notes side projects, Spear (Dudu, Mongezi, Louis and Harry Miller) and Tower of Power-ish Assagai (Dudu, Mongezi and Louis along with London Nigerians Fred Coker and Bizo Muggikana) went down very well with the rock crowd. Mongezi worked with Elton Dean, Henry Cow and Robert Wyatt; he guested on Wyatt's African-jazz-tinged *Ruth Is Stranger Than Richard* album, one of the highlights of which was a version of the Spear song "Sonia" (from the *In The Townships* album). Louis and Harry Miller , meantime, were part of Mike's *Earthrise* multimedia touring project, while Dudu played with John Martyn, and Chris with Alexis Korner and Nick Drake.

Well known as players, they had a strong following beyond the jazz audience, and while their albums *Chris McGregor's Brotherhood Of Breath* and *Brotherhood* may not have made them household names, they sold respectably, providing an entry point to new jazz. Much of their music's broad appeal, especially live and among a post-hippie crowd, lay in the communal atmosphere fostered on the bandstand by Chris's arrangements and the musicians' spontaneous interaction. The group really was a brotherhood; those arrangements were so generous to all members of the band that they were free to interact and spur each other on without having to covet every second in the spotlight. A happy, welcoming way of working, it brought the best out of everybody and communicated itself to the audience, bringing them in to the proceedings rather than placing them as disconnected observers. Like a musical village. All that comes through in the Brotherhood's recordings, and especially their first album, which remains one of the greatest London jazz albums of all time.

This sense of communality, among not only the twelve or so members of the band but also the people who travelled with them, gave rise to another recurring Blue Note/Brotherhood myth – that they drank far too much, in detriment to themselves as musicians and as men. It's even been linked to their exile in London to conjure up an image of the tortured black jazzmen self-medicating into oblivion, and the group as ill-temperedly falling apart. According to Mike, that wasn't entirely the case:

'Everybody drank too much, nobody's going to deny that, but that was the scene. A lot of the previous generation, just before the modern jazz guys – people like Tubby Hayes – were into a hard drug phase which killed some of them off. On the whole with our sort of generation, and this is a generalisation, it was booze and toke. There was a very strong feeling among the Brotherhood of sharing a joint, and the camaraderie that involved was a very important element of it – it was a huge part of the culture of that scene. There wasn't anything sleazy about it, it was about sharing, and it should be told as it really was.

'Of course some did get into drugs. Mike Osborne who was in my band was also in the Brotherhood; he was somebody who was terrifically committed to the sort of *jazz life*, and he did get into heavy drugs. He went crazy and he died a couple of years ago. That wasn't the norm. People would be fairly pissed like you always were, and after a gig you'd be excited so that was part of having just played a good set. And if there was a joint going... there was always a lot of smoking going on.'

SADLY, BASIC ECONOMICS had little respect either for this ground-breaking music or its big-hearted musicians. It proved impossible to keep an outfit that size as a permanent working entity in the UK, so the players gigged all over the place with other bands. While creatively this was a win-win for contemporary jazz – the groups concerned benefited from the injections of South African innovation, and the guys themselves kept fresh by playing in different environments – commercially it still didn't add up. At the start of the 1970s, with jazz in Britain in steep decline, much of the work for the London-based South Africans was on the continent. There, Hazel believes, the music was treated with far more respect:

'Our big beef was with the media. When I first started Ogun [*1974*] and when I was doing the Brotherhood, we had people like Richard Williams, Val Wilmer and Max Jones at the *Melody Maker* writing about jazz, and we used to get immense coverage. I used to fill the *100 Club* or bigger venues... hundreds of people used to come to Brotherhood gigs because we were getting the press coverage. Then it got ignored in the rock boom that came along, and the press completely wrote it off, because the major companies were focussed on pop music and they've got the clout to pay and buy space. We got left out.

'It was different in Europe, the music was never going to be like pop music but that didn't mean it didn't have a place. It was frequently on television on the arts programmes – still is – and you've got 24-hour jazz stations in France and Germany. Here you were lucky if you got half an hour once a week, and hardly any television. It's no different now if it is television – *they think Jools Holland is a jazz musician*! Pffft! It's unbelievable.

'In Europe, jazz was always accepted as a valid art form. The art institutes in Europe recognised the old Arts Council and the Contemporary Music Network over here, and were very appreciative of what we were trying to do. So the media covered it, and so your audiences are bigger, and so people would promote it more [*put on more/bigger gigs*], and they just love it. Chris and his family moved to the south of France in 1973. He said it was for the weather, as London was too cold, but the environment for jazz was much more encouraging.'

In 1975, thanks largely to action taken by Hazel, the Musicians Union passed a motion to give jazz more support with its media profile and promotions. As she admits, however, 'nothing changed'.

The lack of publicity and promotion may well have contributed to what many saw as the premature end of the jazz/rock coalition. Really, though, the Brotherhood belonged very much to a particular era, which was pretty much over at just the time when ideally they would have been consolidating their impact. Prog rock itself didn't last, while those bands that did survive moved away from the previous, improvising brothers-in-arms camaraderie, as Mike explains:

'We were drawn into that sort of area more as a creative thing than a commercial thing. For us, rock music was a kind of musical metropolis, where we used a big band for the first time, and used a bass guitar as well as double bass, and guitar and keyboard as well as normal jazz horns and such things. It was very complex music but, to underpin it, it needed those simple rhythms, and the bass guitar gave it structure. The Brotherhood were part of that, with their township influences used in the same way as my band and others used rock.

'I suppose what one wound up with was jazz/rock. And for a while there was this sort of fusion of theatre and rock music with improvisation, and it was a very exciting time – we did the *Earthrise* tour. We did some very big gigs, but I don't think any of us were serious about it – it was just a phase, for a while. Especially when we got a record contract – we didn't want to be pop music, nobody on our side of the scene did, the whole thing was about freedom. So to cut a very long story short, all that burned itself out and came to an end in about 1972.'

The continental scene was shifting too. First there was a political period as left-wing municipal authorities supported left-field arts:

'There was this political phase in the mid-seventies, when we played abroad quite often and they were communist festivals, run by the communist city councils – Florence was a big one – that were free to the public as a sort of great Utopian vision of modern art and music. It didn't really happen much over here, although the Communist Party did organise one or two events at the *Roundhouse*. We got on very well with the Henry Cow people and played gigs all over France and stuff. It didn't last long, but there was this feeling of being involved with social change and political awareness.'

Brotherhood Of Breath were part of that circuit, given added star status by their South-Africans-in-exile credentials, but they were never fully politically committed. Although their background was now coming through in the music, they demanded total artistic freedom, and weren't going to compromise that to make any non-musical points. When the final sea-change came, it was that approach that finished them off. Mike explains:

'During the jazz phase, particularly in France, there were loads of jazz festivals that European groups, people like us and the Brotherhood, were playing, and they were less American-dominated for quite a long period. European jazz was doing very well. Then it was very significant that the mood changed, and world music became the thing, and you could see the jazz side of these festivals shrinking then, and there were big concerts by African groups who were big stars by then, them and the Cubans. Brotherhood Of Breath overlapped with that because it had that sort of ethos – and you had the international success of Abdullah Ibrahim and

Miriam Makeba, and other exiled South Africans, very much referring back to their native music.

'That took over as world music, and the Brotherhood basically were too uncompromising to be proactive with it, as it tends to be not really improvised. It's more folksy, really, you don't have this wild Cecil-Taylor-style improvising going on, which is the thing people find difficult. So jazz again had sort of come up, and then retreated into the background.'

Chris McGregor carried on with various incarnations of the Brotherhood, from his base in France, until the end of the 1980s. Good as they were, they never reached the improvisational heights of the original line-up, but they kept the big band's flag flying practically up to his death in 1990.

Today, Louis is the only surviving Blue Note. Improvised jazz does still exist in London – Louis still plays here on a regular basis, while Mike, among other projects, writes, arranges and plays in the Mike Westbrook Big Band, and Hazel's Ogun Records flourishes. However, it's nothing like the vibrant, adventurous scene it used to be, and that it gained the foothold it did is massively down to the five South Africans that made the city their home.

CHAPTER FOUR

West Africa in the West End

||||||||||||||||||||||||||||||||||||||||||||||||||||||||||||||||||||||||||||||||||||||||||||||||||

Mods and Afro-rockers

'WE WERE THE FIRST ALL-BLACK BAND to go on *Top of the Pops*, with "Music For A Gong Gong" in 1971, when our album *Osibisa* was at number seven in the charts.'

Sitting in his comfortable Kingsbury front room, Teddy Osei, founder and leader of Osibisa, thinks back forty years to the impact that the legendary Afro-rock band had on British music:

'That was really sensational, not only for us and also for Africans at that time, but for all blacks at that time in England. At that time, all the bands that got on the BBC were either all-white bands or black and white bands, but this was the first time an all-black band had come on. [*That's band as opposed to vocal group*.] We did *Old Grey Whistle Test* as well, and were the first black band to have a whole show devoted to them.

'One of our things was that, when we got onto *Top of the Pops*, we would be wearing African clothes. We always wore them to play our gigs – even the West Indians in the band – but on television it made such a difference. It let everybody see we were a proud band, proud of the music we played, and after that at our gigs, sure the Africans would turn up wearing African clothes, but among the white people all of those who had ever been to Africa would turn up at our gigs wearing something African. That was wonderful.'

Something more than just a sartorial milestone was being passed. When three Ghanaians, one Nigerian, one Trinidadian, one Grenadian and an Antiguan came together as Osibisa, in a Finsbury Park rehearsal space in 1969, they became the first example of the genuine Londonising of an immigrant music. Here was a band aiming, right from the start, to create a sound that came from an African perspective, but was *of* London, rather than simply being *in* London.

'The idea was to come out with a fusion of original African drums and Western instruments. Of African melodies, and also the jazz and rock and the Caribbean music and other Western music … If something like that was ever going to happen anywhere, it would be in this city, London, because everything it needed could be found here.'

This was a major shift: a genuine local fusion, not merely a palatable version of something exotic. The African clothes serve as a deft illustration. Calypsonians – whether suited and booted, or kitted out in a clichéd Caribbean style – wanted to get to the mainstream. Osibisa, on the other hand, encouraged African dress among their audience – all their audience – and wanted the mainstream to come to them.

Not that West African music was anything new in London. Osibisa were not the first African group to make an impact, or even the first band to mix Africans and Caribbeans. Parallel to the African involvement on the jazz scene, highlife had evolved into a healthy cottage industry. It's just that the front door to this particular cottage wasn't too easy to find.

DURING THE FIRST TWO DECADES after the Second World War, by far the greater proportion of Africans who arrived in London were from Sierra Leone, Nigeria and Ghana. Like Teddy Osei, who came to study music and drama in 1961, on a scholarship from the Ghanaian government, they were here to attend university, with engineering, medicine

Osibisa show off their interesting-looking instrument. Left to right: Mac Tontoh, Dikoto Mandengue, Sol Amarfio, Kofi Ayivor, Teddy Osei.

and accountancy as the most popular subjects. That meant their time in the capital was far more insular than that of their West Indian counterparts. Most were middle- or upper-class, and didn't need to work. They stayed in college halls of residence or student digs, so they had much less social interplay with Londoners or other black immigrants. University courses lasted for a fixed, relatively brief period, which further reduced any imperative to engage with London. The usual plan was to graduate and find a good job back home, preferably with a government, not to settle down in London. On top of that, students who failed their degrees were often not allowed to return home; the prospect of enduring another London winter served to keep the young men and women focussed on their studies.

The wave of independences in anglophone West Africa during that time – Ghana 1957; Nigeria 1960; Sierra Leone 1961 – ensured that nationalistic spirit was running high among young people. Their new self-governed homelands represented every opportunity, *African* opportunity, and made the desire to go back as graduates, and contribute to the building of the nation, paramount. This point was much truer among West Africans than West Indians in London; while the same pride existed among the Caribbean diaspora, many were well aware that independence had only been granted because there was precious little of anything left on their islands, least of all opportunity.

Independence also played a huge part in the musical development of each country, encouraging, as with ska in Jamaica, obviously African expression. Thus highlife, which originated in Ghana at the start of the twentieth century but had been all but ignored by the establishment, came to the fore when musicians began to turn away from western music, and it took hold across Nigeria and Sierra Leone as well.

The social lives of African students in London tended to revolve around what was going on in their universities. Most London colleges had groups like the Ghanaian Student Union or the Nigerian Society, usually backed by the relevant High Commission, to deal with welfare issues, maintain contact with home and organise get-togethers. Social events were strictly African in style, recreating as much back-home atmosphere as possible. As music took on a central role in the psyche of each newly independent nation, it became a major part of African life in London. A coterie of musicians who could play highlife – mixed in with a bit of palm wine or juju, depending on whichever union booked them – came together to service this lucrative circuit. There was a certain irony here, because as the musicians established themselves in London, their music evolved in subtle ways. As a result, what audiences celebrated as the genuine article was not really so, but they took to it keenly anyway, because, perhaps subconsciously, it better reflected their new-found sophistication as part of their essential African-ness.

Teddy's first band, Cat's Paw, formed part of this reassuringly familiar entertainment:

'By the early 1960s, there was enough going on around the universities to mean there was a big highlife scene in London. In the summertime it would move to the town halls – St Pancras Town Hall, Seymour Hall, Porchester Hall, Battersea Town Hall – because many students would stay in on London during the break. African students from other parts of the country would come to London for the summer vacation, too, so it would really build up. Every Saturday, there would be a Ghanaian community dance or Nigerian or Sierra Leone … it was a big scene. And it was all highlife, because all of West Africa was highlife – the only part that wasn't playing highlife was the francophone areas, they were playing a type of music with the cha cha cha. All the English-speaking regions were playing highlife, the only difference was the dialect of the lyrics, which is their own. Nigerians have juju music as well, like Sierra Leone has maringa or palm wine, but they are all very close to highlife, and Ghanaian highlife was the most popular across the whole region.

'It was all live bands on that scene, playing versions of the hits from back home. There were a lot of Nigerian bands, Fela was living and playing music in London at the time, I can't remember most of the groups' names because many of them didn't have names! They weren't professionals, but they would get themselves together for the highlife gigs in the summertime – there was a very good band called Black Star, from Ghana, who were big, they were amateur. There were more professional bands as time went on, because musicians were realising they could make a living from this and the recording scene that started up. I had jobs in hotels, cleaning or washing dishes, or in the Post Office, during the breaks, but I went to the Ghanaian embassy here and talked to them, and they supplied some equipment for us to entertain students. So, come the summertime, we all get something to do and everybody is very happy.

Nigerian Ambrose Campbell, a mainstay of Soho's 1950s jazz community, was among the first to mix African and Caribbean players and styles.

'Because the dances were organised by different unions, there would be more Ghanaians at a Ghanaian Union dance and more Nigerians at a Nigerian Union dance, but enough people go to each other's dances to make it a joyous muddle!'

One interesting consequence of this collegiate mash-up was that because stylistic adjustments were aimed at other Africans rather than a potential wider audience, they could develop instinctively without being subject to the whims of the mainstream. The scene was big enough to support a large and perpetually shifting number of musicians, so there was considerable creative growth in London. But it was pretty much an exclusively live phenomenon, and in order to achieve longevity it needed someone to get it down on wax. Not surprisingly, that someone was Emil Shallit.

FROM THE EARLY 1950s ONWARDS, a large number of African musicians were operating in London. Unlike their West Indian counterparts, they tended to stay for relatively short periods, and to travel to and from their home countries far more frequently. They played on jazz, calypso and big-band sessions, indulging in all sorts of cultural intercourse as well as coming together as solely African bands to service the university dances and national association functions, where they made the most money. They started recording in their own right during the 1950s, when Emil Shallit – already introduced in chapter one of this book, as the King of Calypso – shifted his focus to transform Melodisc into the hub around which London's African recording industry revolved.

As Melodisc had already shipped a great deal of London-recorded calypso to West Africa, Shallit knew how the region's wholesale and retail business worked. Similarly, in London, he knew how to sell records through an off-grid network of black-owned shops and small businesses, and was aware that the capital's immigrant market contained many different demands. He had also seen tastes in anglophone West Africa shift away from European music as it geared up for independence, and figured that new music would be in demand. Above all, he had witnessed the modern, more pan-national kind of African music bubbling up in London, and noticed that people seemed to love it.

Although EMI and Decca dabbled in African music, it was recorded in Africa, primarily for African consumption. The small proportion that received a UK release didn't accurately reflect the scene that was establishing itself in London. Shallit, however, with his keen sense of what was happening around him, was willing to commit to the brand of highlife being played in London. Through his dealings in calypso and jazz, he had the hook-ups to recruit the right players, and the experience to get the best out of them in the studio. For a while, too, he had the field to himself.

Ambrose Campbell and the West African Rhythm Brothers, the core of the Melodisc catalogue, cut the largest number of singles and at least one album, going from the ten-inch 78-rpm era of the early 1950s until late in the next decade. Most of Campbell's tunes were easy-going highlife, given Melodisc's trademark jazz swing with piano, clarinet and brass. As when the company started out with calypso, Denis Preston was involved, and events in the studio reflected was going on live. Highlife, juju, palm wine, merengue, calypso and jazz all got mixed together, and so too did the personnel. Trinidadians Rupert Nurse and Russ Henderson often sat in on African sessions. Sierra Leonean Bliff Radie Byne recorded for the label backed by Ivan Chin & His Rhythm Sextet, a Jamaican mento group who appeared in the Melodisc catalogue in their own right as the Ivan Chin Calypso Sextet (calypso being much more saleable than mento). Byne's fellow-countryman Ali Ganda cut highlife for the label, but mixed so much Trinidadian style into it that he became a bona fide calypsonian. Calling himself Lord Ganda, he cut a series of righteously multi-national highlife/calypso mash-ups, including "Freedom", "Freedom Sierra Leone", "Ghana Forward Forever" and "The Queen Visits Nigeria".

The Melodisc roster also included London-based acts like Nigerian Union Rhythm Group, fronted by Brewster Hughes; Lonely Lamptey & the People's Highlife Band, who played highlife with a big-band swing; and Ebo Taylor's Black Star Highlife Band, who were sponsored by the Ghana High Commission. Ginger Johnson & His Afro Band, the predecessors of the African Messengers, gave "Won't You Cha Cha?" a highlife feel for the label, and the master drummer went on to record three albums of jazz-ified highlife for Shallit.

Later, Melodisc hoovered up practically every African act in London, as well as a few that were put together specifically for the session: Billy Sholanke; Tunji Sowandei; Victor Coker & His All Stars; Yesu Fu Adeyeno & His Group; King Jimmy; Enoch & Christy Mensah; Banna Kanukeh; Ad Kinle's Highlife Beats; Suberu Oni; and the marvellously named Adam's African Skyrockets. The mid-1960s electric guitar'n'brass-powered outfit Flash Domincii & The Supersonics was especially interesting – not only did they cut a set of festive songs under the title *Christmas Highlife Music*, but their numbers included both Teddy Osei and future Assagai member Fred Coker.

Arguably even more significant was Melodisc catalogue number 1532, a 1959 single entitled "Agigana". The clue lies in the B-side, "Fela's Special"; these were the first recordings by the man then known as Fela Ransome Kuti. Resident in London between 1958 and 1963, after his family sent him over to go to medical school – his two brothers are doctors – Fela switched to Trinity College of Music in Greenwich, and played a mix of highlife and jazz in the capital's clubs at night. The nucleus of the band that became Africa '70 came together in London at this time, under the name Koola Lobitos.

To promote the music in Africa, Shallit compiled two sampler albums, somewhat audaciously titled *Authentic African Highlife Music Volumes 1 & 2*. Shallit was spot-on as regards the appeal of London highlife in Africa, where the music rode in on the back of his calypso, setting itself up as 'the most modern African music' – precisely the right soundtrack for the most modern Africans. As the reputation of the label grew, some of the biggest names in highlife and juju, including Tunde Western Nightingale, Ayinde Bakare & His Meranda Orchestra and the Rans Boi Ghana Highlife Band (who also worked as the Rans Boi African Highlife Band), either came to London specifically to record, or would incorporate studio dates for Melodisc into European tours. Shallit also pushed the records hard in continental Europe, where Melodisc became the first company to sell African music.

Traditionalists complained that the music was being de-Africanised by the incorporation of precisely the modern instruments they'd been working to get rid of, and that the distinct regional styles were being mongrelised. Mostly, though, the London sounds were welcomed, on the grounds that the new music was making colonial (western) instruments sound African, and thus claiming them for Africans.

That London played such a crucial role in the development of the music was thanks largely to the sheer diversity of its black musicians. Proficient in Latin, jazz and calypso, they made it possible for different styles and approaches to rub against each other in a way that could not have happened anywhere else. African bands flocked to London studios to take advantage of Caribbean session players, arrangers and producers, or just to learn new licks. Thus Ghanaian highlife superstar ET Mensah spent three months in London by himself, in 1955, just soaking up what was going on. His band back home, the Tempos, were huge with their danceable swing-influenced highlife, and he came over to study the arrangements of Edmundo Ros and Lord Kitchener. He was so impressed by the *Paramount Ballroom* that on his return to Accra he renamed his own nightclub the *Paramount*. Similarly, drummer and percussionist Kofi Ghanaba, then known as Guy Warren, moved to London early in the 1950s, where he presented jazz, African music and calypso on the BBC. After he took home Latin/Caribbean percussion instruments – maracas, claves, congas, guiro – as gifts for other musicians in Ghana, they became almost regulation in highlife rhythm sections throughout West Africa.

For the plethora of West Indian-owned/oriented independent record labels that sprang up in Melodisc's slipstream during the 1960s, there was cash to be made from recording highlife. Planetone in Kilburn – probably London's first black-owned record label – Carnival, Giant Records, Masquerade, Pama and Stamford Hill's R&B Records were all putting out African sides. This made good sense, as they were already plugged into the small-shop circuit, and there was considerable crossover in black clubs. London highlife bands drew sizeable crowds in West Indian-owned venues like Count Suckle's *Q Club* in Paddington, the *Four Aces* in Dalston, and the *Apollo Club* in Willesden.

However, all that served to keep the scene insular, whereas Teddy's longstanding dream was for the music to sound African but still reach the mainstream. By the end of the 1960s, when he was looking for record industry support, the company best placed to help, Melodisc, was running its operation down, and Shallit himself spending more and more of his time in France. As late as 1969, Ambrose Campbell cut a reggae-ish cover of the Beatles' "Hey Jude", but after that there wasn't a great deal of anything, let alone highlife, on the label.

On the other hand, though, a new kind of commerce-meets-counter-culture spirit within the music business, first apparent during the 1960s – and also visible in the links between modern jazz and prog rock described in the previous chapter – was becoming increasingly influential in life in general. The post-hippie determination to be open-minded allowed Teddy and his peers to write a vital chapter in the organic evolution of London's black music, which was probably as much social as it was musical.

This important aspect had been developing alongside the lower-profile highlife scene for about ten years before Osibisa ever set foot in a studio, and came out of the same Soho clubs that used to put on jazz. To come to grips with it, it's necessary to go back to before that group even came to London.

Ska legend Prince Buster playing Ambrose Campbell's drums – the two musicians were good friends and frequent collaborators on Melodisc/ Blue Beat sessions.

THE START OF THE 1960s saw a sizeable cultural shift in the UK. The post-war generation was looking for its own way of doing things, and as mod emerged out of beatnik, young English men and women found a different soundtrack in the largely Jamaican-controlled black scene that was moving into the West End clubs. With jazz giving up ground, West Indians, American servicemen and some, if not all that many, Africans were grooving to the far more mainstream-friendly American R&B and the emerging Jamaican ska. Accessible via imported records and newly formed groups, the scene quickly attracted a white following in clubs like *Le Discotheque*, the *Flamingo*, *Sylibles*, the *Bag O' Nails*, *Le Duce*, *Whisky-A-Go-Go*, the *Scene* and the *Marquee*.

This was a lively, dance-oriented crowd, stylistically on the cutting edge and eager to shake off the spectre of their parents' wartime austerity – and just as keen not to go home until the sun came up. Most London mods prided themselves on their racial acceptance, which was another way to distance themselves from their often bigoted parents. Seeking out West Indian clubs for music and dancing, they created the first widespread movement to engage with immigrants on a straightforward level. For ska to share the turntables with R&B was an entirely natural state of affairs – the two styles are first cousins – and many clubs were run by Jamaicans who had operated sound systems in 1950s' Kingston, where the genres happily coexisted.

Once again, Emil Shallit was at the hub of ska in London, among the first to anticipate the potential impact of this new Jamaican music. In 1960, he launched the Melodisc subsidiary label Blue Beat, dedicated to the music and aimed specifically at the young white R&B crowd. He made regular trips to Jamaica to do licensing deals with producers, and with records by the likes of Prince Buster, Derrick Morgan and Laurel Aitken, he cornered yet another market. When Shallit began recording ska in London, he recruited many of the same West Indian and African players that he'd used for calypso and highlife, complemented with local R&B musicians. Prince Buster, for instance, who recorded regularly for Blue Beat in

London, taught his good friend Georgie Fame the rudiments of ska. Often alongside Blue Flames' saxophonist Mick Eve, the organist can be heard on many of the label's tracks. Buster, whose original name is Cecil Campbell, got to know his Nigerian namesake Ambrose Campbell in those same studios. Ambrose sat in on a few of his sessions, and taught the Prince to play the African talking drum – the conga drums the lamé-jacketed Buster is playing in that famous photograph (on p.141) were borrowed from Ambrose Campbell.

Although ska had a dedicated following that extended beyond the Caribbean community, the big record companies got behind R&B instead, and by the middle of the decade it had prevailed. As mod died out, to be replaced by all things

Speedy Acquaye (centre) with Georgie Fame (left) & the Blue Flames. Any apparent sartorial discord went down very well with the band's mod audience.

flowery, homegrown blues started to take over London's music scene, and in doing so introduced Africans *as Africans* to the mainstream. In 1964, the Fourth National Jazz and Blues Festival, held over three days in Richmond, provided a vivid early illustration. Not only did blues supplant jazz in the prestigious evening slots, but these were *British* blues and R&B acts. In front of a crowd of around 30,000, the Rolling Stones, the Yardbirds – at that point, Eric Clapton was in the group, and Jimmy Page was still in the audience – Long John Baldry and Georgie Fame & the Blue Flames had equal billing to Acker Bilk, Ronnie Scott and Tubby Hayes. Of as much significance in our story, Ghanaian drummer and percussionist Nii Moi 'Speedy' Acquaye was also taking part, as a key member of the Blue Flames.

The single most vital connection between London highlife and jazz on the one hand, and the rock world that gave Osibisa their platform on the other, Speedy first arrived in London in the mid-1940s. After initially performing as a fire-eater, a dancer and in panto, he decided to specialise in music during the 1950s. Joining the jazz and dance band scene, he played percussion with the likes of Tubby Hayes, Ronnie Scott and Kenny Graham, and was a featured drummer in Melodisc's highlife recording posse. A familiar, usually smiling face in the black clubs of Soho, he ran into Lancashire-born R&B singer and pianist Georgie Fame in the early 1960s, in the *Roaring Twenties* in Carnaby Street. The two became instant friends. Fame, forever fascinated by different musical styles, had just bought a Hammond organ after hearing Booker T.'s "Green Onions". He brought Speedy's Ghanaian drumming and percussion into his band a couple of months later.

This was a bold move, as the Blue Flames, who at various points included guitarist John McLaughlin and drummer Phil Seaman, had already developed a trademark sound as one of England's finest R&B outfits. Then there were the sartorial considerations. Mods took clothes very seriously, and expected their bands to dress the part; while the Blue Flames obliged with stylish matching suits or cardigans, Speedy would take to the stage in traditional Ghanaian

144

dress. In the event, the audience lived up to their open-minded reputation, embracing the new rhythms along with Speedy's energetic, often unpredictable performance style. His drumming remained integral to the Blue Flames for almost five years, during which time Speedy was responsible for introducing Georgie Fame to the Melodisc operation.

Later still, Speedy gigged regularly with, among others, Alexis Korner, Graham Bond and Cyril Davies. This may not have done a great deal to develop African music in a uniquely London way, but it brought him to the attention of younger English R&B musicians like Rod Stewart, Jeff Beck, Eric Clapton, Ginger Baker, Mick Jagger, Denny Laine, Eric Burdon, Peter Green ... mostly former mods, all Soho club regulars. The evolution of their music from blues to rock coincided with a hippie-friendly urge to explore the music of other cultures as a way to enhance their own musical ideas. The studiously musical rock and folk bands used alternative rhythmic structures and intricate patterns to open up new tonal and tempo possibilities, and add an extra dimension to their compositions. The Beatles, the Stones, and Led Zeppelin all flirted with Indian classical music – which had the bonus of built-in spirituality – while African rhythms proved popular in the London environment. Speedy became something of a 'go-to guy', working with Rod Stewart, the Rolling Stones, Stevie Winwood, John Martyn, the Faces, the Animals and the Small Faces. He became a key member of Ginger Baker's Air Force, and in 1979 was in Paul McCartney's Rockestra, as featured on Wings' *Back To The Egg*.

Speedy was not the only African musician to join the new rock party. Pyrotechnic Ghanaian keyboard maestro Kiki Gyan, who came to London in 1972 to join Osibisa, became a Traffic regular. Nigerian drummer Remi Kabaka played with Jim Capaldi, Paul McCartney, John Martyn, Ginger Baker, Paul Simon and Steve Winwood – these days his son, also called Remi, provides the voice for the Gorillaz drummer Russel Hobbs. Fellow Nigerian Rebop Kwaku Baah gigged with Eric Clapton and became the longest-standing non-founding member of Traffic, before getting in on the beginnings of

Krautrock, working with Can from 1977 to 1979. Before returning to Nigeria to form his own groups, Gasper Lawal was resident in London where he featured with the Rolling Stones, Ginger Baker's Air Force, Viv Stanshall, and Stevie Winwood, as well as Clancy, one of London's original 1970s' 'pub rock' bands.

A couple of members of London's rock aristocracy were so taken with West African sounds that they formed groups around them. In 1972, former Small Face Ronnie Lane produced the eponymous album by Akido, a multi-national Afro-funk outfit of which Speedy Acquaye was the rhythmic force, while a year later Steve Winwood formed the Third World, a trio of himself, Remi Kabaka and Ghanaian Abdul Lasisi Amao. They made one album, *Aiye-Keta*, of intricate Kabaka-written, Winwood-produced Afro-rock. Kabaka and Amao had first met in Ginger Baker's Air Force, and both went on to play in Osibisa.

One high-profile link between Africa and the new rock gods dated back to the Soho jazz world, in the shape of Nigerian drummer Ginger Johnson, who came to London in the 1950s. A regular Edmundo Ros and Harry Parry sideman, he later formed his own Afro/Cuban jazz group, the African Messengers, who recorded extensively for Melodisc, and were on the bill for that 1964 Richmond festival. By the mid-1960s, he was rated London's foremost Afro/Latin percussionist, and his flexible-membership troupe, Ginger Johnson's African Drummers, was in huge demand from rock acts. He'd frequently pop up on stage at underground clubs like *UFO* on Tottenham Court Road, *Middle Earth* in Covent Garden, or Chalk Farm's *Roundhouse*, bringing up to two dozen drummers along to augment whatever happening was already, er, happening. Johnson's group was chosen, apparently by Mick Jagger himself, to be part of the Stones' massive free concert in Hyde Park in 1969, where their contribution to "Sympathy For The Devil" took the tune into a new dimension. Among Johnson's troupe that day was another Nigerian drummer, Jimmy Scott-Emuakpor. He had been on the Soho jazz and R&B scenes ever since the 1950s,

Jimmy Scott-Emuakpor's favourite expression was 'Ob-La-Di, Ob-La-Da, life goes on', and he used to hang out with Paul McCartney in the Soho clubs. Do the maths.

usually in full African dress or with a leopardskin thrown casually over western clothes, topped by ever-present, very dark glasses. Jimmy became good friends with Paul McCartney; his constantly used catchphrase 'Ob-La-Di, Ob-La-Da' ('such is life' or 'life goes on' in Yoruba) formed the basis for the Beatles song of the same name.

Even if all this activity seemed more like a fad than anything likely to develop African music in the capital, it introduced African sounds and costumes to the rock world, and thus paved the way for Osibisa.

BY THE TIME THE STONES played Hyde Park, the 1960s were pretty much over culturally as well as chronologically. A new generation of blue-eyed soul fans had emerged from the post-mod R&B fans and the upmarket hippies. The influential West End clubs were the *Speakeasy* in Margaret Street, just north of Oxford Circus; the *Bag O' Nails* in Kingly Street; *Scotch of St James* in Mason's Yard just below Piccadilly; and the upstairs room at *Ronnie Scott's*. The soundtrack was American soul on the cusp of funk, and the crowds were musicians, English scenesters and black Americans from the suburban air force bases. A live band would still be part of the night's entertainment, and because they were soul clubs that would mean a black band. Ghanaian Wala Danga, future founder of the legendary *Limpopo Club*, was then a promoter, producer, manager and sound engineer. He laughs heartily as he remembers those days:

'Black musicians in London had to learn many styles, because with promoters and club owners back then there was this thing about colour: it didn't matter where you were from, all they saw was you were black, therefore you must be *authentic*. They didn't really care about authentic *what*! Usually they wanted to make out they had an American soul band on, so a group of musicians who could be from different African countries and the West Indies would play soul. Or they'd want a band from Ghana so the same musicians would be that. Once, I remember, when a group turned up with a couple of white session musicians the promoter, who was white, was not happy. He was like, "I don't care who you bring, whether they are American or African or West Indian, as long as they are black! Then I'm happy, but don't bring me these guys, 'cos then my audience don't think it's authentic!" He was right, too, because as a promoter one time I was fielding a band that had genuinely come from Senegal, and they had a white guy playing guitar. The audience – the majority of which were white – were complaining! They were shouting "What's he doing here? We came to see a black band!" Actually I don't think this has changed much today.

'The good thing about it was, it threw different musicians of different styles together. After all, if you've got a gig, you've got a gig … you can always pick up the new style. You needed somebody else for a gig, so you ask around, "Who's good at playing highlife?" OK, this guy is. Whether he was African or not, it don't matter, that he was good was the only thing that counts. And because people pooled in that way in a small scene like London, they are going to bring different things to the band and influence it. If you have a guy who is an expert in something else, but he's playing highlife he might say "OK, what if I do a bit of bass and slam it a bit like this?" and the others would go "Yeah, yeah, that sound good, OK, let's do it." So the music was starting to change to suit the styles that were going into it at the time, and often the audiences like that.'

Little had changed from Russ Henderson's days twenty years previously, and this serves as an accurate description of Osibisa's evolution, as Teddy explains:

'Before Osibisa, when I had the band Cat's Paw, we played in clubs like the *Q Club* and the *Speakeasy*, we had to play soul. This was before reggae came in big, because after that if they came to book Osibisa they'd think we were a reggae band because we were black! But back then, like many other soul bands, we'd play James Brown, Otis Redding, Wilson Pickett, all cover versions, but we'd put in bits of our own highlife, to make us stand out from the other bands. When we play it the people love it, not because they knew anything about what it was, just because they thought "At last, here

Ginger Johnson – fourth from left with drum and stick – and his African Drummers, including Jimmy Scott-Emuakpor, backed the Stones at their 1969 Hyde Park gig.

was a different black band." As we got into it, we'd play a few of the covers that people knew, but we'd put a different rhythm behind it, make it sound highlife.

'When we became Osibisa [*1969*] we started rehearsing in this basement in Finsbury Park, and that's when the Caribbean musicians came to check us out. Wendell Richardson, guitar, Spartacus on bass and Robert Bailey on keyboards; one after the other, they all got interested. We did a single called "Black Ant", which we took to the record companies, but although there had been so many African musicians with the rock groups, nobody was ready for an African band. So we carried on in the clubs where we built up a cult following because we were different – we even looked different, with African clothes and Spartacus, I think, was the first person with braided hair [*dreadlocks*]. Anywhere we could play it was all full up.

'It's through that we got a management from Bronze [*Manfred Mann, Colosseum, Marianne Faithfull, Uriah Heep, Bonzo Dog Band*], after Gerry and Lillian Bron saw us play in a club in north London. We picked up a good rapport with the press – Richard Williams of *Melody Maker* was very keen – and although we had tried the London record companies, our management invited Mike Maitland, the boss of MCA America to come and see us play at the London School of Economics. He came in there, the whole place was jamming, you know, the students jumping up. We didn't even know he was there, then after the show he came to the dressing room and the first thing he said to us was "I will sign you up, worldwide". That's when all our efforts became fruitful.'

Producer Tony Visconti, of Badfinger, David Bowie and T-Rex fame, was so taken with the group after seeing a Ronnie Scott's show that he agreed to produce their first album. He took them into the studio, where they played their set live, and he caught it in one take. Teddy maintains:

'We knew what we were doing. We had developed that sound for nearly a year, we were already playing the set we were going to record ... you know, "Ikobea", "The Dawn", "Music For Gong Gong" and all that. We wanted the same excitement of the live show on the record, and Tony Visconti understood. Also, because we were well known in the clubs and the colleges, when the album came out people already knew the songs. That's why it was a big hit.'

Because MCA marketed the band as they would any rock act – in the colleges – Osibisa reintroduced themselves to their original audience, African students, albeit this time via the mainstream entertainments rather than particular societies. That helped them to build on their London club following, which, as Teddy tells, was almost exclusively English:

'As Osibisa, we didn't start with a black following at all. We, as musicians, had all played the town halls and African student dances, but because of where Osibisa were playing, the West End clubs at the end of the sixties, it was mainly all-white audiences. You'd only get one or two black people ... Americans. Remember, at that time it was very difficult to go out in the night in central London, especially for Africans. They didn't have the money for those clubs, and the vibes weren't right. Many didn't feel it was welcoming for them.

'Once our management started to get us colleges and universities, we reconnected with our African audience. At first our own people knew there was an African-oriented band playing that circuit, but they didn't come out right away because we weren't playing what they considered to be a *typical* African sound. Our following among them wasn't there until they saw us on *Top of the Pops* wearing our African clothes, and heard that what we were playing was African, but could fit into this country. That's when we started to get Africans in the audience at the universities, they plugged into it, as they'd come to a show and say 'Oh yes, we've got our own music now.'

'Everybody was proud, not only Africans but West Indians as well. At that time the West Indians and the Africans weren't together, they didn't get along. There was so much differences, so much ... It wasn't like ten or twenty years before, it seemed we were no longer black people together. Our message was there were no differences, especially in an environment like London. We really hammered it home that we were all one people.'

This last point is important. Teddy is addressing the often-confusing process of racial integration that was going on in London in the late 1960s and early 1970s. A great deal had changed within Britain's immigrant communities during the twenty or so years since the *Windrush*, to produce a frustrating period of transition between the first and second generations. The arrivals of the 1940s and 1950s had accepted they weren't going home, but, for the most part, continued to feel like immigrants, and behaved as such, socialising among themselves with minimum engagement with Londoners at large. That said, they were also very aware of who they were, and how much they had in common with other black arrivals. Their children, on the other hand, were far more integrated, yet in searching for their identity they often identified with lands that many of them had never seen, in much more vociferous ways than their parents.

Hostility wasn't simply contrived between young West Indians and Africans. In much the same way, children of Jamaicans would be scathing about the 'small islander' children of Barbadians or Kittitians, or a guy with Trinidadian parents might sneer at a second-generation St Lucian as a 'chicken waver'. *Osibisa* the album, though, went a fair way towards papering over cracks. It was so proudly black it was difficult for anybody to find fault; it was funky enough to sit alongside Kool & The Gang or the J.B.'s; and the group mixed Africans and West Indians, one of whom had dreadlocks. What wasn't to like? Also, most importantly, it was a cultural expression created in the UK, for the UK, which made it into the mainstream.

At this point, with the exception of Eddy Grant's Kentish Town soul band the Equals, the only black music that was having any impact on the pop mainstream came from Motown, Memphis or Kingston, Jamaica. (London funksters the Foundations' hits sounded so Motown-y they might as well have been from over there.) By the time Osibisa formed, the mainstream British entertainment industry had taken several steps backwards from the 1950s in its approach to race relations. The group's first album was released into a cultural environment best described as institutionally hostile. With the exception of Kenny Lynch, Charlie Williams, Derek Griffiths and Spring – played by a teenage Brinsley Forde, five years before Aswad, on kids' drama *Here Come The Double Deckers* – the number of non-Caucasian British faces on television, other than *TOTP*, was somewhere south of negligible. Trevor McDonald and Lenny Henry didn't hit the screens until the mid-seventies.

Far worse, though, was the casual, often quite vicious racism permeating TV comedy, where 'darkie', 'paki' and 'paddy' jokes were thrown around with abandon. In 1969, the same time as Osibisa were coming together, ITV was airing a sitcom called *Curry And Chips*, written by Johnny Speight, which made the trademark racial abuse of his *'Till Death Us Do Part* seem like Noel Coward. The lead character, known as Paki Paddy, was mixed-race Irish and Pakistani, and played by blacked-up white English comedian Spike Milligan sporting a ludicrous Indian accent. Kenny Lynch was a regular cast member. Even if, as always, justifications were issued as to why such a clearly odious state of affairs was being promoted, that was the tip of a light entertainment iceberg that gave the country at large the licence to a) assume that people who didn't look like them must be foreign; b) that they had little value beyond being laughed at; and c) that it was funny to be rude about them.

Under such circumstances, wanting to sound and look African yet still take that music out of its own environment was a big deal. *Osibisa* was a massive worldwide hit, yet relevant enough to its environment for tracks to find their way into practically every aspect of young black London's clubs and dances. It also opened a few ears, and records like *Fela's London Scene* and Manu Dibango's *Soul Makossa* were better received because of it. Then, almost as quickly as they had seemed to appear, Osibisa all but vanished, leaving London's African music to take another couple of turns.

'OSIBISA WERE QUITE OUTSTANDING as a band, and they had that edge of rock about them with the guitars – they were like Afro-*rock* instead of Afro-funk. The executives of the London record companies were more familiar with rock, so there was something they loved about that sound.'

Wala Danga is explaining what put Osibisa ahead of the pack when it came to getting major label recognition. As they were signed by MCA International rather than the company's UK arm, the album was marketed all over the world to great effect. It was the first African hit in the US mainstream; they gained strong followings in continental Europe, Australia and Japan; and in West Africa they became superstars, even megastars in Teddy's native Ghana. To consolidate the global success of *Osibisa* and their swift follow-up album *Woyaya*, however, the group pretty much abandoned Britain for a couple of years. Surprisingly, no other African groups were thrust into that gap, as would have been normal record-industry behaviour. Wala has an idea why that never happened:

'Because this thing was so unlike what the record companies had been developing or looking for, it took a while for them to get on board and to realise the potential of it. Then by the time they did, they couldn't find the sort of groups they were looking for. There were a lot of bands in London playing Afro-funk, but they didn't want funk – they used to say if they wanted funk they would 'find the *real* people to play funk' and all they could think about was James Brown, not these guys making music in London clubs.

'Really, Osibisa were unique. Although a lot of bands used to talk about trying to do Afro-rock, only Assagai came close to it. Them and a London Nigerian group called Ojah which was led by a guy called, I think, Ian St Louis.'

To this day, Assagai remain the best known of the bands that followed in Osibisa's slipstream. It's not hard to see why. As the group was a side project of three members of the Blue Notes/Brotherhood Of Breath axis – Dudu Pukwana, Louis Moholo-Moholo and Mongezi Feza, supplemented by London Nigerians Fred Coker and Bizo Muggikana – they had strong prog-rock connections. They were signed to Vertigo Records, Philips's left-field rock subsidiary and home to Uriah Heep, Black Sabbath, Gentle Giant and Jade Warrior. The latter group almost adopted the Africans, writing songs for them and guesting on their two albums *Assagai* and *Zimbabwe*. Kwela-ish Afro-jazz and soul, with a healthy dose of prog-rock twiddling, both sets did very well, and the Osibisa-style Roger Dean sleeve art did *Zimbabwe* no harm at all in its chosen market. The London African musicians who joined Assagai on the first album included Terri Quaye, the (much) older half-sister of electronic reggae star Finley Quaye, who has also worked with Osibisa in his time.

Another reason why Osibisa's absence left such a vacuum was that the scene was so informal. Musicians approached live work much like sessioneering; key players would organise bands on behalf of club owners or promoters on an ad hoc basis. As in the jazz days, if you went to the same circuit of clubs at all frequently, you'd see the same players in all manner of permutations. While this provided reasonable job opportunities, Wala believes it held things back. No matter how good these amalgamations might be, there was nothing for audiences or record companies to latch on to:

'These guys were the best bands under those circumstances, because they knew how to get people dancing, but most of the time nobody knew their names. So many of these musicians were concentrating on just playing music, the image thing was coming second. They just didn't bother with "What shall we call ourselves?" and "Why should we call ourselves that?" And these were big bands on that circuit, who have been playing together for ages. I remember asking a band I had booked "What is your name?" They said "Oh, we never thought about that. What shall we call ourselves?", and I think they gave themselves a name just for that night.

'That was very much the London scene, so much that even now it's not changed much. It was not good for development, because it was the ones that worked as groups – proper, regular groups – that by and large would be the most successful, because it meant that the sounds never changed that much. True, if you keep putting different guys together they will bring different things and experiment more, but it has to be able to settle. If there was a unit and the people were working *together* to change the sounds, there would have been more progress. Also, if they stayed together for a bit longer as a group, the professionalism would even get higher – in terms of timekeeping and all of that …

'It meant they could build up a following too, and promoters could advertise a particular group. That's what would get record companies interested, the record companies weren't going to try and track down musicians and then put them together and wait for them to call themselves something.

Roger Dean created Osibisa's iconic flying elephant before he did any graphics for Yes.

Osibisa already had all of that. They even had their songs, and they made it very easy for the record company.'

Such bands largely followed the Osibisa model by mixing London Africans with London West Indians. That the Africans were usually in the majority had a lot to with the centrality of sound systems to Jamaican/Caribbean London culture, as opposed to the much stronger live-music tradition among Africans. Pretty much everything else was changing, though. As the 1970s got underway, clubs were evolving away from the rock/R&B crowd into strictly soul, pushing bands away from African-isms laced with rock-isms, and towards more straightforward funk. In the same way, as described in the next chapter, a soul scene was blowing up quite spectacularly in West Africa, and that in turn hastened the decline of the university high-life dances as hip young students wanted to give up the funk. The more traditional music had evolved into a looser circuit of club nights and one-off dances at places like *Billy's* in Meard Street, the *Country Club* in Belsize Park, and the Winchester Road Community Centre in Swiss Cottage.

Being more about the desire of promoters to attract the largest regular clientele than about particular national organisations hiring venues, this scene resulted in a greater blending and cross-fertilisation of music from all over West Africa and from London. What's more, the fact that events would mix live bands with records, or even be deejay-only, made it much easier to mix the music up; deejays would, within the context, play whatever would move the crowd. By this time, there was an audience for this very modern presentation of traditional music, as a generation of young Africans was growing up in London who presented themselves to the outside world as *African* rather than of a particular nation.

AWAY FROM THE CLUBS, an ad hoc network of African music outlets, whose approach to stock control veered between quirky and downright anarchic, was fuelling this scene. This had its roots in Emil Shallit's distribution channels, which serviced as many black-owned hairdressers, grocers and cafes with calypso, ska and highlife as they did actual record shops; Shallit had quite rightly realised that black people across the board tended to patronise the same establishments. By now, though, records were being made in West Africa and brought into London, along with foodstuffs, cosmetics and bolts of Kente cloth, by the more aware African importers.

The prime movers in this area were the Oti brothers, based in their large supermarket in Balham, who would import food from all over West Africa for wholesale to shops across London, and simply added records to the operation. According to Wala, who bought his first-ever Fela record there, *Oti's* was for a while the only place to find a good selection of African music. It became something of a Saturday pilgrimage for Africans from all over London, who came down to sort through crates of records stacked next to boxes of yams. Spotting the opportunity for some vertical expansion, the brothers set up a licensing operation and, briefly, a record label.

At much the same time, another general-goods emporium, *Stern's Electrical Supplies* on Tottenham Court Road, established a reputation in this market. Being close to several universities, it did very good business among African students who needed things fixed and bought valves, electrical parts, small appliances and other household items. Staff would often accept records brought from home instead of cash for repair work. The resultant boxes of random singles became so popular with browsing students that the shop introduced a dedicated record counter at the back, and began to order in from the Oti brothers. In similarly opportunistic fashion, it also stocked a sizeable selection of gaudy but inexpensive lingerie, which often caused casual customers to raise an eyebrow, but was simply a response to demand from the thriving red-light district in Fitzrovia to the west.

In its new incarnation, *Stern's* came to play a crucial role in London's African music scene. Music sales – African music sales – had become the largest part of the business, and when old Mr Stern sold up at the end of the 1970s, the new owners concentrated on that side of things and kept the name. During the next twenty years, *Stern's* became Europe's largest distributor of African records, with a truly massive mail-order department, and even had its own label. The retail operation remained the key, however, especially after they expanded into bigger, dedicated record-shop premises in nearby Whitfield Street.

Stern's was as much a social club as a shop. Every Friday, African music aficionados of every stripe – musicians, writers, journalists, deejays, punters and the merely curious – would gather to swap information about clubs, sessions, tunes or just life in general. With so little media space given over to African music, this was where you had to go to find out about the scene, which while simmering nicely was doing so entirely under the radar. All manner of different demographics would happily rub shoulders. The new improved *Stern's* still bought records over the counter, so a student might stagger in with a huge suitcase of records he'd lugged over from Nigeria, in the hope of making a few quid.

Or an ambassadorial limo might pull up, and its occupant step out to buy some sounds and stay on to enjoy the banter. Or a deejay might be twitchily waiting for a box of brand-new tunes to arrive. Or a doctor might just pop in to buy an album as a birthday present for his dad.

Then there was downstairs at *Stern's*. If the street level was the club, the basement was the VIP Room. Technically a stock room/office space, it held a sound system, television and sofas, and was usually occupied by musicians, both resident and visiting and their entourages – not that you'd necessarily be able to recognize them through the smoke. The local off licences and pubs always did very well out of *Stern's Music* on a Friday afternoon.

Although the scene seemed healthy throughout the 1980s, it was losing focus. Changing dancefloor tastes in London were pushing the music to incorporate more soul and funk, and it might well have evolved itself out of existence. Wala, though, had an idea of dazzling simplicity: run an African music night at the Africa Centre. 'It was something we felt needed to be done', he chuckles.

THE AFRICA CENTRE FIRST OPENED in 1964, at 38 King Street, Covent Garden, WC2 – the same location where it remains today. What's now Covent Garden Piazza was then London's main fruit and vegetable wholesale market, and the Centre took over a tomato warehouse that, somewhat ironically, had once housed auction rooms specialising in Benin bronzes. The idea behind the Africa Centre, as conceived by English Africa enthusiast Margaret Feeny in 1961, was to foster non-governmental relations between newly independent African nations by bringing people together on neutral, apolitical ground. It would also maintain informal cultural links between Britain and her former colonies, while offering a friendly meeting place for Africans living in London. Student-oriented, it held a lecture theatre, a library and a conference room as well as a bar and a restaurant, plus an art gallery and a performance space to showcase the emerging nations' culture.

An immediate success in almost every respect, the Centre seemed to treat music as a kind of anthropological 'experience', rather than a casual social occurrence. While it provided a suitably cerebral hangout, therefore, it neglected that other important aspect of student life: the Friday-night knees-up. Or at least it did, until Wala thought up the *Limpopo Club*:

'The Africa Centre was unique. One of the first places that people from different African countries really used to mix, because for a lot of the African students it was like a home away from home. They could go to the bar or get some African food. For a social thing it didn't matter what country was hosting or doing a show, where there was some kind of celebration everybody could join in, even if you weren't from that country.

'Because it was in the centre of London you'd not only get people from the universities, but people from the north, the south, the east and the west of the city – that helped to mix it. And being in the West End, there would always be other people who have wandered past the building just dropping by to see what's going on, there would be quite a few English people in there too. But although it was mixed, it was still community based – a Ghanaian night or a Congolese night – so the band and the music tended to be from that country and only on certain nights. There was nothing on a consistent level that was open to everybody. This was the middle of the seventies, and we felt there wasn't so much of an organised *African* music scene at the Africa Centre, or anywhere in London. We started the *Limpopo Club* to be able to put on all African music on a regular basis, for everybody.

'We did it on every Friday night and at times on Saturday nights too. Occasionally, when we got a really big band on, we'd take Thursday as well. Although we didn't formalise it as the *Limpopo Club* until 1983, we started the regular night in 1975.'

These club nights were an inspired move, establishing a pan-African vibe at the Centre thanks to the democratic turntable policy of Wala and his fellow deejays, Ugandans King Maslo and Bossa:

'When we started we were sourcing records straight from Africa. African students would come in with their own records and say "This is the club record they are playing back home right now, would you play this for me?" And if the crowd enjoyed it we would also ask them to order copies for us from their country, and it didn't matter which country that was. So it was very much people bringing the music to you, then you going back to Africa to source it out. Very informal.

'Then I went out to make kind of bridges with the record companies in Africa, so I started getting new records, I was on their mailing lists. It meant we were always up to date with whatever sounds were being played in Africa, and I could ask for back covers and things like that.'

The Centre believed it was important to have a live band on each club night and Wala's random approach to booking the groups further helped African musical solidarity. He supplemented acts that were based or had originated in the UK, like The Funkees, BLO or Assagai, with African bands visiting Britain to play the community dance circuit, cajoling them into doing a date as they arrived or left the country, and he'd also put together pick-up groups that knew how to keep the groove. All of which meant that the club's only booking policy was that there was no booking policy.

In keeping with the welcoming atmosphere of the venue, the *Limpopo* looked beyond expat Africans, and aimed to enlighten a wider audience by offering workshops, seminars, classes and discussion groups on African music and dance. Debbie Golt, who now manages and promotes African acts, and deejays African music at club nights and on the radio, was among the English people who were made to feel welcome at the Centre:

'When I came to back to London in the early eighties, from living in Manchester, for somebody who hadn't lived here for a long time, the Africa Centre was a mecca to find music and to socialize. There was a mix of Africans from all over, and for the Friday nights [*Limpopo*] there were quite a few English people there. For me, this was strange, because in Manchester it wasn't mixed at all – on the African scene there was hardly any English people, and the only way you'd get an introduction would be if you worked for Zimbabwe Solidarity or something like that. The Africa Centre was always much more relaxed.'

Limpopo became one of the hottest African clubs in Europe, as Wala achieved his goal of mixing up African styles with a spontaneity that would appeal to a broad crowd. A huge factor in this was that *Limpopo* was presented by an *African*, with a fundamental understanding of the music, the culture and how things knitted together. He was making his decisions based on a prospective audience of Africans, not as an outsider trying to second-guess what his peers might want for or from African music. That meant *Limpopo* was the real deal, and ensured that people of every stripe loved it.

It quickly became *the* most important venue for anglophone African acts, too, so Wala was no longer limited to capturing acts at one end of their tours. Indeed, any African artists with even half an eye on the world stage also had *Limpopo* in their sights. As a showcase, it was second to none: Baaba Maal, Kanda Bongo Man and Salif Keita played their first European shows at the Centre, while Angélique Kidjo and Thomas Mapfumo made their UK debuts there.

Naturally enough, a consistent diet of such exciting, glamorous African music, presented in an ideal setting, swiftly attracted the mainstream music business. In the wake of punk and Rock Against Racism, mainstream types were freshly aware of the commercial potential of ethnic music, and coming to terms with the idea that Bob Marley's passing in 1981 might have put an end to their Jamaican adventure. The prospect of that new gateway to the world sparked an unprecedented explosion in African bands during the 1980s, particularly in Zimbabwe, Zaire and the Congo. Although only the likes of Kanda Bongo Man, the Four Brothers and the Bhundu Boys made much of a dent in London, literally hundreds of bands back home were trying their luck. The vibrancy of those Africa Centre gigs was a true reflection – albeit in microcosm – of what was happening in Africa.

For about twenty minutes in the early 1980s, the mainstream recording industry went Africa-crazy.

While it might be a bit ambitious to credit the Africa Centre with responsibility for the world music boom of the 1980s, for anyone exposed to an evening at *Limpopo*, it was hardly going to take a series of marketing meetings to work out that African could be 'the new black'. So to speak.

ISLAND RECORDS, BOB MARLEY'S LABEL and previously the UK's biggest investor in reggae, got in first, signing Nigerian juju sensation and Africa Centre regular King Sunny Adé to a long-term deal. The 1981 release of his first Island album, the totally infectious *Juju Music*, was accompanied by a hefty dose of Marley-type marketing – treat it like a rock album, and push it squarely at the mainstream. The press duly lauded the LP, and several scribes, with a staggering lack of self-awareness, dubbed this charismatic Nigerian 'the new Bob Marley'. Suddenly big record companies were in a sub-Saharan scramble, signing up acts like Salif Keita, Chief Ebenezer Obey, Gasper Lawal, Angélique Kidjo, Youssou N'Dour, Ali Farka Touré, Ladysmith Black Mambazo and the Bhundu Boys. That in turn opened the door for specialist independent labels like Stern's, Earthworks and World Circuit. Radio deejays Charlie Gillett, John Peel, Andy Kershaw, and Gilles Peterson took African music to the airwaves, and the mainstream press featured the records and artists alongside their regular rock coverage. Then a new generation of rock stars started showing an interest in all things African: Brian Eno, Malcolm McLaren, David Bowie, Talking Heads, Peter Gabriel ...

Jumbo Van Reenen, a perpetually genial South African and lover of music from all over that continent, who arrived in London at the start of the 1980s, founded the Earthworks label in 1983. He remembers those growth years:

'We started when *Stern's* was still just a shop, and the African wave was starting to break into the mainstream. As well as the rock acts playing around with African sounds, hip-hop acts and post-punk groups like Rip, Rig + Panic were listening to all sorts of stuff, and going on their own excursions with African experiments. Earthworks had the intention of doing wholly African things, which was never easy in England but at least back then you felt you had a chance. There was some interest from magazines like the *NME* and *Sounds*, they all started to write a little bit about it – if you gave them something to write about.

'Also at that time there was a healthy thing revolving around the festivals and African bands crossing over to the rock side for those events. And there was the GLC [*the left-wing Greater London Council, later abolished by Mrs Thatcher*] who, through subsidies, would enable promoters and all sorts of people to bring all sorts of bands over from Africa to play gigs in London. We could bring bands in, and people used to wander down to the South Bank, or wherever, and see a band, then tell their friends and maybe want to buy an album. In the beginning we used to get a lot of West Indians at these things, because we'd advertise them in *Black Echoes*, but then we started to attract more and more of an English audience.'

While it seemed that African music couldn't be any stronger, the problem was that to reach the mainstream audience it had to be part of the mainstream business. That upset the delicate balance maintained at clubs like the *Limpopo*, where guys like Wala Danga were losing control as a new high-profile scene was tailored for wider tastes.

King Sunny Adé's tenure at Island was a vivid example of that sort of cultural engineering. A huge star in Africa, and a supremely gifted performer, he took great exception to the expectation that he would Europeanise his style. Understandably so: he's not merely the King of Juju, but an *actual* king as well, and parted company with the label because of their demands. Wala remembers acts he had brought to major labels, whom he was then asked to produce:

'They'd say "Why don't you put the guitar solo in there?", not even thinking about whether we had one planned for anywhere in the song! Because that was the way they heard the music in their heads, regardless of how it sounded.'

Jumbo describes how an ultimately self-defeating big-company mentality took over:

'Once the major labels got involved, they were always looking for that quick pop-star business, because that's really all the people working there understand. And it didn't always work for something like this – I could sell more records out of the back of my car, very often, than they did at Island, dealing with the sales force who are just looking at it from a pop point of view. You know, "Is there a sales point?" "Is there a video?" and so on.

'Then with all these things factored in, you have to play that game to make it work; if you don't, or it doesn't work, you're gone. Even if it does work, it didn't guarantee you anything, because then the next thing comes along and everything becomes geared up to that. It wasn't like these artists were used to doing these things, they were used to building up a following and then working to keep it by developing and moving forward.'

The term 'world music' came into play around this time. No one who was involved in African music, then or now, has anything particularly good to say about it. Debbie explains how it worked, or rather how it *didn't* work:

'I have mixed feelings about the whole world music thing, Once the term established itself, retailers racked African music alongside Latin, Turkish, Bulgarian and so on, reducing its presence. You had music from *everywhere* totally diluting it and losing any direction for it … you won't get a band like Taxi Pata Pata racked under their own name, they'll just be 'Congolese' or 'soukous' within the World section, so they won't easily be found.'

Graeme Ewens, who co-owns RetroAfric Records – kind of African rare groove specialists – still splutters at the introduction of the world music category:

'I believe it was the worst possible umbrella for African music at that time. African and Latin music were building solid and separate fanbases, and had established a touring circuit of small venues in London and around the UK. Then world music gatecrashed that party.

'It may have brought a short-term increase in exposure in high-street record stores, but African culture was diminished by being lumped in with Mongolian throat singing and Bolivian nose flutes. Even using the name *Africa* itself was too general. There was already a wide variety of African genres. The big-selling music from Nigeria, Congo/Zaire and Cameroon was urban dance music, not the plinky-plunky stuff that now proliferates. That is "folk" as far as I am concerned, and it is still being traded on its exoticism. Now we have "urban" to cover all black music but are there no cities in Africa? Cameroon, for one, is a whole culture/country that has been erased from the musical map. I still find that whole scene patronising to the point of racist.'

African music in London, whether local or imported, appeared to have hit a wall.

IN PRACTICALLY ALL RESPECTS, the Afro-rock of Osibisa and Assagai was *the* pioneering London black music style. Rather than simply limit its evolution to its own internal ideas, it was always making moves to consider its new musical and social surroundings. It hadn't simply adapted itself to suit an existing London audience, it had deliberately set out to represent the changing face of the city and make a point that went beyond performance. Yet it was unable to maintain any thrust, and nothing had followed up on it during the intervening couple of decades.

The biggest barrier was that there was no London African-controlled scene to incubate such a style, or what there was wasn't big enough, exclusive enough or young enough to properly get it going – unlike, say, lovers' rock reggae. That scene, as we'll see in chapter six, was totally exclusive, deeply underground and with a teenage demographic desperate for a music that represented both their ethnicity *and* their British-ness. Under these conditions, players and producers could generate enough finance to evolve imported reggae into what a new audience expected, away from outside pressures.

There was no equivalent process with African music, despite the fact that a sizeable second generation of children of West African immigrants were now building their lives in London, thanks both to economic migration and civil wars back home. Instead, the capital's young black population was growing ever more Jamaicanised, as, pre hip hop, Jamaican identity became the cornerstone upon which any identifiable black London character was being built. In the interests of fitting in, most kids were not overly inclined to pursue their African-ness beyond their own front doors – it was actually possible to know kids for years and not realise they were African until you met their parents. Also, the fact that black youth culture already existed in London – in the shape of the soul and reggae scenes – greatly reduced the need for anyone to start a scene of their own.

By the 1990s, even though African-owned clubs had for years been crucial to the establishment of self-regulated black music in London, it would have been virtually impossible for even the relatively high-profile African-owned/run venues to nurture a London sound and still stay in business. As Wala explains, it was all to do with 'authenticity', and the situation was hardly unique to African music:

'I, and others here, were working to try to create stages for African musicians in London, so at least they can come and showcase and be heard and develop a unique sound – something African and London, but contemporary. But the record companies and the media were looking to get groups in from Africa, and would look on anything being done in London as not being authentic, and there is something they feel is inferior about using guys who are local. Which is quite interesting because a lot of these guys who were making the London music had been playing with those groups in Africa that the industry was going wild over! Many of them had come here on tour and decided to stay over. So it is really the same musicians [*he chuckles richly*] but because they now live in London, people just look over them. It was quite ironic, because we could mix up different African styles and countries, as long as it was African. But it made it very difficult for us promoters to attract the crowds we needed by putting on local bands.

'It was the same thing with reggae. That's why the first record that Matumbi did, they put a white label on and pretended it was a Jamaican record – that's how they broke into the charts. Then they told people "No, actually we're from London!" and the reviewers had to admit "Ha! You're good then". But they had to force their way like that, and deliberately put nothing on the label and said this is a new band and the copies have been smuggled out of Jamaica. It worked.'

Subterfuge like that could only work because there was a huge underground reggae business. The London African bands had little choice other than to go to the mainstream record companies. Where there was little joy to be found, even if many such groups epitomised world music, incorporating influences from three continents and players from all sorts of countries, and having developed in response to the shifting population of the city. Behind the 'authenticity' aspect lay a fiscal consideration. Signing acts from abroad is a much lower investment, as it's usually a matter of licensing in finished product rather than paying for a young local band to develop a career. In this case the practice was to scoop up a few more or less finished African albums on an A&R safari, throw some marketing at them, and see if anything stuck. As Jumbo implied earlier, the inevitable hit-and-miss results did little to convince the industry that the genre had a commercial future.

The demise of the GLC was the final nail, as the loss of subsidised venues and sponsored festivals meant that groups who might have had a bright future at the start of the 1980s were struggling. Debbie tells how the options were closed off:

'As far as promoters like myself went, the GLC going made a vast difference. So many of the shows we'd put on just weren't viable without them, but they were always very well attended so the people of London must've been happy with them. After about 1984 or 1985, it was down to the local authorities and the Arts Council, who started from the point of wanting operations to have self-sufficiency. They'd support you to a certain extent, then when you looked like you were self-sufficient they'd say "Oh, you're making too much money therefore we can't really fund you." They'd withdraw their tranche of money, which would mean suddenly it didn't add up, so then that crumbled. It became harder and harder to get the public-money support to put things on.

'This had a knock-on effect in other areas, because the music business wasn't supporting the development of the acts. We could only self-release so far, and we could only get press coverage so far, but then when we came back for the second round, without the exposure from live work the media and audience moved on to the next thing. It was very hard to build a fanbase. A lot of artists got out of music or went back to Africa.'

TODAY, THE AFRICAN SCENE SURVIVES in London, even if it's not really thriving. The town hall dances are still there, as are a few local groups; individual artists rather than whole bands come in; Wala's *Limpopo Club* is still in existence, if no longer at the Africa Centre; and Debbie's Outerglobe promotions present regular nights at Notting Hill's Tabernacle. There's also a circuit of underground all-night warehouse parties in London that tend to be nation-specific rather than pan-African, a kind of post-rave-culture version of the town hall dances, which usually feature live music and frequently pull in crowds upwards of a thousand.

Wala still believes that African music can gain serious ground in London:

'I still think it's going to happen again. There'll be somebody, another group maybe, and it will take a lot of convincing for these other record companies to jump in. But I believe it can happen like it is in France, where they've kind of adopted the African music as their music to export. African music is the music they can sell as French music all around the world, so you get Youssou N'Dour and Salif Keita and they become bigger than all the other African artists, because the French have adopted them and the record companies in France have embraced them. They probably have realised all they have got is Jean-Michel Jarre or Frank Zappa to sell, and then there's what? The Rolling Stones? So they said "Oh all right, why don't we go with this one?"

'That is why the French have moved to reggae in a big way. They are the guys controlling most of the reggae catalogues from before, and touring a lot of the reggae acts. So I think that is just the positive attitude needed over here.'

CHAPTER FIVE

Basslines, Brass Sections and All Things Equals

||||||||||||||||||||||||||||||||||||||||||||||||||||||||||||||||||||||||||||||||||||||||||||||||||||

London gives up the Funk

'IN 1970, THERE WERE LOTS OF THINGS HAPPENING, worldwide. One of which was the Black Power movement already established from about '69 in the States, and that was sort of percolating into the British black scene. People were taking positions – some positions intransigent, as in the case of Michael X and guys like this – but the Equals were caught in the middle of this by virtue of being a mixed band. We've never had issues of race with the band, I've never had a racial argument with anybody within the band, as a matter of fact there weren't that many arguments to start with, we seemed to be *sorted*. But there was this thing in the air that there was going to be a change.'

At the tail end of the 1960s, when Osibisa were retooling African music in Finsbury Park, Eddy Grant, the bleached-blond Afroed leader of the Equals, was a mile or so away at the top of the Holloway Road, and similarly about to shake things up. Eddy was still at Acland Burghley school in Tufnell Park when he formed the group with two local English lads and a pair of Jamaican immigrant twin brothers. He actually straddles several aspects of this book: his dad was a professional trumpeter who played with Russ Henderson among others; Eddy started off in a trad jazz group with schoolmate and future *Playaway* star Derek Griffiths; he produced London African and reggae acts; and he always strongly supported calypso in the capital. His soul band, though, which played an exuberant Caribbean-flavoured pop soul, had a number one in 1968 – "Baby Come Back" – and several other chart hits. By 1970, a couple of less successful releases had come and gone since they'd livelied up the top ten with "Viva Bobby Joe", and now Eddie Kassner, boss of President Records, wanted to know how they might change things. Eddy continues the story of the band's single "Black Skin Blue Eyed Boys":

'I said I've got this great song, and it will change the way people look at the Equals and it will change the way people will look at music in this country. He asked me to play it. I had it on a demo and gave it to him. He listened and said "*What*?!?! I'm not going to have *anything* to do with this! You can't sing about black anything to middle-class white audiences – they'll bury you and I'll be the one they blame when it's released! I want nothing to do with this record!"

'As a group we paid for the making of our records – that's how the business is structured – but this time he wasn't even going to forward the money to make the record. OK, I'll do it! The making of the record was totally in my hands at this time – I wanted to *compete*, I wanted to have the sound that I wanted to have. I decided we were going to record sixteen track, which we'd never done before, the most we'd done before was either two four tracks or eight track, so I booked the studios and paid for it. I got a couple of my friends in – Gasper Lawal played bongos.

'This record was really significant in terms of the Equals' future – that's when I burned the wig and cut off the hair, as much as I could without going bald [*as well as his white afro, Eddy sometimes wore a blond wig*]. I got a friend in to help promote the record, because it *needed* promotion as it was a total change in the image of the Equals, much

The Equals, left to right: Pat Lloyd, Dervan Gordon, John Hall, Lincoln Gordon; Eddy is the shadowy figure lurking at the back.

more aggressive. We travelled up and down the country, to everywhere they would listen to us – or, in particular, listen to me – talking about it. I went out with a whole new political concept, a whole different political attitude.'

The gamble paid off. The label's fears proved groundless, and the pop-music audience bought the record to such an extent that "Black Skin Blue Eyed Boys" was a top ten hit. More than that, Eddy believes, they also bought *into* it, further confounding corporate assumptions:

'I think Eddie Kassner was behaving like any other record executive would have behaved at the time, because there was not a political plethora of those records coming out. That didn't happen for quite some time thereafter. You have to remember, my good friend Stevie Wonder, for example, who's become a massive campaigner for all sorts of things, was still writing '*Baby I love you*'. So the question is whether Eddie Kassner was even qualified to judge a record like "Black Skinned Blue Eyed Boys" ...'

Interestingly, Eddy and the group had previous in this area, with the rather self-explanatory "Police On My Back" as a track on their first album – a song that the Clash deemed worthy of a cover a decade or so later. But did he think they underestimated the British public?

'There was a little of that. At that time the British public were, through the medium of radio and television, getting certain messages from the street, and that allowed a record like that to go through. Don't get me wrong, it was a really hard sell, but people seem to buy what they innately may not have wanted to buy! [*Eddy laughs*] I think generally, with good music people become blind, they don't become deaf, but I suppose by encountering whatever it is the ears are hearing the eyes become blind and the sensibilities tend to change. I mean why did the British public buy "Living On The Frontline"? I don't know? [*He laughs again, hard*] I mean why did the British public even buy "Gimme Hope Jo'anna", when England, under the Thatcher government, was not supportive of anti-apartheid? I don't know. Nor do I know if anybody else could've got away with it!'

In 1970? Probably not. Or not as far as the music industry and media were concerned. Over forty years later, "Black Skin Blue Eyed Boys" may not seem like the most incendiary political statement, but this was before socio-political awareness became an expected facet of black music anywhere. James Brown had "Say It Loud I'm Black And I'm Proud" in 1968, and there had been a flurry of Civil-Rights-related sounds in the mid-1960s – "Keep On Pushin'", "Respect", "Mississippi Goddam", "Alabama", and so on. In the UK soul music wore matching suits and worried more about precision than protest; reggae was, beyond the sound systems, a stringed up pop party; and the closest thing to political statement was Blue Mink's "Melting Pot". A white pop group with a black girl singer, Blue Mink had a huge hit in 1969 with this hymn to racial harmony, the lyrics of which, even in those dark days before political correctness, astonished many listeners by speaking of 'Red Indian boys', and rhymed 'Latin kinkies' with 'yellow chinkies'. However, the public themselves deserve some credit.

Race relations in London at the time of "Melting Pot" were being defined by the trial of the Mangrove Nine, a deliberate attempt by the Home Office and the Metropolitan Police to undermine black community organisation. The *Mangrove Restaurant* in All Saints Road, Ladbroke Grove, was a Caribbean hangout where the area's black residents mingled with left-wingers of every stripe, from the arts world in particular – Vanessa Redgrave and Richard

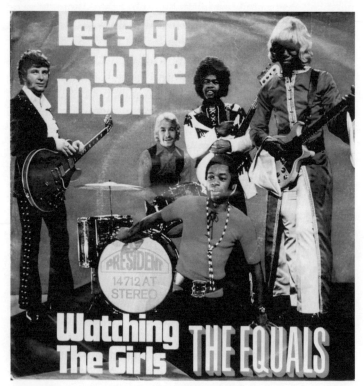

To drive home his point that the Equals weren't a regular funk band, Eddy Grant (right) would often sport a blond wig on top of his blond afro.

Neville were regulars. It was also the base from which the local community newspaper *The Hustler* was published. Concerned that the restaurant was fostering the sort of black political subversion that had so altered America's social landscape, the authorities launched a campaign of coordinated harassment that brought a dozen heavy-handed police raids between January 1969 and July 1970. Coordinated by Special Branch's recently appointed, if not officially acknowledged, 'Black Power Desk', each invasion was looking for drugs, although no evidence was ever found and the *Mangrove*'s owner, Trinidadian former musician Frank Crichlow, was very anti-drugs. In August 1970 a couple of hundred local black residents taking part in a march to protest the raids were met by nearly four times as many police officers. Confrontation was inevitable, and nine demonstrators, including Crichlow and Darcus Howe, were arrested on charges including incitement to riot.

During the high-profile Old Bailey court case that followed, several of the nine defended themselves. Unsuccessfully demanding an all-black jury, they centred their case on politically motivated police harassment and allegedly fabricated police statements. The authorities' campaign was intended, as Home Office documents would later reveal, to 'decapitate' any black organisation. They even discussed deporting Crichlow, a twenty-year UK resident and former Commonwealth citizen, but couldn't quite make the legal justification. The event was used to discredit black radicalism as being inherently felonious, and the *Mangrove* described as a haven for 'criminals, ponces and prostitutes'.

The magistrate threw the charges out after discarding substantial portions of certain police statements. Outraged, the Director of Public Prosecutions opted to have the nine charged with the same offences once again, and had them re-arrested in a series of aggressive dawn raids. The second trial went ahead, and hinged entirely on whether the jury believed the police statements. They didn't. The nine were acquitted of all charges, and the Metropolitan Police tried to get the judge's closing statement, which referred to racism within the organisation, withdrawn. It wasn't.

Rather than whip up public condemnation of black self-help, the trials highlighted police misbehaviour, and elicited sympathy from the majority of ordinary British people towards their black counterparts. Not long after the success of the Equals' "Black Skin Blue Eyed Boys", Bob (Andy) & Marcia (Griffiths) reached number five with their reggae version of Nina Simone's "To Be Young, Gifted And Black".

The Mangrove Nine was a landmark case in the UK, revealing the establishment as demonizing a large group of British citizens purely on the basis of what they looked like. The Equals' single was even more notable. "Black Skin Blue Eyed Boys" was the first recognisably black British statement – a song that saw itself as being of this country in both words and music, and announced that London's indigenous black soul music was entirely self-sufficient. And it had become a mainstream success beyond music industry control.

LONDON HAD WHAT MIGHT BE CALLED a soul scene from the first half of the 1960s onwards. However, it said virtually nothing about the city itself, and barely left a footprint. Primarily a live phenomenon, its initial wave dovetailed with the emergence of the capital's beat groups, and grew out of the musical legacy of the mod movement, which presented US soul music to the UK as a legitimate, mainstream-friendly pop music – in the case of Dusty Springfield and the *Ready Steady Go!* special *The Motown Sound*, quite literally so. As the generation of British R&B players spawned by mod had migrated to new-style rock, the youth themselves never evolved their own soul groups. To a large degree that was left to the record industry itself, which, with a stupefying lack of imagination, figured that the future of British soul must, in fact, be American.

With the licensed-in sounds of Detroit and Memphis all over the British charts, a club scene built up in London. It catered especially to American servicemen stationed around the capital, who expected a funky live group as part of their evening's entertainment. Before long, these same service-men actually *became* said funky live groups – many first took to the stage while on weekend passes, and later made a go of it on demob. Among the best known was for-mer GI Herbie Goins, who arrived in London to sing in front of the Nightimers, a band that included Mick Eve and Speedy Acquaye, for-merly of Georgie Fame's Blue Flames, and Bar-badian trumpeter Harry Beckett, who went on to join Brotherhood Of Breath. Goins took over the spot from another

demobbed US serviceman, Ronnie Jones, who had previously fronted Blues Incorporated and continued to work solo in London clubs. While Goins enjoyed little recorded success – a single and an album that set nothing alight – he became a top draw at venues like *Whisky's*, the *Flamingo*, the *Telegraph* or the *Dome* at the *Boston Arms*. The undisputed king of this club circuit was Geno Washington, formerly of the US Air Force. Washington and his all-English Ram Jam Band were the most exciting live act in London – even the Rolling Stones were said to have thought twice about trying to follow Geno.

Away from the military, PP Arnold came to the UK with the Ike & Tina Turner Revue in 1966, and stayed on after Mick Jagger recommended her to the newly formed post-Mod Immediate label. She took over Ronnie Jones's backing group the BlueJays, when Jones was spending increasing time in Europe, and her big, blues-drenched voice made her a sensation on stage, which translated to the recording studio. Arnold's original take on "First Cut Is The Deepest" was a top twenty hit, and she was the first artist in the UK to have a hit with "Angel of the Morning".

The most serious contender for Geno's crown was Jimmy James, who wasn't American but certainly wasn't English either. Having come over from Jamaica in 1964 with his group the Vagabonds – which included the later-to-be-legendary Count Prince Miller – he recorded ska and rock steady, and even had a chart hit with a reggaefied version of Neil Diamond's "Red Red Wine", before Tony Tribe. However, the group worked out that they could make more money by sounding American and playing soul music, and did so to great effect both as headliners in London clubs and opening acts for the likes of the Who, the Faces and the Stones. Another West Indian on the circuit was Guyanese Ram John Holder. Now better known as an actor, he came to London in 1962 as an accomplished musician, and built a considerable following in the blues and R&B clubs. His *Black London Blues* album centred on the immigrant experience in London. While most of its self-penned numbers are tales of social injustice, racial prejudice and hard times – "Brixton Blues", "Wimpy Bar Blues", "Notting Hill Eviction Blues" and so on – it still finds room for the hilarious "Pub Crawling Blues", which does little other than name-check apparently random alehouses. Holder was something of a rarity in London's clubland, post-calypso, in that he sounded distinctly Caribbean, but this may be because he started out as a folk singer, and was part of the Greenwich Village scene before coming to London.

Record companies had long found it convenient to more or less to clone US acts. Earlier in the decade, both St Lucian former doo-wopper Emile Ford and South African soulster Danny Williams were funnelled into Johnny Mathis impressions, to the extent that the latter was even billed as 'Britain's Johnny Mathis'. A few years later. PP Arnold was Tina Turner 2.0, while the Foundations, a horn-heavy multi-racial group formed a couple of years after the Equals, perfected the classic Motown sound with hits like "Build Me Up, Buttercup" and "Baby, Now That I've Found You". This sort of lack of control did much to hamper the development of any unique British soul scene, as once acts had become caught up in someone else's trajectory, there was nowhere for them to go when trends changed. The arrival of the beat groups confined Ford and Williams to cabaret; PP Arnold moved into musical theatre, where a big voice is a huge asset; and the Foundations were packed off to the US and Motown to open for the Temptations. Having failed to make any impact, they came back to find their audience was moving on from a sound which had been dated from the very beginning.

Only a minority of black London soul acts actually had recording contracts; in an echo of the chitlin' circuit in the US, quite a few actually chose not to. Perhaps not surprisingly, many performers preferred the direct approach of getting paid cash in hand by a club owner to dealing with a white record company via a white manager. In those days, before big advances and transparent(ish) accounting, the better bands could earn a great deal more doing ten gigs a week on the road. Geno Washington was a vivid example: he resisted the overtures of record companies and persuasive friends alike, believing that he knew what his strengths were and he'd do best to stick to them. He wasn't wrong, either; when he did finally sign a deal, it was for a live album, *Hand Clappin', Foot Stompin', Funky-Butt... Live!*, which was released in December 1966 and still in the top forty in July of the next year.

As more London players got into the scene, it began to open out creatively rather than simply clone American soul. The original acts therefore found themselves pushed onto the Northern Soul circuit, where they reached enthusiastic audiences in clubs like Manchester's *Twisted Wheel* or the *Mojo* in Sheffield.

Besides taking on Caribbean influences, soul music in the capital was paying attention to what was happening else-where. That made it far more accessible to the mainstream pop world, in much the same way as 'Trojan Explosion' reggae. Londoners Joe E Young and the Toniks, who sprinkled their footstompin' soul music with pop psychedelia, earned a con-siderable following with their *Soul Buster* album, before Joe took over from Clem Curtis in the Foundations. Black Velvet, a

powerhouse trio led by a deeply funky Hammond organ, and previously known as the Raisins or the Black Raisins, played soul music that was so openly reggaefied it was as much downtown Kingston as downhome Memphis. In demand at both soul clubs and underground 'happenings', they supplemented their live work with half a dozen dancefloor hits, including the enduring cult favourite "African Velvet".

One significant but oddly overlooked contributor to this sixties scene was the Ferris Wheel, a band who readily embraced the embryonic hippieness of soul music to evolve a London-gutsier, Fifth Dimension-type sound. The band was fronted by singer Diane Ferraz (hence the name), an arrival from Trinidad. Her entry into the music business came in 1965 as half of the duo Diane & Nicky. A curiosity for the time as a black and white pairing, they were also the first act managed by future Wham! svengali Simon Napier-Bell. Diane's new group, though, bridged the old wave and the emerging pop soul that became part of the rock world. The line-up included George and Dave Sweetnam, the half-brothers of Emile Ford – saxophonist George, along with Ferris Wheel drummer Barry Reeves, had been in Ford's backing band The Checkmates – as well, later, as Dennis Elliott, who become Foreigner's drummer, and Jim Cregan, destined to join Steve Harley's Cockney Rebel. When Ferraz quit the music business in 1968, her spot in the band was taken over by a pre-*Hair* Marsha Hunt, who was in turn replaced by Linda Lewis. Although the Ferris Wheel never managed to turn their live success into record sales, their *Can't Break The Habit* album remains a Brit Soul gem.

Another integral part of the transition to an indigenous London soul sound was Root Jackson, who came to the UK from Curacao as a youngster, and settled in Huddersfield before he moved to the capital at the end of the 1960s. Together with his singing cousin, he formed Root and Jenny Jackson, a self-contained band in which Root started as drummer before moving up front to share vocal duties. Big at first on the Northern Soul scene, then causing a stir in the London clubs, they were at one point the highest-paid non-recording band in the country. Despite that, and a few hits after they signed to Beacon Records, trying to establish the notion of a unique UK sound was a constant struggle. Root thinks back to those days as we sit in the *Map Café*, a funky little spot hidden away behind Kentish Town High Road which thanks to the rehearsal rooms and studio upstairs has a strong connection to London's black music. Somewhat appropriately, when this big smiling figure first walked in, the "Theme From Shaft" is playing on the music system:

'In the beginning, with Root and Jenny, because we used to do a lot of that duo stuff – like Charlie and Inez Foxx or Ike and Tina – people used to think we were American, so we were always telling them 'No, we're from London'. We started doing US covers for the club gigs, because that was what the crowds expected, but we always had a distinct Caribbean flavour going on. I come from a steel pan background – that was my first instrument in the Caribbean – so as the band's drummer I would always have a kind of Caribbean rhythm underneath everything else that was going on.

In the beginning we had to compete with the Americans, our first record in 1968 was "Lean On Me" and was very American [*this is "Lean On Me" by deep soulster Tony Fox, written by Teddy Vann, not the Bill Withers song*]. We had another hit in the Northern Soul clubs with "Save Me" [*an Aretha Franklin original*], but I was writing from the beginning, our B-sides and album tracks, and that's where I come from, our experience over here, rather than try to ape the American sound.

'The thing was, the Caribbean sound did well, even if people didn't acknowledge what it was – Black Velvet were on Beacon Records same as Root and Jenny, and they were very Caribbean; and Eddy Grant's sound was too, "Baby Come Back" had a very Caribbean sound to it. But back then people associated soul music so strongly with Americans.'

During the 1960s, another aspect of the Caribbean was having a far more noticeable effect on London's music, and indeed London in general. Recalling, with considerable relish, a remarkably patronising incident backstage in a south London pub, Eddy Grant explains:

'At that time, England was a pretty dark place ... the English environment was extremely dark, musically and in every other wise. I remember there being really only two colours in England – brown and cream – all the houses were painted like that. In fact they actually brought that tradition to the Caribbean, where everything was brown and cream for a time! But it was the West Indians that basically changed England; the Greeks had a hand, the Indians had a hand, but ostensibly it was the West Indians, because it was the West Indians that were fighting. And they are the ones who bought colour to England.

'Take the Equals, they personified the Caribbean in dress. People talk about Bowie and Marc Bolan as having changed the dress code and dress mode of then-current popular music and culture, but the Equals really were the first. The Shadows wore suits, and everybody else, *even the Beatles* wore suits ... and they were all dark suits. I remember playing the *Witchdoctor* in Catford with a group that was Dave Dee, Dozy, Beaky, Mick and Tich, who everybody likes to say brought colour to the music business – *total rubbish!* We were dressing in lime greens and pinks and blues and yellows, things that were unheard of on the stage in England in pop music, and they were wearing – for the record – brown corduroy jackets! When they saw us in our brightly coloured uniforms they laughed, it was [*Eddy affects cockney accent*] "Oh look at that lot, look at that lot, poor chaps!" They didn't know what really was happening. There really was going to be a change and a massive change in the way people looked at black people from there on.

'All of that Carnaby Street issue too, I don't know if Colin Wilde is still alive, but it was on the Equals he tried out all his odd materials and whatever. I would go in there and have him draw whatever it is, and we'd wear it.'

Wilde, who died in 1988, was the co-founder of one of the first tailor/boutiques on Carnaby Street, the *Carnaby Cavern*. Its clientele was to include Jimi Hendrix, the Kinks and Alvin Stardust, as well, strangely, as Benny Hill. Eddy continues:

'You know the history with the Bay City Rollers and those trousers? Those trousers were mine! [*He chuckles*] If you look back into the history there's enough *Top of the Pops*es there with me wearing Bay City Rollers trousers!

'This is one of the reasons why there wasn't a wave of London black music that came through after the Equals. There were many great bands, some even better than the Equals, but pop music requires a certain bravado, a certain upfront in-your-face kind of attitude, and the Equals had that. We showed it straight off in how we dressed, and from a cultural standpoint there's never been anything like the Equals.'

AS THE SIXTIES BECAME THE SEVENTIES, London's soul scene made a dramatic shift. With funk now the way forward, it was no longer influenced by American soul alone, and began to incorporate elements from English prog rock. That turn of events allowed much more of a London flavour to come through, according to Root:

'We had just come back from Europe and the mood was very progressive, and it was general for people to take a bit more interest in *music*. The bands were not just taking the American sound but creating something that was distinctly British ... using the influences from Africa and the Caribbean as well as the States. I remember doing a gig as Root and Jenny in the West End, at the *Valbonne*, a very hip place at the time – it had a swimming pool in the middle of it. Spartacus was down there, he's related to Jenny [*Spartacus*

R was Osibisa's first bass player]. He told us about this new band he had, and then Osibisa burst on the scene, and then came Cymande ,and we were taking what we were doing into F.B.I., a much more progressive situation [*F.B.I. were a nine-piece, horn-heavy, very modern funk outfit*].

'F.B.I. was a band that, at first, was a backing band for Americans when they came over and couldn't bring their own bands – the first tour we did was with Eddie Floyd, we did Percy Sledge, Jimmy Helms, Ben E King. You step up a gear for that kind of gig because they'd come in one day and you're on the road the next – one rehearsal and *bang* you're ready to go. Soul ... blues ... funk ... all of that, you really had to know your shit to get the feel right, because they weren't going to take any old stuff. But there was discipline involved, so when we were doing our own stuff we couldn't fail to keep it tight. That meant we could experiment more, be more progressive, and it meant our own influences could come in. Not only our Caribbean influences, but telling our own story of being in this country – we'd been here since the sixties, from the street, fighting with the Teddy Boys, and all that came through the music.

'This was at the very end of the 1960s, and we'd taken a lead from what was going in the rock world. Now it was all about *playing*. We were kind of showing off, because it was all about competition, but in a nice way! It was a real change from the singer-and-backing-band situation. Us, Kokomo, Cymande,

we were groups who had singers, but it was led by the musicians who used to practise so much. You'd spend hours just jamming and swapping licks – that was the jazz element coming out – so you'd really be able to cut it, in any situation. We always had a good show, we knew we had to compete with anything that came in from America when we started opening for them. Then when you'd be in the studio you'd record live, and you could do it, that's why those albums still stand up today because they have that energy about them.'

The timing was just right for such musical adventures. In London at the start of the 1970s, the pub rock scene was getting going in boozers like the *Hope & Anchor* in Islington, the *Red Lion* in Fulham, the *Dublin Castle* in Camden Town, the *Half Moon* in Herne Hill and the *Torrington* in North Finchley. In the beginning, they carried over from the largely London Irish and calypsonian tradition of music on a Sunday lunchtime or a Friday night, or in the case of Kentish Town's *Tally Ho* moved from a jazz-only policy. Then this circuit became augmented by enterprising landlords who liked a bit of music themselves. A couple of years into the 1970s, this no-frills, usually R&B/rock'n'roll-based antithesis to glam rock was a fully fledged movement.

It was pub rock, via groups like Kilburn & The High Roads (Ian Dury's first band), Dr Feelgood, Bees Make Honey and Squeeze (featuring Jools Holland on piano), that laid the back-to-basics, DIY groundwork for punk. It opened up small informal venues once again, stimulating live music to such a degree that for a while it seemed the only way to sell drinks was to have a band on in the back room. Audiences weren't necessarily too fussed about what the band was, provided they could play and never strayed into self-indulgence. Crowds wanted easily accessible drinking music that might well facilitate a bit of a dance, and London's new wave of funk bands fit the bill perfectly. The circuit of established clubs like the *Q*, the *Marquee* or the *Country Club* was now supplemented with big, or sometimes not-so-big, pubs. Root continues:

'You could earn decent money from those gigs, because there were so many of them, then there was *Dingwalls*, and even bigger places like the *Roundhouse* was still having regular bands. You'd complement that with the university gigs, because the university circuit was kicking for musicians at that time, as they had the budgets and they used to book bands on a regular basis. There was nowhere without a band.

'We had a large, I'd call it, *underground* following. Everywhere we played, us and a lot of other London bands on that scene, was packed, people were hanging from the ceiling, and the sweat and energy was something else. It helped us all grow as bands, being able to play to audiences like that without the pressure of having to always look for the wider appeal.'

Root is spot-on in this respect. These audiences and their expectations played a huge part in shaping London funk. Although above all they wanted it tight, with plenty of *playing*, the clue is in the name 'pub rock' – crowds were usually inebriated enough to accept all sorts of ideas and accents. Developing with far greater freedom than much of the US equivalent, these funk groups were closer in spirit to Funkadelic or Rufus than the more conventional outfits. The heaviest and most black radical of them all was Noir; Kokomo, possibly the capital's best-ever white funk band, were jazzy; Gonzalez, who had evolved out of guitarist Bobby Tench's Gass and featured the ubiquitous Mick Eve, had a vivid Latin tinge to their rock-y funk; and as for Root's F.B.I. (it stood for Funky Business Incorporated), think Tower of Power after a very long holiday in the Caribbean.

The most remarkable band of all, though, was Cymande. These eight musicians were to West Indian music what Osibisa were to West African sounds; they created the perfect fusion of Caribbean and funk structures, with a nod to contemporary rock, but did it from a deeply spiritual Rasta perspective. That could only have happened in London – all the players lived here, but were from assorted West Indian backgrounds – and it came before roots reggae had become remotely fashionable. Their first album, *Cymande,* was an astonishing and astonishingly London funky take on the smoky Jamaican jazz of Cedric Im Brooks or Count Ossie.

At a time when it was still considered cool to have a live band as part of the clubbing experience, these groups were a valuable component of London's funk scene. Alongside

London Caribbean/African funk group Cymande, whose 1972 album *Cymande* was one of the earliest musical examples of Rastafari in the capital.

them on the capital's small stages – less innovative, perhaps, but never stinting on the driving rhythm – was a funky result of the spate of contemporary independences in West Africa.

HEAVYWEIGHT AMERICAN SOUL STARS had been taking their revues to West Africa since the mid-1960s. This was prompted as much by the desire to send cultural envoys to satisfy the newly independent nations' thirst for self-assured black expression as by the opportunity to open up lucrative new markets. These acts, and their subsequently imported records, made a deep impression on local highlife, and arrangements started to incorporate western ideas such as horn riffs and big bass guitars. The 1966 Nigerian album *Super Afro Soul*, in which Orlando Julius & His Modern Aces created a supremely funky blend of highlife, Sam & Dave, James Brown's Famous Flames and jazzy brass tinges, is probably the earliest prominent example. Through the rest of the decade, the continent's love of soul music grew. James Brown set a concert attendance record in Lagos in 1970, while the Soul To Soul Festival in Ghana the next year, organized by Maya Angelou, brought together Wilson Pickett, Ike & Tina, Roberta Flack and the Staple Singers with native Ghanaians Guy Warren, ET Mensah and the Damas Choir, for a 14-hour concert in Black Star Square, Accra. A documentary of the event is available on DVD.

By the start of the 1970s, legions of groups had become so consumed by this music as to be virtually James Brown or Otis Redding tribute bands. Yet more studied the American riffs and arrangements to recreate soul songs, but then put African lyrics on top. Ghanaian star George Darko coined the term 'funky highlife' around this point, and a great deal of the very best can be found on compilations like Strut Records' *Nigeria 70*, Superfly Records' *Afrofunk Expressway*

and Harmless Records' *Africafunk: Return To The Original Sound Of 1970s Funky Africa*. These albums show off a level of soul sophistication that could have given groups like Mandrill or the Bar-Kays a run for their money. Acts like Shina Williams, Orlando Julius & The Afro Sounders, Tony Sarfo, Afro Cult Foundation, Ebo Taylor, the Sahara All Stars and Monomono were local heroes, and provided serious competition for the more enduring Gasper Lawal, Tony Allen and Sunny Ade.

EMI Nigeria latched onto this music, and with remarkable appreciation for its value in 1971 the company brought Fela, the undisputed king of what he called 'Afrobeat', over to London to record. As a mark of how highly he was regarded, they installed him and his band in Abbey Road studios. While here, Fela hung out with Ginger Baker, and gigged in clubs like the *Four Aces* in Dalston, the *Q Club* and the *100 Club*. It was in these jumping, capital-city sweatboxes that he soaked up London's unique multi-national black funk vibes before recording *Fela's London Scene*, which many believe, with good reason, to be the greatest Afro-funk album ever made. Arguably precipitated by the album, London came to play a huge part in that music during the 1970s.

Although most West African countries had well-equipped recording industries, releases were often sent to London for final mixing and mastering, particularly when multinationals like EMI, Phonogram or Decca were involved. Another trend, reminiscent of how Jamaican reggae was 'stringsed up', was for string section overdubs or extra orchestration to be added to Afro-funk in London. This was especially prevalent among Nigerian producers, whose desire for sophistication gave their funk a kind of Philly-Sound flavour.

As a result, London became the place to be for modern African recording. Osibisa were massive in West Africa by now, and bands wanted to catch some of that vibe. So much money was sloshing around the West African recording industry – particularly in oil-rich Nigeria – that whole groups would be flown over just to cut a couple of tracks in costly studios like RAK or Olympic. Such jaunts had the added bonus of London's clothes shops: many of the vertiginous platform boots and the shirt collars measured in acreage that grace Afro-funk album sleeves were bought in Oxford Street or the King's Road. Bands like Congo's Super Mambo 69, Nigeria's Ofo The Black Company, and Ghana's Ebo Taylor and CK Mann flitted in and out to record, but many opted for longer-term stays. The Funkees, one of Nigeria's most popular Afro-funk acts, moved to London en masse in

Many Nigerian funk bands who came to London to record in the 1970s spent as much time in Kensington Market as they did in the studio.

1973; fellow countrymen BLO and Apostles arrived a little later; South African multi-racial exiles Hawk assembled in the capital in 1974; Kenya's Matata built quite a career in London; and both Super Combo and Sabanoh 75 came from Sierra Leone on tour and decided to stay.

Although their recordings were more or less exclusively shipped back home, these groups enjoyed a tremendous amount of interplay with the capital's West Indian, African and English session players, both on stage and in the studio. Wala Danga remembers this as being as much of an attraction as top studios or alarming wardrobe, and it became a defining factor for making the move:

'It used to work for even the more traditional African bands when they came to London, because whatever they did would have bits of soul and funk in it, and that was every African musician's journey – to find out where their music had travelled to. American soul was from the same tree as African music, which was easy to see from the cross-fertilisation going on when they arrived here.

'It was common for them to mix it up with West Indians, and easy to make it work. There was something about the music being from the same stem root, as it were, that the West Indian musicians didn't find it at all difficult to cross over to play it. It was as if they instinctively knew, and it was good for the African musicians to look at what they were doing from another angle. The musicians that came in to work with bands would have listened to music like calypso or funk or reggae at home, and be infusing whatever knowledge they had of those types of music into the African situation. You know, 'Why don't we try some of this in it?", and then find out it works. That was proved in the case of Osibisa, where you had people like Wendell [*Richardson, an Antiguan*] singing some of the songs and composing some of the songs. Or Spartacus R [*Grenadian*]. They were very much a part of that sound.

'In live gigs, the audiences in London loved it, because there were elements they could easily identify with – say if a group over here played one particular strand, like fuji, which is a Nigerian kind of deep roots music, many people would probably get lost a bit. I used to have lots of white friends always asking me "where is *the one* in this music?", but if you get them playing kind of crossover funk they were quick to find where the beat was and could identify with the music. It made it easier, [*he starts chuckling*] or more palatable for their ears. Not just English audiences, but the West Indians too.'

These musicians were building a very progressive and unique brand of funk, as their intrinsic understanding of how a groove worked could probably challenge George Clinton, while they also knew more about polyrhythms than most Americans or Londoners could shake a stick at – or a shaker, for that matter. Just as African acts were employing London-based players, so these musicians were learning another dimension to their music. Conspicuous in Cymande's work, that's also noticeable in a great deal of what F.B.I. and Gonzalez did.

Playing live, the bands that were in London for the long haul had no trouble fitting in and building a following beyond their own national crowds. While most gigged largely in clubs, those that crossed over to venues like the *Nashville*, the *Greyhound* or the *George Robey* acquired fanbases as broad as any London group. Matata, for instance, became entrenched enough in their new funk environment to enjoy huge club hits with "I Feel Funky" and "I Wanna Do My Thing". Many London fans who bought their 1974 *Independence* album assumed they were a local band.

As the 1970s progressed, the keys to the buoyant Afro-funk recording industry were two of black London's biggest music-business movers and shakers, Eddy Grant and Akie Deen. Following his incapacitation in 1971 due to a heart attack and collapsed lung, Eddy no longer toured and had built a musical empire in Stamford Hill, North London. His state-of-the-art Coach House Studios had top-notch mastering facilities, and he'd even bought his own pressing plant – the first black-owned manufacturing facility in England. He was well known in Africa from his time with the Equals, and now African bands in the capital were seeking him out. Wala remembers what he did for the capital's Afro-funk:

'Eddy Grant was one of the main people behind the recording in London. I pay my respects to him because he did a lot of groundwork and really got things started. He was always very keen on Africa, especially in his wanting to go back to Africa and play in Africa. He really kept the links between London and Africa.

'He had his Coach House Studios, and a lot of these guys would find their way up there to record in his studio with him. Because then Eddy was most well established as a black musician in London, so really if you wanted to aspire to be successful in London you had to aim to be like Eddy. He had had a number one chart record, "Baby Come Back", and all those other hits in the sixties, so there was a lot of aura around Eddy even then. So all the musicians were kind of looking up to him – him and Errol Brown from Hot Chocolate – but it was really more Eddy because he stayed with that kind of rootsy sound, fusing the African and the Caribbean sounds together. He gave the groups a lot of help too, he'd reduce the rates if you didn't have any money and he was always giving advice, which you took because by then he had done it all. It

Eddy Grant relaxing on the veranda of his Barbados villa.

helped them get record deals too, when the companies knew Eddy Grant was behind these bands.'

Wala is understating Eddy's role. He operated a hugely benevolent regime at the Coach House, and it was rare for a black band – African or otherwise – not to be able to cut their tune regardless of the state of their finances. As in-house producer he often got involved, giving advice or assistance or even acting as uncredited, de facto producer. He feels it was his duty to assist London's black music community:

'Help a bro! … I wanted to change England – in a great regard I did – and having the recording studio wasn't just for me, in fact it was never just for me. It was hoping to change the way black musicians operated. Those days you were getting stuff from Jamaica, you were not making stuff, and if you were you had to compromise all the time. I was forever talking to people, trying to bring them away from the status quo, trying to show them there can be another way. People from every different area of black, I interfaced with them – if it was that they needed studio time then so be it, if they didn't have any money then so be it. Everything with me was an open-door basis down at Stamford Hill.

'What was important was that we were able to drive the culture through, to create a black presence … a black way … We were able to create history, and that history is now being shown in all sorts of ways as there is now an accommodation made for us in Britain.'

Not everything produced at the Coach House was Afro-funk, but Eddy created a fertile, style-swapping nursery for London funk, soul and reggae that drove the style's journey in the capital. The premises became the same kind of musical information exchange that Melodisc had been ten years previously and, as Wala stated, helped many Afro-funk acts to get signed.

Eddy produced Matata, whose first album was on President, the Equals' record label. Vernon Cummings and Keni St George took their London-formed, trans-national Afro-funk bands, Dante and Ozo – both were considered serious rivals to Osibisa at one point – to the Coach House, and they were signed by Epic and DJM respectively. The supremely funky 32nd Turn Off also released a Coach House-recorded LP on Jay Boy, while the UK's first black power-blues trio (ie embryonic heavy metal), the Sundae Times, featuring future Osibisa member Wendell Richardson, made an album there for Joy Records, entitled *Us Coloured Kids*.

Later in the decade, Sierra Leonean concert promoter and music business entrepreneur Akie Deen came into the business. Having built a name for himself back home by bringing over major American acts to share billing with West Africa's finest, he came to London because he believed it to be central to developing the international potential of African music. He also reckoned the situation here to be wide open, and followed the Emil Shallit model, utilising the capital's resources and players but with an eye on both the West African and the expat market. His strictly DIY approach used the network of small studios and disc cutters that were then springing up. Drawing from the capital's pool of African and Afro players, he started out recording straight-up maringa and highlife, but became better known for mixing these traditional musics with disco, reggae, calypso, samba and rhumba. The results would go out for sale in London through the Oti brothers' retail network on one of his own labels – Afrodisc, Rokel or Sabanoh Sounds – or be exported or licensed to West Africa.

Deen didn't limit his recordings to London musicians either. It became more or less obligatory for any popular African act touring or even stopping off in the UK to detour into one of Deen's sessions and cut a few sides for him. He could also afford to bring groups over specifically to record. In 1976, he started running songwriting competitions in Sierra Leone, with a first prize being a trip to London and a recording session. Such was the status of this contest that when the first winner, Big Fayia, came over to cut his winning number "Blackpool" (about a Freetown football team), he was accompanied by Sierra Leone's biggest band, Afro National. Often, presumably to get around contractual obligations, Deen would record visiting bands under different names.

Deen's London productions blended musicians and styles for something he called 'discocalypso', putting highlife, juju and maringa into an irresistible soundscape of thumping disco beats and super-slick production, and then stirring in liberal splashes of reggae, soca and funk. It made such an impact that you could barely go to any club or party in West Africa, or any decent disco in London, between, say, 1978 and 1982, without hearing a plethora of Akie Deen productions. His artists included Teddy Davis; Super Combo; Miatta Fahnbulleh, a Liberian R&B and jazz diva, who had narrowly missed success in the US; Sabanoh 75 (who also called themselves Sabanoh International and Wagadu Gu, and were really Afro National after they had moved to the capital); Jimmy Senyah (whose professional name was an anagram of his real name, Haynes); Afro Akino (in reality, famously, the Ghanaian stars Nana Ampadu & the African Brothers); the conservatory-trained Martha Ulaeto; and Emmanuel Rentzos.

Super Combo were one of many West African funk bands that took up residency in London during the 1970s, to earn a good living on the club circuit.

Deen reached a personal peak with Bunny Mack's "Let Me Love You", a calypso-ish/highlife-ish disco track that became a worldwide dancefloor smash, making a massive impression in West Africa, North and South America, and the UK. His big mainstream hit came a couple of years later when he produced Odyssey, formerly of New York but relocated to London. Giving them the Lamont Dozier song "Going Back To My Roots", and adding his trademark rhythms, he correctly calculated the African market would love the sentiments. The tune was huge there, a number four in the UK, and gave the group their first US club hit for several years.

Many purist guardians of the African music flame chose to discount Deen's achievements as 'not real African music' – that word 'authentic' cropped up frequently, usually coupled with 'not'. The truth is, he was a businessman and a music lover who reacted to what Africans all over the world let him know they wanted, rather than attempting to sell them what he might have figured was best for them.

The music that came out of England during the five years from 1977 – not just Deen's productions – was so influential in Africa itself that the period became known, completely without prejudice, as 'the London era'. It also seems relevant that "Let Me Love You" was voted Record of the Year in several African countries, won gold discs, still figures on compilation albums, and has its hooks sampled on a regular basis. At the time of writing, Akie Deen was Sierra Leone's Trade Commissioner for the United Kingdom.

WHILE THIS AFRICAN FUNK INVASION was going on under the radar, the British bands had been finding ways into larger UK labels. Just like Osibisa before them, this was down to their live performances, more a matter of individuals' enthusiasm than A&R policy, and usually involved overseas rather than domestic deals. Cymande were a case in point: long-time British pop producer John Schroeder (he co-wrote "Walking Back To Happiness" for Helen Shapiro in 1961) happened across them rehearsing in Soho when he was looking for a rock band that he was supposed to meet. He was so impressed that he did a deal with them, recorded a single, "The Message", and on the strength of that got them signed to the US label Janus. When the tune was an American hit, that convinced Pye, who had a licensing deal with Janus, to put out their first album in the UK.

The Olympic Runners, in 1974, were an equally happy accident, courtesy of veteran English blues producer and label boss Mike Vernon. The group members were all session regulars at Olympic Studios in Barnes, where Vernon was using them to back a blues artist. Waiting for said singer when he was late for a recording, the players messed about with some funk grooves. Vernon recognised quality when he heard it, and recorded it as "Put Your Music Where Your Mouth Is". Signed to London Records in the US, it became an instant club hit, and eventually brought the band to the attention of the UK side of the company.

Perhaps the most fortuitous of all were Root's F.B.I., who owe their recording contract to a north London pub, a children's TV show and someone who did rather well out of Woodstock. Root explains:

'We were playing the *Hope and Anchor*, and the producer of this kids' TV programme, *Magpie*, was in the audience. He really liked us and came down again to see us, and after that put us on the show. When we did *Magpie* a friend of mine saw us on it, Alvin Lee of Ten Years After, the blues group from the

era before. I knew him because we used to share the same agent up north, from back when I was in Root and Jenny, and we'd become friends. He phoned me up and ended up becoming our manager.

'Alvin had made a lot of money from Ten Years After and Woodstock and all of that [*the group played at the festival and were featured in the film and on the soundtrack album*], and had invested in this studio complex near Henley, [*Hook Manor*] on acres and acres of land. It was beautiful, and he invited us down to record there, to make the F.B.I.'s album in what was the perfect creative environment.

'Alvin totally understood what we were about, and he'd got us an English producer. We were dead against an American producer because we didn't want that sound, we wanted to remain true British, but he'd come up with this guy Chris Kimsey. He was only 21 but already he'd been working with Pete Frampton, Humble Pie and those bands from Alvin Lee's era – he went on to produce the Rolling Stones. He got it straight away, he was full of energy and he wasn't afraid, nor was he intimidated by us as a band. We were really lucky to get him because he knew how to record live music properly, which not every producer did. He knew we knew what we were doing, so he'd put stuff down, and when he'd had enough he'd say "Oh, fuck off!" and go off into the snooker room and leave me to it. When he'd come back, he'd balance it up perfectly.'

The result is the *F.B.I.* album, probably the finest example of London's take on classic funk, a storming set of brass-laden songs that never let you forget they're from the Caribbean. It spawned several club hits and quickly become a cult album that, to this day, is usually available on somebody's catalogue.

Even if strong live followings and dancefloor hits were enough to sustain London's funkateers until the middle of the decade, however, they weren't nearly sufficent to get them through what came next – disco. By taking the accent firmly off *playing*, disco reversed the ideals of this generation of bands, and virtually killed London's live funk scene. It now made far more commercial sense for venues to employ deejays rather than book bands. As relatively little disco was made in England during the genre's early years, UK record companies relished the notion of licensing in from abroad, instead of dealing with irksome bands and their managers – something that would become a trend (as the next few chapters will show). Although the perpetually optimistic Root roars with laughter when he talks about 'the time when everybody had a band on,

Post-F.B.I., Root Jackson was never less than dynamic as a solo artist.

and although they had a deejay, that deejay knew his place' he still splutters when he talks about what happened next:

'I thought it was a great insult to music, when you've got venues that were making good money taking their stages out. The music was being made instantly, and nobody was helping anybody to develop a career. It all became short term, as the record companies started seeing it as *records*, not *artists*, or *singles* not *albums* – nothing like it used to be.'

Really, the problems with the record labels lay with their never properly knowing what to do with black British acts, as so few people within those companies had got their heads around the notion of black people or black music being anything other than foreign. It was no coincidence that so many of this chapter's bands were signed to US or International departments or smaller labels – F.B.I. were on Good Earth, the label owned by Tony Visconti, who produced the first Osibisa album. Now, with disco, the business thought it had a neat pigeonhole for these bands. This served further to infuriate Root Jackson:

'Once the disco thing started happening that made a lot of difference, because here we are, musicians coming from the sixties with all that tradition, all that energy from the music that was coming from everywhere, *and they throw disco at us*! I've always been dead against that mentality – the sheep mentality – when everybody sounds the same, and there was no individuality in the music when disco came along. Before that if you hear Pickett you know it's Pickett, if you hear Otis you know it's Otis ... they all had an individual sound. But then suddenly we're fighting a battle because the record companies all want disco music, they're saying to us "You're a black band, why don't you do something that sounds like that?"

'It was one of the reasons the band split up, because some of them wanted to go that way. I definitely didn't, I wanted to keep the original energy going ... I'm still here!'

Some funk bands did make the switch. Gonzalez adapted very smoothly, and had their biggest hit in 1979 with "I Haven't Stopped Dancing Yet"; similarly the Olympic Runners had "Sir Dancealot" and "Get It While You Can". Otherwise there were a few other successes – Bob Dylan used Kokomo on sessions for his *Desire* album, and Cymande had quite a career in the US. That said, while outfits like the Breakfast Band and Morrissey-Mullen formed the bridge to London's new wave of jazz/funk, little London funk made an impact after the Equals' churning, Eddy Grant-penned "Funky Like A Train" in 1976.

ALTHOUGH LONDON'S FUNK ERA seemed to come and go relatively quickly, two by-products that it left behind proved significant in the early days of the march of the city's black music towards self-empowerment. As we'll see, Eddy's Coach House set-up provided a template for many who came later, and inspired a great deal more – it was not unusual for black acts to set their sights simply on 'being like Eddy'. It also served as a vivid illustration of what was and wasn't possible; even if Coach House recording studios and produc-tion facilities were viable, Eddy admits that perhaps he went one step too far in creating his own pressing plant, primarily for his Ice Records label's product:

'Setting up the studio was one thing ... you can't imagine what it was like trying to find out how to build a recording studio when there isn't one – it was like Columbus stepping over the horizon. I always had available to me somebody else's recording studio, and when I left the Equals I no longer had that, but nobody will tell me [*how to build a studio*] because then I wouldn't be using their studio. But we built it.

'When it became critical was with the pressing plant, because the bastards at the major companies would use my plant for their overruns – Christmas is coming or Elvis's birthday or something. They would use my facility and wouldn't want to pay; there was a particular time when the music business was in such terrible straits that they wouldn't pay me. So I had on the one hand the brothers who *couldn't* pay me, and on the other hand the white companies who *wouldn't* pay me. And on top of that I had the white companies that were providing vinyl and the other necessities, like if a stamper broke or one of the extruders broke or something, they wanted cash for it – I had to pay cash for everything. So I was fighting an impossible war.'

Although he didn't keep the pressing plant as long as the rest of his Stamford Hill set-up, the whole exercise demonstrated how important it was to gain control over what you were doing.

Root also felt the way forward was greater control, but looked at it from an inside-the-existing-business point of view. On one side he saw black music being squeezed by disco, and venues vanishing; on the other, artists unable to take advantage of the recording side because so few understood the business they were in. They weren't maximising their publishing; they weren't collecting all the monies due to them; they were signing restrictive contracts with record and management companies; and often they didn't have the money or the wherewithal to get professional advice. It's not much different for a lot of young white bands, but black bands feel it more acutely as they tend to have a limited range of industry options. In 1985, together with Byron Lye-Fook – Omar's dad, who had been in Root and Jenny – Root founded the Black Music Association. Launched on the same day as Live Aid – and gaining a fair bit of PR mileage as the aid-for-Africa concert had virtually no black presence – the organisation was dedicated to educating black musicians as to their rights within the business, not only in the UK but across the Caribbean and Africa too.

The timing was fortuitous, because the GLC had just commissioned a report on London's black music industry and found it to be particularly lacking on the business side. Between them and Camden Council, the BMA raised enough grant money to get going the ball rolling. Root remembers:

'After F.B.I. split up, I had a bit of knowledge about the industry from them and Root and Jenny, and I wanted to find out a bit more. It didn't make any sense to me at all that so many of us were just making music, with no knowledge of the business that we were in. You hear all these stories about how so-and-so didn't get that or so-and-so didn't get this, so the primary purpose of the BMA was to educate musicians about their rights. We figured if we could do that then they would up their game as far as the business side of things went.

'It was modelled on the old American organisation that had Miles Davis and Stevie Wonder in it, and we started going to [*mainstream*] music business seminars ourselves, to find out what it was they knew that we didn't! The first one we went to cost £600 per person, and there was the BPI, PRS, the Musicians' Union, the Music Publishers Association and PPL, all sitting on this panel, and they charging that sort of money! I said to Byron, "This is designed to keep musicians out!" So we went to all of those organisations and we explained what the BMA was, and we asked them to send representatives to our seminars. Which they did, and that kicked it off straight away.

'The BMA ran courses on every aspect of the music business – journalism, marketing, management, manufacture, PR … And we'd negotiate with record companies for artists, get them legal or accounting help, look over their contracts and give them any help they needed. What we really wanted to do was to get musicians to start looking at their careers as long-term things, and the only way they could do that was if they understood every aspect of it and could prepare for the future. At one point we had over six hundred members.'

One of those members who benefited hugely from the BMA was, not surprisingly, Omar. Root and Byron negotiated a deal for him that saw his debut album *There's Nothing Like This* come out on their own Kongo label, and sell over thirty thousand copies, which put them in a very strong position to negotiate with the major labels for it and any singles.

EDDY RELOCATED TO BARBADOS around thirty years ago, where he built a state-of-the-art studio and accommodation complex that's used by some of the biggest names in music. He still records and tours, pretty much to his own schedule, but his real energies go into promoting ringbang, a fundamental pan-Caribbean black musical style that dates back to slavery. Found in the basis of the region's different genres – mento, rhumba, kaiso and so on – the music allowed the different styles, and therefore different people, to communicate. It is, Grant believes, an important aspect of the Caribbean and its diaspora:

'I spent my time trying to make musical statements that are good for people, and ringbang is good for people – it's good for us black people in particular. I didn't make it as a racist thing, though. Just like how the Japanese or the Chinese would make karate or talk about Zen, it comes from them and they're proud of it, but it's for everybody. Ringbang comes from us and I'm proud of it, it's about stretching the borders of what is good for us.'

Root has remained much closer to home. He continues to run the BMA and Kongo Music, and remains totally true to his beliefs with one of the funkiest scenes in London – every Sunday night, at the *Prince of Wales* just off Kilburn High Road, whichever veteran funkateers are in town and fancy a jam turn up and play. Regular participants include Tim Cansfield, Mick Eve, Richard Bailey, Winston Delandro and Mel Gaynor; the funk they create is little short of astonishing and admission is free. And even better than that, during the half-time break, on really good nights, the landlady brings out platters of complementary fried chicken.

2

Nobody's going anywhere

'We were the second generation of black people over here and did what came naturally to us. Whatever had been thrown into our pot went into making lovers' rock.'

Janet Kay, *Queen of lovers' rock*

CHAPTER SIX

The Whole World Loves a Lovers

‖‖

Lovers' rock sells reggae to Jamaica

IN JULY 1979, AFTER JANET KAY had performed her hit single "Silly Games" on *Top of the Pops,* the *Guinness Book of Records* hailed her achievement as the 'First British Female Reggae Singer to top the UK charts'. In fact, they'd got a bit ahead of themselves – the single peaked at number two. Kay herself wasn't nearly so carried away. The next day she phoned Rank Xerox's offices in Wembley, where she worked in the personnel department, to ask if it would be all right if she came in a bit late: 'I was on *Top of the Pops* last night', was the excuse. 'And I'm a bit tired.' Her bemused boss gave her the whole day off.

Although both Janet and her distinctive pop-reggae style appeared to have come from nowhere, young men and women who called themselves 'black British' had by this point been creating and consuming massive quantities of light, soulful reggae for more than half a decade. Having started in the capital, lovers' rock reggae, as the genre came to be known, had spread to cities like Birmingham, Leeds and Bristol, and indeed anywhere with a sizeable second-generation black population. While a significant proportion of the records commented on black life in London, the most common subject matter was young love in all its guises, and the melodies owed almost as much to the sounds of Philadelphia and Detroit as to Kingston, Jamaica.

Over the course of the 1970s, lovers' rock had developed quietly, and pretty much independently of the higher-profile 'roots' end of reggae. Centred primarily on sound systems, it evolved organically as the music that best reflected the concerns and preoccupations of those youngsters.

That a music form could thrive for so long, so far removed from any mainstream spotlight, is not totally surprising – such things have happened time and time again among London's various tribes. Quite *why* it evolved, however, given that Jamaican music provided its fundamental building blocks, is remarkable. To a significant degree, lovers' rock originated in the widespread dissatisfaction of its audience with what was going on elsewhere in reggae.

WHILE IT MIGHT NOW SEEM downright churlish, a large proportion of black teenagers – whom you'd expect to have formed the primary audience for reggae – became disgruntled during the mid-1970s. This, after all, was the time when such giants of the music as Culture, the Mighty Diamonds, Augustus Pablo, U-Roy, Max Romeo, Johnny Clarke, Big Youth and Burning Spear strode the studios; Lee Perry was at the peak of his powers on the bridge of the Black Ark; and Bob Marley was honing his output down into *Exodus*, which *Time* magazine was to proclaim 'Album of the Century'.

It was reggae's Golden Era, a jamboree of roots, culture and creativity brought to prominence when the left-field edge of the rock audience embraced the sounds and social consciousness of Jamaican music.

Much like Afro-rock, as described in chapter four, roots reggae first found mass favour in the universities – indeed Osibisa played a considerable part in opening the ears of the rock crowd to ethnic styles. With its student-friendly combination of militancy, marijuana and danceability, roots reggae was a reggae movement that could be taken seriously.

The Queen of Lovers' rock, Janet Kay, circa "Silly Games".

That it shifted into the wider mainstream as a partner-in-disaffection to punk was entirely predictable.

Even if reggae at the time enjoyed its highest-ever status, the truth behind the enthusiastic acclaim of the UK music press was that many sons and daughters of the Caribbean simply couldn't relate to those records. Their disconnect with what was ostensibly 'their music' provides a vivid example of how the relationship of black music to black Britain has always been too complex to be taken for granted.

Even if the UK at large tended to view its black population as a single homogenous group, several different black youth tribes were emerging in the 1970s, each under the radar but easily identifiable to anyone in the know. Just like white kids, really. With black Britain undergoing the most significant shift in its demographics since the early days of mass immigration, the notion of a one-size-fits-all playlist was becoming less relevant than ever. A sizeable wave of black teenagers, born in the UK, was coming of age. These were the first black Britons to approach their lives from a social perspective that related to the Caribbean or Africa as well as Great Britain, and saw their blackness as being qualified by both. Exposed to cultural influences ranging across a broad cross-colonial spectrum, and of course to the US as well, via TV, this generation was characterised by a huge internal diversity. Jamaican music was especially prominent in the mix, and formed the basis of the first totally British black music.

SKA AND ITS PREDECESSOR, JA BOOGIE – the late-1950s' Jamaican take on US R&B – fetched up in the UK at the start

of the 1960s, almost immediately after it established itself in Jamaica. Independence Fever was mounting in London, with the Union flag due to be lowered on the island for the last time in 1962, and national pride among Jamaican expats was running high. As increasing numbers of Jamaican records began to arrive in London, to be sold in all manner of black-owned commercial establishments, Jamaicans embraced their music with a patriotic gusto that kicked calypso,

R&B and jazz off their turntables, to become black London's soundtrack of choice.

Beyond the sheer number of records being made, or the size of the potential audience, the key component in this Caribbean musical shift was the sound systems. Trinidadians may have made an instant impact in London, introducing calypso as a ready-made musical culture, but to get it to the ordinary people they had to rely on the sound systems, and those were almost exclusively controlled by Jamaicans.

A distinctive product of the Jamaican ghettos, sound systems were invented in West Kingston in the late 1940s as a way to provide exciting entertainment for the masses who could not afford orchestral dances or radios. Pioneering sound-system owners like Coxsone, Duke Reid and Prince Buster used powerful amplification and banks of massive speaker cabinets to put on open-air dances that became the focal point of downtown life. Competition between sound systems was so intense that continual musical innovation was the only way to survive. To ensure that the crowds kept coming back, the operators had to identify what their clientele wanted before they even knew it themselves, then serve up hot new tunes that would be guaranteed to go down well. What distinguished the top systems from the rest was their ability to play obscure R&B dance records, sourced from shopping trips all over the eastern United States. For a sound system to get hold of a song that a rival outfit had previously been spinning as theirs alone, was a cause for wild celebration.

When the American music business shifted, and the smoother sounds of soul began to replace R&B, the music favoured in Jamaica began to disappear. The bigger soundmen responded by hiring local musicians to record their own approximation of R&B – JA boogie. Thus, prompted by the need to maintain their supplies of exclusive tunes, and keep their dances unique, the sound-system owners became Jamaica's first large-scale record producers. In other words, Jamaica had a fully operational music business before it had any of its own music.

Naturally, things didn't stay that way for long. With so much desire to keep the music evolving, the producers experimented with tempo and sound changes or vocal techniques. It didn't take long for JA boogie to become ska, for ska to become rock steady, and so forth. Every shift in Jamaican music, indeed – reggae, deejay, dub, dancehall, ragga – originated with operators trying out new ideas on the sound systems. They'd record direct onto one-off acetate discs in the afternoon, and air them at the dance that night, where audience reaction was noisy, instant and determined everything. If a tune went down well, the soundman would try more of the same, refining the productions as he went along; if it didn't, it would never be heard of again.

It was merely a matter of time before these enterprising souls started to look beyond their own dances. Tunes that were particularly well received were soon being pressed up on vinyl. At first this would be for jukeboxes in bars and cafes, but as the number of gramophones on the island increased, they started to put records on public sale. The best way for producers to publicise their new releases being at their dances, the sound systems remained at the centre of the Jamaican music business. Apart, obviously, from the open-air element, that way of doing things was imported into the UK all but unchanged.

LONDON'S FIRST JAMAICAN-STYLE sound systems were built not long after the first Jamaican sound-system operators arrived in the 1950s. Ironically, even though so much of the equipment they'd used in Jamaica was shipped in from the UK – Wharfdale and Eagle speakers, KT88 and KT66 valves from GEC in Holborn – English companies didn't take their gigantic specifications seriously, and the only person they could find in London to build big enough amplifiers was an African engineer. At first, they played R&B and jazz imported from the US, and calypso recorded in London; then, once the Kingston recording scene got going, they switched to mento and JA boogie brought in by sailors, friends or relatives.

These soundmen swiftly instituted an underground circuit of blues dances, house parties and shebeens that became a vital aspect of West Indian social life in London. Although Soho, as described in chapter one, held a handful of Jamaican-owned nightclubs, those were out of reach for many recent arrivals, while venturing as far as the West End from, say, Stockwell brought its own set of concerns about personal safety. A few London pubs welcomed Caribbean customers, and engaged sound systems at the weekend, but with outright racial hostility never far from the surface, much of the city's nightlife was effectively closed off to black men. For most ordinary black Londoners, routinely refused entrance to just about all the capital's regular dancehalls, the only options were unlicensed, pay-on-the-door dances in basements, empty houses, and school halls, where West Indian caretakers would make premises available after hours.

No one was making a fortune out of these dances, but the soundmen, who often had day jobs, would play them just to keep the back-home spirit alive. As welcoming and familiar environments, full of people who looked like each other, the dances had the significant effect of bringing expatriates from different islands together. After an unforgiving week at work, a house party complete with curry goat and rice, bottled stout or rum, made it very easy for different nationalities to realise that, in London, they had much more in common than was keeping them apart. Veteran Ladbroke Grove soundman Jah Vego remembers:

'Ska came over here in a rush! It was like the whole era came in at once, as we got everything that had gone before at the same time. This was because it took the people back home a while to realise there was such a market over here, but it was what so many of us had been waiting for. I am a jazz man, but when ska came it just lick jazz clean out my head. Many people felt the same, because it was something from our own Jamaica, and that meant so much if you was living in England. You could relate to it more. As a deejay on a sound system you could see it, as soon as you start to spin the Jamaican tunes *everybody* would be up dancing.'

Lloydie Coxsone (right) and his fellow giant of London's lovers' rock sound systems, Fatman, get ready for a dance in the early 1980s.

Ska became enormously popular. The mods who came to the Soho clubs where Vego and other Jamaicans were deejaying also enabled it to make inroads into English youth culture. Emil Shallit's Melodisc set up a ska-dedicated label, Bluebeat, licensing from Kingston and recording ska in London with Georgie Fame as a regular contributor. However, even though Millie's exuberant "My Boy Lollipop" reached number two in 1964, and Prince Buster's "Al Capone" went top twenty in 1967, ska never had a sustained impact on British music until Two Tone came along almost twenty years later. Much like calypso, it came and went leaving only a very shallow footprint.

GIVEN THE TIDAL WAVE of superb dance records that flowed out of Jamaica in the 1960s, and the growth of UK sound systems, the island's music bossed things at street level. So much so, that by the end of the decade, rock steady and reggae had seeped into the working-class end of London youth culture, thanks to black and white kids who grew up together on inner-city estates. Trojan Records, launched in 1968, licensed on a large scale from Jamaica's booming music business, and several London-based labels recorded reggae over here specifically for the domestic market.

Soon enough, the music was fulfilling its pop potential. In the 'Trojan Explosion', at the turn of the decade, Brit-friendly, 'stringsed-up' reggae – tracks imported from Jamaica, then remixed to add strings and other sweetening – gained mass acceptance. While reggae classicists often dismiss this jaunty, satin-suited reggae as pretty much worthless – pure pop'n'polyester – acts like Greyhound, Bob & Marcia and Nicky Thomas were in reality a deeply compelling expression of that particular time and place. With their flares, 'fros and upbeat attitude, in the context of London circa 1970 they were hugely aspirational – remember, at this point in time, if you saw a black face on television you'd shout for the rest of your family to rush to the living room. Glamorous black pop, as valid and as valuable to a lot of youngsters as the Jackson 5 or Chairmen of the Board, this music deserves to be lauded for its success in tailoring a foreign sound to take its place in the wider world, and appeal to those who were brought up with British pop music playing in the background. It was really something of a triumph, albeit a short-lived one.

When the likes of Desmond Dekker, the Upsetters and the Pioneers were making it onto *Top of the Pops*, so too were the Temptations, the Supremes, Johnny Johnson and the Bandwagon, and Marvin Gaye. Then, once the 1970s rolled around, *Shaft* ushered in blaxploitation, James Brown's *Sex Machine* kick-started a funk revolution, and imported TV shows, building on the success of *I Spy* and *Julia*, stopped ignoring African-American actors. When it came to images of cool black people – most of whom weren't Caribbean, let alone Jamaican – this generation of British youth were spoiled for choice. Visuals played a major role. The attitude in the Jamaican music industry that photography was an unnecessary expense meant that few Londoners had any idea what reggae stars looked like, whereas black American music stars always put effort into presenting an image. For boys and girls alike, hair styles and hats assumed holy-grail status. By the time these kids hit the party circuit, many were looking beyond the sound-system dances. Once roots and culture took over, that disconnect increased all the more. With little apparent room for compromise, this new reggae was all about Jamaica, indeed all about one aspect of being Jamaican – sufferation.

So, while there's no disputing how musically creative and spiritually directional the magical era of roots reggae proved to be, subject-wise reggae was turning in on itself. Faced with a wide array of black cultural templates, London teenagers did not unequivocally embrace it. Yes, of course they liked reggae, but not this reggae, or not to any great extent. Janet Kay explains:

'Although I'd grown up hearing reggae music, I'd also grown up watching *Top of the Pops*, listening to Motown and pop music and the Beatles or Michael Jackson. Acts

218

like the Supremes, Bob & Marcia, or the Jackson 5 were the acts I looked forward to seeing. When I was young, I used to idolise singers like Lulu and Dusty Springfield, because they were who was on TV and the radio. I used to buy all the Motown records, and the Philadelphia Sound, or Earth, Wind & Fire, Deniece Williams and Candi Staton. Anything with nice harmonies and melodies – I could've sung soul, but I was handed the opportunity to go into the studio with a reggae singer/producer [*Alton Ellis*]. Then once I was doing reggae, I wanted to do the sort of reggae that took in my other influences.

'It was a natural thing, very pure because at the time the singers just went out and did it how they felt. So many of us loved reggae music, but didn't feel part of the Rastafari movement, of roots and back to Africa. I understood what it was about, but I didn't feel it related to my life and my surroundings. So it wasn't as if we had anything to follow, there was no image thing, we were the second generation of black people over here, and we could do what came naturally to us. It was organic, whatever had been thrown into our pot went in to making lovers' rock.'

Janet's husband, lovers' rock icon and successful actor Victor Romero Evans, expands:

'We had a lot of different musical influences, and those of us that recorded, we all could've been soul singers ... could've been anything. All we wanted was to sing as good as our heroes, and in my case that was Teddy Pendergrass and Marvin Gaye as much as John Holt or Dennis Brown or Slim Smith. But because of the predominance of Jamaican culture in London, at the time of my generation and my parents' generation, reggae was the dominant music. Even though my parents are from St Lucia, when they had a party the music would be reggae. There was so much of it out there.

'Although lovers' rock was our interpretation of what we heard all around us, also it was influenced an awful lot by where we were and who we were. Like Janet says, although we could appreciate the sufferation that was being sung about, it didn't really strike a chord – we were young and falling in love. That's what so much of the soul and pop music was about, and so it was a kind of reggae pop that lovers' rock came out of.'

Janet continues:

'That's why Motown was probably the biggest influence on that first generation of lovers' rock singers, bigger than the reggae at the time. Because Motown songs were about us – falling in love, having our hearts broken – so they appealed so much to us as young kids, growing up and finding our ways in the world.'

This separation between the sounds of sufferation that were coming out of Jamaica, and the lush love songs being listened to in London, makes a fitting metaphor for what was going on in life in general. When Janet talks of 'finding our ways in the world', she could be referring to the social evolution then taking place between the first and second generations in Britain, as the seeds of a black middle/professional class were beginning to germinate.

Although, economically speaking, the first half of the 1970s is usually remembered for the oil crisis, the three-day week and the stock market crashing, for the sons and daughters of the first big wave of Caribbean immigration it was nonetheless shot through with a fair degree of optimism. True, Britain was never any sort of land of milk and honey – and police harassment was at a level best considered routine – but back then a British education was still worth something and, even if employment opportunities were far from equal, with so much yet to be computerised a wealth of clerical jobs were on offer. Most black teenagers seemed content to buy into the fundamental reason why so many of their parents had set sail from the Caribbean: for their children to do better than they had themselves.

This was a time of strong family values. The original immigrants were largely establishment-sympathising churchgoers, who prided themselves on maintaining 'good homes', and most children were close enough to their parents to appreciate what they had gone through to get this far in a strange country. Despite Britain's niggling levels of residual racism, the overwhelming sense of alienation or frustration that became such a factor a decade or so later did not yet exist. There was a strong all-round sense of community. Of course there was inter-generational friction, and while this frequently resulted in young men 'locksing up' – Franco Rosso's movie *Babylon*, in which Victor played a character called Lover, pretty much nailed that situation – there wasn't really any more rebellion than you'd expect in any other segment of society. By and large, the ideals that had made the crossing from the Caribbean were handed down mostly intact – especially to the girls.

This was a significant factor in how many youngsters initially took to, or *didn't* take to, Rasta. Their now-middle-aged, work-oriented parents simply didn't get the notion of not combing your hair, smoking vast amounts of ganja, and not wanting to be a part of society. To them this made even less sense in London than in Jamaica – what were you here for other than to get a job? These people came from an environment in which Rastas were outcasts, and were subject to 'trimming' – a process that went way past humiliation, in which Jamaican police would haul Rastas into police stations and hold them down while their locks were hacked off. Then there was the straightforward religious aspect: as churchgoers, many so deeply resented the perceived blasphemy of Rastafari's appropriation of the Bible that the mere notion of dreadlocks filled them with, er, dread. That was without even taking into account the Old-versus-New-Testament debate. Those of these upstanding citizens who were not Jamaican were likely to be even more horrified by Rastafari, which at that time had not yet surfaced on other islands.

All in all, it's hardly surprising that London's take on reggae music was far less confrontational, and had a lusher, more conventionally pop-and-soul vibe, than what was being made in Jamaica.

BY THE TIME JANET AND VICTOR came into lovers' rock
– they both began recording (separately) in 1977 – the genre
had already existed on the sound systems for several years.
The first lovers' rock classic, Louisa Mark's "Caught You In A
Lie", was produced by one of London's top sound-system operators, with another soundman leading the band that played
on the session. For all its shiny, pop-tastic approach to reggae, lovers' rock was still reggae, and as such conformed to
reggae's rules. When sound-system owner Lloydie Coxsone
launched the style, he did it in exactly the same tried-and-
tested manner as employed in Jamaica. That explains why,
although reggae became increasingly fashionable after the
1972 release of the Jamaican feature film *The Harder They
Come*, lovers' rock came about without the rest of the UK
music business noticing.

Lloydie Coxsone is no relation to Jamaica's Coxsone Dodd –
his choice of stage name is a mark of respect, and shows how
closely London sound systems allied themselves with those
back home. Like his counterpart, his Coxsone's Outernational
sound system was and remains among the very biggest and
best in town. However, contrary to received wisdom, back then
his massive set-up of powerful amplification and wardrobe-
sized speaker cabinets was never a strictly reggae state of
affairs. In true soundman spirit, he responded to what his
crowd wanted by mixing in soul and (old-style) R&B, while also
producing specials that had a softer, poppier feel. This meant
his dances always had a strong female crowd, something that
was not always the case in the often-macho sound-system
world. One of his regular forays north of the Thames was
Wednesday nights at the *Four Aces Club* in Dalston, during
which he ran the Star Search talent contest. It had a citywide
reputation, and hopeful vocalists would come from all
over the capital to sing on his sound system over specially
prepared instrumental backing tracks – riddims. Audience
reaction determined the results; winners were invited back
next week, and eventually competed in a grand final, with the
prize of a recording session and single release. These vocal
sessions at dances were another imported Jamaican-ism;

Dennis Bovell today. Astonishingly, he's not laughing.

live singers have always been a major attraction on sound systems over there, while talent contests had long been a part of the Kingston scene in theatres as well as dancehalls. Many of reggae's superstars got their start at the talent shows, but at Lloydie Coxsone's Wednesday-night affairs something far bigger was going on – a whole new style of reggae was emerging. From the audience itself.

Coxsone and Dennis Bovell, leader of reggae band Matumbi and operator of the Sufferah HiFi sound system, had reacted to the mostly female contestants singing smoothly reggae-fied versions of pop hits by creating suitable riddims for the contest, and matching vocal specials for the sound system. In 1975, a sweet-voiced fifteen-year-old from Shepherds Bush, Louisa Mark, devastated the competition week after week before going on to win the final, and Coxsone and Dennis prepared her prize in singularly Jamaican fashion. At central London's Gooseberry Studios, they built the riddim of their choice for her recording session, and only when that was completed to their satisfaction did they ask the singer in to do her bit. The tune they constructed was a cover of Robert Parker's 1967 Southern soul gem "Caught You In A Lie". Dennis remembers the session as one of those happy accidents that litter reggae's history:

'It was an important decision for Lloydie Coxsone to use that tune, because it was his sign-on piece, the first record he'd play when *he* came to the turntable, so it had particular significance for his followers. Because of that, although he came to me looking for a reggae version of it, I knew he wouldn't want to lose the flavour of the original. Now at this point there weren't any lovers' rock records – the girls used to sing on the sound systems to pre-recorded riddims – so while that means you can do anything you like, you've still got to get people's attention somehow, with something familiar. At the time there was a song that was killing it – "Curly Locks" – it was on rewind on every soundman's turntable. I decided to attach a soundalike bass sound on the beginnings of this "Caught You In A Lie" – *duum du dud u baah bad dah dah* – to make it sound as if you were about to listen to another version of "Curly Locks", but then switch to another tune. The original melody, though, a horn riff, seemed a bit dry against that bassline, and we wanted to create something unique. Robbie Shakespeare was over from Jamaica and in that studio at the same time, and I had a Moog synthesiser in there, which was unheard of in reggae, so I was showing off to Robbie – "Look, you ain't seen one of these in Jamaica yet, mate. Listen to this!" I was making those electronic sounds with it to impress Robbie, and while running the track I came up with *awah wah wah wah waaah* ... Just to show what you could do. But Lloydie Coxsone was sold on it and shouted 'Yo! Dat sound good, yuh know, dat sound like the intro! Don't rub that off!' All I could say was 'Yeah, OK, you like that ... there you go!"

With the backing track finished and Louisa's vocals in place, Coxsone rushed it up to the *Four Aces*. As he remembers, the reaction surprised even him:

'Immediately I cut it on a dubplate, and that first night took it back to the club. From the first time I played it, the whole place went haywire. More than just because this was *their* tune because it came out of *their* club off *their* sound system. They *loved* this record, because the young teenagers in London have never heard themselves before on a record with a good production like a great musician like Dennis Bovell coulda given it. I knew I had to release it, and it's with that record that lovers' rock truly started.

'In the beginning, it was only people in London that came to my dances knew it was an English record; as it started to go wider when people first heard it they thought it was Jamaican. It was when the publicity began to go on around it, and people found out it was English, that's when it really take off. It was a massive reggae hit, the biggest ever English-made record, and it immediately started to inspire a generation of singers as people realise that this young lady is only fifteen years old, from London just like them, and make such a good tune! I think all the other young ladies were saying "Well I could do better ... I'm older than her and I believe I have a better voice!" It sparked one big competition in the reggae field as so many young ladies all over England start singing.'

"Caught You In A Lie" sold tens of thousands of copies in the first few weeks of release, but very few in chart return shops, and did not trouble the mainstream music media in the slightest. Louisa herself cut a couple more successful records for Coxsone, then gave it all up for three years to concentrate on her school work. Before that, she had such an effect on her black British female contemporaries that once again the usually self-assured Lloydie Coxsone was astounded:

Louisa Mark, whose "Caught You In A Lie" kick-started the lovers' rock recording industry in 1975, died mysteriously in the Gambia in 2009.

'It was a surprise so many came forward. I knew it was a special record when we made it, but I don't think I fully realised what the demand for something like that was out there. Every time you make a song you do your best because you *think* it will do well, but you don't know where it's going to go. But these young ladies identified themselves in that song, which had never happened before, and they took to that straight away. Then if a record does do something like that, then right away you have to recognise it.'

Dennis recognised it to perhaps a greater degree than anybody else. At that same session, on the same fundamental riddim as "Caught You In A Lie", he cut two more smooth reggae songs with his band Matumbi, "After Tonight" and "The Man In Me". Both were huge hits, and the latter got the group onto *Top of the Pops*. Far more important than that, though, he turned this new brand of reggae into a London cottage industry.

AWAY FROM HIS DAY JOB AS BASS PLAYER and leader of Matumbi, Dennis enjoyed a prestigious residency with his Sufferah HiFi sound system at the Metro Youth Club in Ladbroke Grove, and played dances all over south London. He had been observing changes within the London reggae scene from two different angles, and knew that something like "Caught You In A Lie" had been on the cards for a few years:

'If you look back to the sixties and early seventies, black kids in London just liked black music – it could be James Brown or Otis Redding or Nicky Thomas or the Pioneers or Kool & The Gang or Betty Wright or the Equals ... The old-time soundmen wouldn't dare to play out without a few soul tunes in their record boxes, just like the soul clubs all played a bit of reggae during the evening. My sound, Sufferah, used to play a regular Sunday-night dance at the Lansdowne Youth Club in Stockwell and we'd be in the hall with TWJ, a soul sound, playing half the dance each. That would be unheard of today, soul and reggae setting up in the same dance, but the place was *rammed* – the doors opened at seven and if you weren't there by seven forty-five, you weren't getting in. That was how the black youth in London used to go raving, there was always a mix-up, but as we got into 1973 and 1974 clubs and sound systems started getting separatist:

'With soul it was all about American influence – Motown, Philly, disco, funk … America was flexing its muscles over here, reminding us that they'd given us the Jackson 5 and they were coming back to claim this territory! The disco stuff was coming back, with their hairstyles and their hair products, and the girls were wanting to be Americanised. And America was ahead of everybody in the video race too – people over here were *seeing* black people in American music and it was glamorous, they weren't seeing reggae people up there, so of course it drifted and ended up getting navigated towards America and the soul sound.

'Then at the same time reggae had become hard – it was all Rastafari and dread and I and I, which is all right, but with that it had become introverted and was all about Jamaica and all about men. The whole vibe at reggae dances in London was changing, it got darker and oppressive, and as the music became more about roots and rockers it became very macho and male-dominated. Women used to talk about "Rasta-for-*him*, not Rasta-for-I", and dances used to be full of a whole heap of man and jus' two gal. But then I could understand that, what woman wants to spend two hours in front of a mirror getting ready to go and stand in some dark sweaty basement? Also the style of dancing changed so it didn't include the ladies any more. That rockers style had come in so the guys were dancing by themselves and inventing their own elaborate styles of dancing solo, running backwards and forwards and flinging their arms about in an outlandish way. This could cause fights when they accidentally hit somebody who might not take kindly to it.

'There always used to be a lot of to-ing and fro-ing between the styles, because reggae and R&B are long-time brothers that have borrowed stuff from each other. By the time lovers' rock was ready to start hitting the sound systems, though,

Dennis Bovell's Matumbi were more or less the lovers' rock house band. Dennis stands in the centre, in the cap.

the reggae world over here seemed to have closed its eyes to what was going on in disco and soul – by then it was only Sly [*Dunbar*] who seemed to be actually listening to disco. Us sound-system operators, or the older guys, at least, like Sir George, Fat Man and Lloydie Coxsone, wanted to bring back people to the dance the way it used to be, so by this time we were looking for several things. How to get the women back to sound systems, because if you get the women the men will follow, and then there's always less chance of fights if it's not all men. Then once we got the women to come back, we had to get the men and women dancing with each other again, up close, because, ultimately, that's what you go to the dance for – grab a gal and rub off some wallpaper! And, importantly, we wanted to do reggae for people who liked reggae but weren't Jamaican.

'That was what I wanted to achieve as a soundman. As a musician in a band, I wanted to write proper pop songs with verses and choruses – which traditional reggae riddims didn't have – make music that would get us on *Top of the Pops*. Lovers' rock, when it burst with "Caught You In A Lie", ticked all those boxes.'

Artistically, Dennis was not alone. Nearly all British reggae of the 1970s was put together in that more conventional pop-song type of way, which was a major factor in the wider success of Matumbi and other groups like Misty in Roots and Aswad. Birmingham's Steel Pulse actually went so far as to create an album, *Handsworth Revolution*, with a central narrative thread – even Bob Marley's reggae didn't do that.

While the music being created for lovers' rock may have been influenced by the UK mainstream, however, every other aspect of the business was straight outta Kingston.

THE HARDEST-WORKING WORD in the history of reggae is 'opportunism'. So much of its development was the result of some sharp-witted operator taking advantage of a situation that had happened as much by accident as by design. Jamaicans must be among the most resourceful people in the world, and sound-system operators were among the most resourceful Jamaicans. In London it was no different. Sound systems like Sufferah and Coxsone Outernational used their crowds as focus groups, and the reactions to those first lovers' rock records was enough to convince those involved that this would be massive.

Where Coxsone saw his business primarily as a sound system, and only sporadically recorded music for release, a plethora of tiny London reggae labels, some formed right there and then, began cutting lovers' rock records with local musicians and the girl singers who were beating a path to their doors. Small-scale operations like Third World, Safari (Louisa Mark's label), Lucky, Charm and Morpheus put records out on a strictly parochial level. Then Dennis Harris, a Jamaican-born entrepreneur got involved. He owned property and supermarkets in south London as well as the reggae labels DIP International and Eve, which he ran in conjunction with his wife Yvonne. In early 1975, in the wake of Lousia Mark's success, they licensed Susan Cadogan's Lee Perry-produced, Jamaica-recorded cover of the Millie Jackson hit "Hurt So Good". Textbook lovers' rock, it topped the reggae charts for several weeks. From there the song was picked up by long-term reggae fan and future Stock-Aitken-Waterman founder Pete Waterman, who knew Lee Perry from his frequent trips to Jamaica. Now, as A&R for the pop label Magnet Records, he licensed the track from DIP and gave it a bit of a pop-music polish. While Louisa Mark was rocking the sound systems, Susan Cadogan's breezy tones got to number four in the national charts.

The Harrises never repeated that degree of pop success, but that record, and other sound-system hits including the huge "Last Date" by TT Ross – unique at the time as a white lovers' rock singer – convinced Dennis Harris to sell one of his supermarkets and invest heavily in this new reggae style. He had an eight-track studio built in southeast London, and employed Dennis Bovell as in-house producer, sound engineer and musical director, responsible for bringing in the musicians, who as a rule would be Matumbi or his other group, the Dub Band. The idea was to build a lovers' rock production line that wouldn't leave too much to chance. Bovell remembers:

'Lovers' rock was going down well in the dancehalls that had a reputation for playing it. So producers knew there was a demand, but they hadn't narrowed it down any more than that – in the dance everybody reacts to a nice tune. But because Dennis Harris didn't have a sound system, all he wanted to do was sell records, and to do that he had to know who was *buying* them, not just dancing to them. Dennis and I did actual market research and went round record shops looking at who was buying what. We'd talk to the customers and the guys behind the counter to find out was it men or women, how old were they, what sort of things were each group looking for in a record …

'Initially, what we discovered surprised us because it was quite a lot more girls than boys buying singles. Then when we thought about it we realised that although the young guys would get off on the riddim of a record at a blues dance and enjoy dancing with a woman to it, he wouldn't want to own it. The girls, however, would listen to the lyrics and they would want to take it home because it would mean something to them. And they preferred songs sung by other girls because they felt like they were talking to them, and there was hardly any women in reggae at that time. Or blokes would buy these type of records to give as presents to their girlfriends, but that was practically the same as the girls themselves buying them. What we needed on top of our easy reggae beat was nice sweet melodies, with lyrics about being young and in love – either if it turns out well or badly, 'cos they all go through both – sung by girls. It didn't actually matter even if it wasn't sung too well or the sentiments seemed naive, in fact that all helped as it brought it even closer to the audience.

'Also we knew we needed a lot of it. A whole heap! Because in order to get the bigger shops or distributors to take you seriously you have to have a catalogue with clout. And for that you need to be putting out about half a dozen singles *a week*. If it's just two or three a month, nobody will take any notice of you. But we had this studio ready to go, so we thought "Right, let's start pumping it out".'

Spreading the word that they were looking for girl singers, they used the standard Jamaican studio strategy of open auditions every Sunday morning. Young hopefuls would line up for the chance to sing a cappella for the two Dennises, with the successful entrants invited to hang around and go again with a dubplate or live music accompaniment – and you thought Simon Cowell thought it up. The best of those were put in the studio to record a single, which, if it did well, could lead to a follow-up. There were no contracts beyond the recording being done at the time. Although the music was done and dusted before any singer got near a

Sound systems were vital to the success of lovers' rock – even the record shops needed serious set-ups.

microphone, Dennis varied this operation from what was becoming the norm in Jamaica by getting his singers to sing over live musicians rather than a pre-recorded backing track. He believed that to establish themselves as *the* London reggae production house, it was important to create as much original music as possible, rather than recycle riddims – dub versions aside, obviously. Their south London set-up further likened itself to Motown's production line, as opposed, say, to Jamaica's Studio One, by deciding who should sing what by focussing on the artists rather than the song or the producer. Dennis would frequently stop a session because he realised an artist would do better with a different song, or the song being recorded would sound better sung by somebody else.

This was vividly illustrated by the hit group Brown Sugar. After trying to record each member solo, he put three girls together who barely knew each other, and formed one of the most successful acts in lovers' rock. As the first girl group in a genre designed to appeal to Motown fans, the trio quickly assumed iconic status. They have since passed into legend, because one of them was Caron Wheeler, who went on to became the voice of the Soul ɪɪ Soul hits "Keep On Moving" and "Back To Life". Back then, though, they were the first to release on Dennis Harris's new label, which was so embryonic it didn't even have a name. Dennis explains how in thinking one up, they came to identify the genre:

'We knew we had to have this on a label by itself, removed from any of Dennis's other stuff, and it would need to have an identity people would recognise straight away, something iconic. Dennis Harris came up with the name Lover's Rock, which was the title of an Augustus Pablo record we all liked. We thought the two words sat well together, but really it summed up exactly what we were doing. Then Dennis came up with the logo, the pink heart with the arrow through it, and although that was a bit obvious it was probably all the better for it. Which is when the guitarist, John Kpiaye, had this song called "I'm In Love With A Dreadlocks", which said it all, and the trio I put together, Brown Sugar, sang it.

'That was the first record on the Lover's Rock label, and we were away. Because we were putting out so much stuff, and it was all of the same vibe and high quality, girls would go into record shops and ask for the new Lover's Rock single or ask a deejay if he had any Lover's Rock. Pretty soon that was what everybody was calling the music.'

ONCE THE GENRE HAD DEFINED ITSELF, and enough of it was out there to give it a presence, lovers' rock boomed. Within months of "Caught You In A Lie" being recorded, this new style had turned London's dancehall scene on its head. Sound-system operators and club owners swiftly came to terms with the potential spending power of a smartly turned out crowd for whom Saturday night was all about impressing the opposite sex. The single-red-bulb-over-the-control-tower blues parties gave way to brighter, less daunting environments, while the systems themselves rebalanced their sound away from the extremes of weight (bass) and treble to incorporate the entire sonic spectrum. And although it would be ridiculous to imagine that roots reggae sound systems became an endangered species, by the end of 1976 they were vastly outnumbered by set-ups touting themselves as 'Strictly Lovers' or 'For Lovers Only', while more than a few kept their options open with the billing 'Roots & Lovers'. It was around this time that dancehall flyers started to feature silhouette drawings of couples dancing close, instead of the almost regulation rootsmen skanking.

All of which had a knock-on effect on record sales. Lovers' rock singles would routinely sell tens of thousands, while the big hits like "Six Sixth Street", "Tenderness", "Let Me Be Your Angel", "Love Won't Let Me Wait", "Last Date", "Fallin' In Love" and "It's True" nudged into six figures. There were,

relatively speaking, only a very small number of lovers' rock albums, but sets like Carroll Thompson's *Hopelessly In Love*, Louisa Mark's *Breakout* and the Investigators' *First Case* all shifted the sort of numbers that under different circumstances would have got them into the lower reaches of the charts. Meanwhile, the reggae charts compiled by the newly launched weekly newspaper *Black Echoes* were so overrun with lovers' rock singles that other more roots-centric reggae labels successfully lobbied to have them confined to their own separate listings. Ironically, though, it was precisely what made lovers' rock such a huge parochial triumph that held it back from more general success.

The music had been created within and shaped by an enclosed world, and devotedly serviced the needs of that demographic. As a result, it enjoyed all the benefits of that environment. The sound systems did more than just invent lovers' rock, they sustained it by serving as its primary marketing tool. It was in the dance that these new sounds reached their prospective buyers directly, and as it flourished it found its own world was big enough. Sure, as Dennis stated, everybody wanted to get on *Top of the Pops*, but not at any price.

When Janet Kay's "Silly Games" – a tune that Dennis wrote and produced – made it into the national charts, it did so entirely on its own terms, with no remixing or watering down. In fact Dennis was astonished that particular vocal had been used, because he wasn't entirely happy with it and wanted to re-record it. When Janet went on TV, she genuinely represented a culture that had reached a point at which it had no need for the mainstream.

Victor Romero Evans, who was a sound-system regular long before he got into the business, remembers these promotional methods as being perfect for the situation, but never really being through choice:

'Reggae was still being treated as a novelty music by the BBC radio. There might have been one or two reggae hits a year, usually in the summer, but they were never taken as being part of anything bigger. This was before Rodigan, and there wasn't any black pirate radio back then, so the only reggae you got on the radio was an hour on Sunday afternoon, *Reggae Time* with Steve Barnard, then Tony Williams took it over. There wasn't any press for us either, except *Black Echoes*. The regular music press didn't like lovers' rock, and by then the other black magazine, *Black Music*, went for the stuff that was on regular release, like Bob Marley or Burning Spear. So it was pure sound systems playing lovers' – Sir George, Fat Man, Admiral Ken, Sufferah, Neville the Enchanter, Chicken, Sir Biggs, Lloydie Coxsone, Soferno B, Santic Romantic, how can you go wrong with a name like that?

'That worked too. Made it seem like *ours*, because there wasn't an outside influence. Kids would hear a tune at a dance and get excited by it and ask for it in the shops the next day. They might have to quote the lyric or just recognise the artist, but the guy behind the counter would know – maybe he was at the same dance! Then the producers that had sound systems could whip up the demand for a tune by keeping spinning it and having the crowd loving it, but not releasing it. Just let the demand for it in the shops build up, then they know they've got a hit on their hands.

'The best thing about this was that the crowds made the hits. They could hear the tunes in the dance and then react to them, and only the very best would get through. It wasn't like in the mainstream, where it seems like you can be force-fed a tune and find yourself liking something you know is rubbish because it's everywhere all day. A lovers' tune was something you heard once a week when you were raving, so if you like it then you knew that tune was wicked. As an artist it was good to get feedback by going to sound systems, and, really, although we might not have had *Top of the Pops* or radio play, when you were raving in the club and your tune came on and people jump up, *bo*! and you can see they really like it, boy, that was the best feeling in the world.'

The manufacturing process of lovers' rock was similarly DIY. As well as the proliferation of tiny recording studios around the capital, there was also a multitude of disc-cutting houses. Disc cutting is a vital stage in the analogue recording pro- cess, during which the  sounds on the tape are grooved on to metal disc to make the stamper that actually presses out the vinyl. Dub maestro King Tubby began his musical career as a disc cutter for Duke Reid, and skilful disc cutting is vital for clear and faith- ful reproduction. The cutting house favoured by London soundmen was Hessle's, a remarkable business in which the cutting lathe was set up in a corner of operator John Hessle's front room at his house in Barnes. On Fridays and Saturdays, neighbours in this quiet semi-detached street would be treated to queues of black guys bearing tapes of music they wanted for that night's dance. Frequently he would shut up shop at about nine, curtly telling them "That's it for tonight. No more! This is my home!"

London also had a cottage-industry network of pressing plants, usually manually operated and ready to produce small runs of seven-inch 45s on a quick turnaround. Although the prices at the big factories were lower, London's reggae labels would routinely complain that their relatively tiny orders were sidelined every time a big one came in from a major label. The reggae industry's more imaginative executives did manage to save a few quid, however, by driving their vans over to the Republic of Ireland, where record pressing was much less expensive. Getting several titles done at once would make the journey worthwhile.

As the bigger London sound systems travelled to play dances outside London, they formed alliances with clubs and other sounds in cities such as Leeds, Bradford, Bristol, Birmingham and Coventry. Lovers' rock thus went nationwide pretty quickly. Distribution was vital, but before independent distributors Jet Star or Rough Trade came along, no mainstream operation would touch it. The industry's answer was typically pragmatic: to get lovers' rock to the customers, you had to go to where those customers were, and take the records with you. Dennis remembers a day-trip he took with Buster Pearson, father of the eighties pop-soul siblings Five Star, which had all the hallmarks of the operations of Emil Shallit some twenty years previously, or of the Oti brothers described in chapter four:

'We had to be responsible for distribution, because it was all about little outlets that were either record shops or else they were where records were being sold as part of another business. They were all black owned, and they were places where black people went, that's what you had to know about.

'One Saturday morning I had nothing else to do and went on a ride with Buster Pearson, because he had a record label called KB – K was for Kay, his wife, and B was for Buster – and I'd made a record for it called "Run Rasta Run", on which I called myself African Stone. He had a Hillman Hunter, and this Saturday he loaded up with records and we drove from London to Leeds, via north London and all these towns in the Midlands. We stopped off at positively seventy-five shops, leaving records and collecting cash for the tunes he'd dropped off the previous week. It was all cash. None of those record shops was an *Our Price* or *HMV* – some of them weren't even record shops, they were grocery stores or barbers or travel agents, anywhere black people came – but we still offloaded about twelve hundred records, he kept all the cash in this satchel thing. And that was just that trip, on other days he'd go through south London and down to Bristol, or west London and on to Liverpool and Manchester.

'It was so successful that when we had the Lover's Rock label we got one of those Volkswagen camper vans and decked it out inside with shelves for records – it was a record bus. A friend of mine, Vivian Allen, would drive that van all over the British isles from Sunday night to Friday night, distributing records and collecting cash. He'd be back at the depot on Friday night, pay the cash in, have Saturday off, get a new stock and go back out again on Sunday. He'd sell thousands of records. That was how Susan Cadogan got her hit, "Hurt So Good", because it was first distributed like that. It became mega when Dennis [*Harris*] took it to Magnet because they had access to the chart shops, but it was always a big record before then – no matter what Pete Waterman says.'

While this sound-system exposure elevated acts like Janet and Victor, Jean Adebambo, Sandra Cross, Peter Hunnigale, Winsome, Brown Sugar and Deborahe Glasgow to cult status, lovers' rock existed almost exclusively on recordings, with very few live performances. As the records were largely singles with no pictures on the sleeves, and there was no conventional media publicity, the singers remained virtually unrecognisable, even to their fans. That explains why Victor was able to hang out at dances and listen out for his records, and how so many lovers' stars still lived normal lives: Janet worked at Rank Xerox; Carroll Thompson was studying pharmacy; Jean Adebambo worked in health care; Louisa Mark was still at school; and so too were 15, 16, 17, a trio whose name was decided by their ages. Astonishingly, many stars of lovers' rock didn't get to meet their audiences until twenty years later, as Janet explains:

'I didn't do hardly any live work, the whole lovers' rock industry wasn't geared up for that so none of the singers did. I didn't go out to clubs either, my parents wouldn't let me go to anything that wasn't connected with the church – that was the same for a lot of the girl singers because they were so young. But we knew there was a big scene out there, because when we did do performances the people would turn up in droves. Because there was so little chance to see the people they'd been buying records by, they'd be so enthusiastic.

'Victor used to go to sound systems, and he's told me about clubs like *Phebes* and *Cubies* getting so packed when they had a lovers' rock sound system on that girls would faint

At the age of 15, as half of the girl duo Love & Unity, Sandra Cross spent four weeks at number one in the British reggae charts with a song she wrote, "I Adore You".

and have to be carried out. But I don't think most of us were really aware of how deep an impact it was having, because we never saw any of that week in and week out. It just became something you didn't really worry about.'

LOVERS' ROCK MAY HAVE STRUCK a resonant chord with young black Londoners, but it found itself at odds with the roots reggae that was then enjoying such a high profile. In Bob Marley's slipstream, record labels like Island and Virgin were marketing acts like Burning Spear, Max Romeo, Lee Perry, Big Youth and Culture to rock fans, and shifting serious amounts of albums. The music media gave unprecedented space to reggae, as large sections paired it up with punk to promote an apparent alliance of the oppressed. While Jamaica had imposed itself squarely on the map, however, what was happening just down the road was all but ignored. Janet believes this new roots reggae crowd simply 'refused to acknowledge the lovers' rock scene, it wasn't even like real music to them'.

But it wasn't really a musical thing. It was more about the changing perception of black music within the British music media: post-Motown, black music wasn't supposed to be frivolous. To be taken seriously in the 1970s, it needed to have a purpose, which usually meant being an expression of pain and suffering or a protest against injustice. That kind of patronising, enforced street credibility reflected an emerging attitude to black people in general – while struggling against obvious disadvantages, there was somehow honour and glamour in being life's perpetual victims. Around this time the first two British-made feature films by black directors – Horace Ové's *Pressure* (1975), and *Burning An Illusion* by Menelik Shabazz (1981) – were released. Both were artistically superb and technically excellent, but they were produced by the very establishment British Film Institute, and consequently toed the sufferation line. The former was enthusiastically described as '… the black experience in Britain today, including the cycle of educational deprivation, poverty, unemployment and antisocial behaviour'; the latter, a poignant story of love and

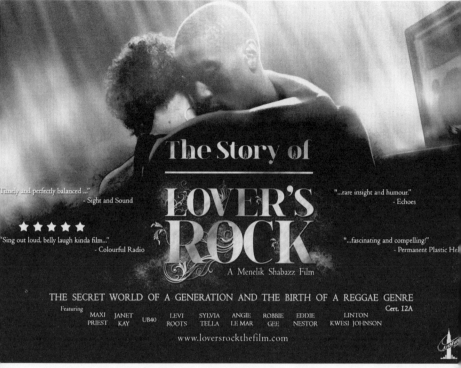

In 2011, lovers' rock reggae became a feature film, selling out cinemas in London and Britain's major cities.

ambition starring Victor Romero Evans, looked to be taking a different direction, but spent its final half-hour wallowing in how the system was holding us down.

While such attitudes may have been overflowing with good intentions, at a time when black people in the UK were starting to take charge of their own destiny, they could come across as almost colonial in their denigration. The hostility to lovers' rock summed this up, as its middle-class aspirations, happy, sophisticated music and celebration of dressing up and having a good time didn't display a great deal of obvious disadvantage. Indeed, its self-sufficient success should have been acclaimed, but Dennis isn't really being flippant when he says 'as soon as they had to stop feeling sorry for us, they didn't want to know.'

Given what lovers' rock had been able to achieve by itself, this shouldn't have mattered too much, but the lingering sense of missed opportunity still rankles. UK record companies were looking to sign reggae acts at that point, but their perspective was skewed by post-Marley press coverage that centred on dreadlocks, chalices and the sounds of sufferation. Of course this had its plus side, in ensuring major-label releases for the London-based but dedicatedly JA-styled Aswad, and thus allowing such works of genius as "Three Babylon", "Warrior Charge" and "Back To Africa" to find a bigger audience. (Stories circulated about the group using industrial heaters to warm up tin baths of water in the studio in order to recreate steamy Kingston conditions.) Southall rootsmen Misty in Roots deservedly came to prominence, and were mainstays of Rock Against Racism,

The King of lovers' rock, a vintage Victor Romero Evans, communes with his subjects.

while Steel Pulse had a huge hit with the aforementioned *Handsworth Revolution*, a masterclass in how to marry an English rock-band structure to a set of reggae songs.

At the same time, there was also a degree of confusion among London's reggae fraternity as to why such a vital part of its output was being ignored, especially when they couldn't see what the problem was. There was always a big crossover in the studio between roots and lovers' players – Aswad's rhythm section of Tony Robinson and Drummie Zeb were in demand for soul and jazz/funk sessions as well as lovers' rock. Indeed, it's Drummie playing on Janet's "Silly Games", and Dennis credits him with the pauses in the drum pattern that he believes made the tune so uniquely London.

Victor is more generous than Dennis about the attitude of the mainstream media. With hindsight, he believes that too many people pronounced upon the reggae scene without coming to grips with its entirety – that they were outside observers, who only saw what was put in front of them:

'There were those that were in on the sound-system scene, who actually went to the dances, and those that weren't. In the dance everybody liked the intimacy of lovers' rock at that time, whether it was a lovers' dance, a soul dance or a roots dance. You wanted to dance with a woman and the women wanted to dance with men, it was like when we used to go to our parents' parties, and men and women used to dance with each other. Every dance and sound system would have a slow jam session and that would be some slow soul like Al Green, or, more than likely, some lovers' tunes before you'd be back to the jump up.

'But you had to be in the dance or part of that scene to know that. It used to make me laugh that people who never went to the dance would say how lovers' rock wasn't *authentic*, I'd be amazed at some of the hostility it would bring out.'

For 'authentic', you can often read 'Jamaican' – and it wasn't only the new reggae crowd that made a fuss about this. A vociferous contingent believed that unless reggae was made in Jamaica, it counted for nothing, and if it was made by non-Jamaicans its value was even less than that. To give some idea of the Jamaican tyranny within the UK reggae scene, there was an informal 'don't ask, don't tell' policy as regards heritage. Janet expands:

'The thing is, you never knew the people you were working with weren't Jamaican. We all assumed we were all Jamaicans and nobody bothered to correct anybody. You'd never have known Dennis [*Bovell*] was Barbadian by the way he spoke, you'd naturally think he was Jamaican. You'd never have known that Drummie or Brinsley from Aswad weren't Jamaican by the way they spoke. But they're Grenadian and Guyanese.'

Victor – who was born in St Lucia – saw that as a positive, as it consolidated the notion of a black British music style as opposed to an imported style merely produced in the UK:

'That is the beauty, to me, of lovers' rock, the fact that we all came from different backgrounds and different heritages, but we were all youth in London. But with the Jamaican thing, because they had all that bravado they did sort of define black culture, and because there were so many, a lot of your friends were Jamaican, so it was natural to aspire to that. Also, reggae, which was the music we were doing, was Jamaican, and it had that strong tradition, so we just sort of went along with it, because that was what we thought being a reggae singer was all about.'

What made a mockery of the idea that London-produced reggae was somehow less than the genuine article, was that this new sound went down very well in Jamaica. Right from the start. Lloydie Coxsone licensed "Caught You In A Lie" to Gussie Clarke, a top Jamaican producer and label owner, for whom it was a big hit, and, in true Jamaican style, 'versioned' numerous times. Ironically, lovers' rock found favour in Jamaica because, by concentrating on roots reggae, the British record companies had unbalanced the domestic industry.

In response to frenzied chequebook-waving from across the Atlantic, the rock steady and early reggae staple of singers singing love songs had been all but abandoned – but local sound systems still wanted music to which men and women could dance together. Similarly, as the 1980s rolled around, and in Jamaica roots was being replaced by dancehall with its computerised brashness and deejay vocalists, the demand for couples-dancing hadn't gone away. That left a great deal of room for lovers' rock reggae. For any Kingstonian crooner looking to maintain a recording career, London suddenly looked very attractive.

DENNIS REMEMBERS THE WAVE OF JAMAICAN singers and players who installed themselves in London, either to record with British musicians or to learn lovers' rock techniques and take them back home:

'Lovers' had been getting attention in Jamaica since the beginning, since "Caught You In A Lie". There's a lot of soul music in Jamaica and people liked this soulful sound – Brent

Sugar Minott came from Jamaica to make London – and lovers' rock – his home.

Dowe of the Melodians did a version of Matumbi's "After Tonight", Harry J did a version of "Caught You In A Lie" ... Remember, men and women over there go to the dance for exactly the same reasons we do. Then people started coming over here to grab a bit of what we had, because as we'd changed up the drum patterns and the riddims to create this new reggae sound, we were actually *leading* Jamaica from over here.

'It was not unusual for a singer to arrive in the morning with a set of songs they'd written, I'd get a band together in the afternoon, we'd go into the studio all night, and they'd be on the plane back to Jamaica the next day with a set of master tapes. And they'd have paid in cash, thank you very much. Then there were those who stayed longer.

'Sly Dunbar was here all the time, he had been for a while, but he is probably the Jamaican reggae musician with the most open mind – he listens to anything and takes his influences from everywhere. Jackie Mittoo, probably the greatest reggae organist ever, came over to learn our playing and shuffles, and his vast knowledge of organ playing was very welcome, of course. He practically lived in East Street Studios, where a lot of lovers' rock was made – so many of those tracks on the Lover's Rock label have actually got Jackie Mittoo playing organ on. Max Edwards, drummer with the Soul Syndicate and Zap Pow, was here, Chinna [*legendary reggae guitarist Earl 'Chinna' Smith*] was here for a while doing stuff, so was Lloyd Parks [*the Revolutionaries' founder and bass player*].

'A lot of Jamaican musicians came to learn what we were doing, and some actually put down roots here because there was more opportunity to play more music. Then there was the singers like Dennis Brown, who moved here and set up his own record labels, and Gregory Isaacs who *practically* lived here, and Johnny Clarke and Johnny Osbourne both recorded here, Sugar Minott found his groove within lovers' rock here, so did Barrington Levy. It was the only time that reggae in the UK was in charge, and it felt good that they were coming to us and taking what we'd invented back to Jamaica.'

Maxine Stowe, a mover and shaker in the Jamaican and American reggae industries, managed Sugar Minott at the time. In describing his coming to London, she sums up the relationship of lovers' rock to the rest of the reggae world:

'There had always been a migration of reggae artists from Jamaica to the UK, especially London, because they found it was a better way of doing business than in Jamaica. They were more likely to earn some money. But because, back then, there was hardly any communications between the UK and Jamaica – you couldn't just make a phone call – many found it easier to stay on. Dennis Brown, Gregory Isaacs, Johnny Osbourne, Sugar and, to a lesser extent, Freddie McGregor, all wanted to do more slick reggae, but the way it was going in Jamaica was mostly deejays like Yellowman and Eek-a-Mouse. In Jamaica, everybody knew that the British-born kids were very much into the American soul, and when they came up with the lovers' rock that was perfect, because it was like a bridge between the soul and the reggae.

'It suited those singers who wanted to cross over with love songs – "Night Nurse", "Money In My Pocket", "Love Has Found A Way". Until they started coming to London they were seen as roots singers, even though they were more into love songs, which is what they could do in London.

'Sugar, now, had recorded roots material in Jamaica and he was known for that, and it was on that success that he travelled over to London – he went there with roots material. But once he got there, the marketplace was such that in order to be relevant in London he had to start recording lovers' rock songs. That was what the scene was, and he just rode on that whole lovers' rock energy. It became him, and he had hit after hit in Jamaica as well as England.'

LIKE ALL REGGAE STYLES since the dawn of JA boogie, sound-system exposure meant constant evolution, and lovers' rock developed to meet the wider demands of its audience. Dubwise takes on tunes became de rigueur, as lovers' sound systems competed eagerly for unique cuts of

popular riddims, but these never neglected
the melodies, and instrumental versions were
always very popular. Jamaican horn players such as Dean
Fraser, Bobby Ellis and Vin Gordon became popular choices
in the London studios, creating sophisticated, jazz-tinged
music. Toasting evolved on the lovers' sound systems, too, as
the more tuneful deejays provided breezy commentaries on
love and life in the dance. It was this decidedly unportentous
toasting that gave rise to what became known as sing-jay in
the mid-1980s, as dancehall deejays such as Half Pint, Tenor
Saw and Anthony Red Rose rocked the sound systems with
their swinging, half sung/half rapped style.

Lovers' rock also started to commentate on different aspects
of the lives of the people who sung it and bought it. Victor's
biggest hits were his observational trilogy about going raving
in north London: "Slacks And Sovereigns" (getting ready);
"At The Club" (what was going on when he arrived); and "I
Need A Girl Tonight" (self-explanatory, really). Then there
was the sub-genre known as 'conscious lovers", which flew

in the face of criticism that lovers' rock was divorced from realities of being black. The lovers' industry wasn't shying away from anything; they simply approached it from their own perspective, which didn't involve a great deal of Rasta or out-and-out sufferation. Kofi's album *Story of a Black Woman* consisted of ten tracks that dealt with her life in London; 15, 16, 17 had a hit with "Black Skin Boy"; and Janet Kay and Carroll Thompson did a tribute song for the victims of the New Cross Fire. One of the biggest and most fondly remembered of all lovers' songs is Brown Sugar's "Black Pride":

'Black is the colour of my skin
Black is the life that I live
I'm so proud to be the colour God made me
Black pride for all to see ...'

Janet still speaks of it as: 'Such a beautiful song, that addressed the way we felt with the riots and suss laws and so many things going on politically. It meant a lot to a lot of women out there, and a lot of men too, but I guess it got overshadowed by the Aswads and the Steel Pulses.'

As the 1980s progressed, and the initial excitement started to wane, the success that lovers' rock had achieved proved not quite sufficient to sustain it at the same level of productivity. The 'informal' business practices of many small labels meant that disputes between artists and producers over money were commonplace. The singers' relative youthfulness was a factor in that respect, as many were at the stage in their lives when they needed to be thinking about careers, and if the music wasn't paying it ceased to be an option. Meanwhile the older women were putting careers on hold to have families, only to discover there wasn't much of an industry left by the time they came back.

Victor believes that the lack of mainstream success was a factor in turning singers away from the style, as "Silly Games" was the exception rather than the rule:

'Disillusionment is what happened. Many people found they weren't making a living out of being singers. Sure, people were always telling you you were really talented and you should go far ... but then what? Nothing. And because your songs weren't being played on mainstream radio you knew you could only get so far. Once in a while somebody would sneak through because they got their tunes onto national radio, like the Cool Notes had a couple of hits, so did the Investigators, then a couple of years later there was Trevor Walters, and Sugar [*Minott*] had a hit when he lived here, Maxi [*Priest*] did very well. But ultimately it wasn't enough to keep you in the business, because you couldn't survive. A lot of people just drifted away from the music industry – I went back to acting.'

Janet points to a combination of artist naivety and the reluctance of large UK record companies to invest in local black talent:

'The major record companies in the UK weren't actually signing any black acts. The majority of the black acts that got through and into the charts were licensed, usually from America but sometimes from Jamaica, so there was no real

investment in the artist as all they had to do was put out the record. It meant nothing was long-term, and there was never any nurturing process.

'Then from the side of the industry we were in we weren't taught how to do interviews, we weren't taught how to perform, we weren't taught how to present ourselves ... We weren't taught anything! Everything that we did was completely organic, completely coming from ourselves. And in terms of knowing what we were entitled to and what we weren't entitled to, in terms of recording and rights and that, we were not given any information. There were no contracts, no pieces of paper, we were really, really young and green, and just happy to sing a song that people liked – if you got paid a few pounds that was bonus. Remember, I had a job so I was really happy.

'But really, everything was done by trial and error. And more of it was error, in terms of the artists anyway!'

LOVERS' ROCK NEVER DIED COMPLETELY. As artists like Peter Hunnigale, Donna Marie and Mike Anthony provided a sound-system alternative to dancehall and ragga, so the mainstream seemed to open itself up a little more. For the ten years from 1986, Maxi Priest, a former singer on the south London sound system Saxon, was never far from the top forty. In waist-length dreadlocks and Paul Smith suits, this charismatic performer was a *Top of the Pops* regular, delivering lovers' rock versions of pop classics like "Some Guys Have All The Luck" and "Wild World", and his own jaunty compositions such as "Close To You" and "Strollin' On". Likewise Aswad set aside the roots posturing to cut chart-friendly pop and lovers' rock reggae, including a number one hit with a cover of Tina Turner's "Don't Turn Around". Then there were actual pop stars doing it. Lily Allen followed the example of Culture Club almost twenty years earlier by installing an album of pure lovers' pop songs in the charts. That came as no surprise to Dennis:

'That's what she likes. Her dad [*Keith Allen, the actor/ comedian*] is a definite reggae lover, a real hardcore collector from back in the day. She would have grown up listening to Keith's records, so it's only right that as a young girl wanting to sing she'd do it in a lovers' rock style.'

The most interesting recent development is the lovers' rock revival that has been sweeping the UK during the last few years. Original artists from the 1970s and early 1980s are in huge demand on concert packages, and Carroll Thompson even runs a regular London club night called the Lovers' Lounge, featuring old skool tunes and live performances for a mixed-age crowd of ravers. Janet is particularly pleased by these developments, as it has given her the chance to interact with the fans she never met thirty years ago:

'What was amazing was when the lovers' rock revival started, around the end of the nineties, that was very much a live thing, all about concerts with artists like us and Carroll, Sandra and Peter. That was when we really came face to face with the people, and I got to know what an impact it had been having. At the shows now are the original lovers' rock fans, who are now middle-aged women, and they can sing every word to every song. It's incredible. Then talking to them at shows, they're telling me their experiences and what they were doing when they first heard a song, or how they felt, or what they felt when they saw me on *Top of the Pops*. Back then, they were falling in love or having their first baby, and our music was the backdrop to all of that, and now the concerts were taking them back in time. It was all very emotional.

'Although I was unaware of so much that was happening at the time, now I'm very proud to be part of something that was quite revolutionary for black people in this country. We all are.'

CHAPTER SEVEN

Living for the Weekender

BritFunk chanting down the discos

AT THE SAME TIME AS LOVERS' ROCK was in the ascendant, a vibrant London soul scene became established in much the same way as its reggae counterpart, via sound systems and low-profile clubs. While it didn't tick enough boxes to trouble a mainstream music business then fixated on prog rock, glam rock and punk rock, this provided the other great musical expression for those second-generation Commonwealth immigrants who saw no problem in taking America as their cultural touchstone. While the music of black America has influenced black Britons ever since its earliest days, during this era its films, TV and literature were being eagerly absorbed in a Britain that was also constantly regaled with news footage of a very glamorous-looking social and cultural revolution. Given that London schools still had pretty decent music programmes, black churches had bands, and popular organisations like the Boys Brigade and the Cadet services' marching bands provided access to brass instruments, it didn't take long for the scene to start producing its own groups. Budding musicians who were immersed in American funk, but determined to show that they weren't American.

Kenny Wellington played trumpet for two of the scene's best-loved bands, Light Of The World and Beggar & Co. Still active on the jazz circuit and as a music teacher, he is sitting in the music room of his canal-side east London flat, occasionally tootling on his trumpet as he recalls those times:

'Although we took as our models the self-contained groups like Kool & The Gang and the Blackbyrds, the thing we did from the outset is we never spoke with American accents. That was always important – we didn't sing with American accents, and we didn't talk on the stage with American accents. A lot of bands before us used to go up on stage, and even if they were from just down the road here, because they were playing soul they'd feel obligated to talk to the audience with fake American accents. We were happy to say that we love the music, but we're from London.

'We were the first of a generation of youths of colour from England, that the man on the ground – not just people of colour, but white people as well – could look at and say "Well OK, this is the generation that are actually from here, that speak the same language that we do, in that our accent and our *syntax* is essentially the same." Not only a linguistic syntax but a musical syntax as well, so people knew we'd listened to the same things they had, and enough of them thought "Oh well I can do that too!" That was very important at that time, because it meant younger people could believe in what they actually were instead of looking for something else. It's why the scene took off so rapidly.'

Although this offered a viable alternative to large numbers of black youngsters who were never fully committed to reggae, it would be wrong to think there was any real animosity between the musical tribes. Such was the paucity of black icons back then that nobody could afford to discriminate, and everybody grabbed hold of the same things: the Temptations *and* the Pioneers on *Top of the Pops*; Brazil's football team; West Indies cricket; *I Spy*; Derek Griffiths; Angela Davis's afro; *The Harder They Come*; Clyde Best ... Funk deejays saw lovers' rock as an integral part of couples-dancing time, just as a lovers' sound system would throw a few Philly tunes into its mix. Heck, *Blues & Soul* magazine even had a column called *The Buzz on Reggae*.

The original TFB (Typical Funk Band) in the back garden of their Cable Street rehearsal premises. Left to right: Lipson Francis, David Walker, Kenny Wellington, Camelle Hinds, Earl Okai, Norman Walker, Henry Defoe; kneeling in front, Errol Kennedy.

David Joseph, singer and keyboard player in Hi Tension, the first of this wave of funk bands to get a record deal, remembers:

'We always spread ourselves. In fact in the beginning, we probably played more reggae – we never said we were a total jazz/funk band, we'd say we were a *black* music band, because there were all sorts of different tastes going on within our lives and the lives of our audiences. We were more together as a community then, so we played *our* music, and that was soul, reggae and calypso – not just Caribbean calypso either but calypso from West Africa too – because that was how it reflected us and where we were growing up. London people connected to that.'

BEFORE THE BANDS, this scene was all about records, American import records, available from a few ultra-specialist outlets that carried US imports within days of their American release dates. These West End shops were the scene's entry level, where people accessed the music, got their faces known and found out where the cool clubs were. The rule seemed to be that if you were cool enough to be there, then you were cool enough to be included in conversations. However, it was unlikely you'd just stumble across the shops; this was such a word-of-mouth experience that not only did you have to know *where* to go, but what time to get there.

In the early 1970s, if you wanted seven-inch singles you'd head for Hanway Street, behind Tottenham Court Road, where John Abbey, the proprietor of *Blues & Soul* magazine, owned the *Contempo* shop. Actually, to call *Contempo* a 'shop' is to flatter it – it was a tiny room above a bar called *Bradley's* (no relation!), reached by a creaky, windy staircase that, today, would be some sort of health and safety cup final. Inside, there was a counter across the middle, with a booming sound system beneath it and shelves stocked with funk behind it. Friday afternoon was when the new music arrived, and punters could spend hours anxiously hanging about while the guys who ran the place took phone calls and tried to reassure the packed room: 'The boxes have just cleared customs, they should be here in an hour or so'. Hardly anyone was going back to work.

Extended cuts or lesser-known tunes meant buying albums – twelve-inch singles were not yet commercially available – for which the shop of choice was *One Stop* at the Oxford Street end of Dean Street. Specialising in soul and jazz, it held comfortable listening booths and a hugely knowledgeable staff. Even if it might not have had every US album on the day it came out, the racks were a treasure-trove of back catalogue – it really didn't matter if something wasn't actually new, so long as it was new in Wood Green.

Other shops worth checking included *Ray's Jazz* in Shaftesbury Avenue, *Cheapo Cheapo* in the Rupert Street end of Berwick Street Market, *City Sounds* in High Holborn, and

Dobell's in Charing Cross Road, but *One Stop* and *Contempo* were the cornerstones, with *Groove Music* taking over later. Further afield there were such black music emporiums as *Sunshine Records* in Turnpike Lane, *Moondogs* in Manor Park, and *Record Corner* in Balham, but although they became hubs of local scenes, they were little more than satellites of what went on 'up West'. *Dobell's*, incidentally, was owned by Doug Dobell, whose record label 77 (the street number of the shop) released records by the South African and modern jazzers described in chapter three.

Because the scene revolved around American imports, the UK industry was not involved, and the British music media never plugged into it. Of the specialist press, *Black Music & Jazz Review* came out monthly, and thus couldn't stay on top of weekly singles schedules, while the weekly newspaper *Black Echoes* didn't launch until 1976. Press coverage therefore rarely went beyond lists of US record releases cut from *Blues & Soul*, and taped to the wall in *Contempo*. Thus, in the same way that Stern's served as the hub of London's African music community, these shops were vital to the cohesion of the funk scene, probably more so than the clubs. Soho, which had previously hosted the old R&B scene, was the centre of the clubbing circuit, with places like *Upstairs at Ronnie's* (the first-floor room above Ronnie Scott's jazz club), *Columbo's* (formerly the *Roaring Twenties*) in Carnaby Street), and *Whisky's* (previously the *Whisky-A-Go-Go*, later the *WAG* in Wardour Street – *W.A.G.*, geddit?), supplemented by *Hunters* in West Kensington or the *Birds Nests* in Paddington, Waterloo and West Hampstead. The shops, however, were more accessible, conducive to conversation and focussed entirely on the music. Kenny remembers the part they played:

'If you wanted to be part of that scene you had to go to those places, there was no press coverage. Because we formed bands locally there were bands like ours all over London. It was only because we all met in the West End that we got to know about each other, and realised there was something going on beyond the end of our roads.

'I'd check *Contempo Records*, and I'd meet people. It would be like this person's in that band, or there would be David Grant who, I think, was a journalist at the time, or Leee John who goes to the clubs I do but also other places like *Maunkberry's* and the *Embassy*. Or that guy in the corner is Dez Parkes, I know him from Forest Gate, and he's got a massive record collection, he's a walking encyclopaedia of music. But he's with other guys, *his* friends who are Noel Vaughn and Trevor Shakes, they're all fantastic dancers and move all over the scene. So then we find out about some new clubs or places we might get a gig, *and* you could check out all the tunes by the groups like Ohio Players or the J.B.'s.

'It was inspiring for a lot of the people getting into bands or setting themselves up as dancers or deejays, because it let you think "I can do that". It wasn't as if to make funk music you had to come from across the water, or have gone to the Berkeley School of Music.'

Dez Parkes, who started off as a dancer but became one of the original scene's most influential deejays, recalls how small it was when it started out, and why it was so important:

'It's funny, because at the time people were under the impression it was really heaving with thousands of people – it wasn't! You could go to several different clubs during the course of a week, but you were seeing the same faces because it was no more than about two or three hundred people. Everyone kind of knew everyone because they would all go to the same places. *Columbo's, Ronnie Scott's,* and *Crackers* for the clubs and *Contempo's, One Stop* or *Dobell's* for records – *Dobell's* was brilliant, it was run by jazz buff Doug Dobell and was like some sort of speakeasy! It had a grand piano on one level, then you'd go down the circular stairs to these booths left over from the sixties, where you'd listen to the records you'd picked out. It was like a timewarp. The West End was where we got to know each other. It was the only reason a lot of people met their spouses, who were from a different part of town – I met my first missus in *Crackers.*

'The thing about this scene was that most of our age group [*mid-teens at the start of the 1970s*] had come out of the

Dez Parkes and friends limber up in Wardour Street for a Friday lunchtime session in *Crackers*.

reggae scene, because there hadn't been much choice. Then when a different type of soul scene came along – with James Brown and with Curtis Mayfield – and as a worldwide people we were moving out of the oppression of the fifties and sixties, where we didn't really have a voice, we moved into the seventies where we could rejoice. All the tunes that were coming out were deep and meaningful and speaking to us as a people, it was trying to uplift us, and wake us up. Some did get woken up, but some didn't because a lot of people at the time didn't quite understand it.

'A lot of people looked at the soul scene as a cop-out or a sell-out, because of the way we dressed and the way we danced, and because it was more *Europeanised* or upwardly mobile. But those artists that were coming out of America were major speakers for us at the time, while those like Roy Ayers were expressing a message of joy and putting us in a happy place – especially for the future generations to bounce off. It gave us exactly the same voice as the nyah man. That's why the scene grew so quickly.'

THE SOUL SCENE WAS ALWAYS going to produce its own bands, too. That took a while, because few black youngsters felt part of a pop process that dictated white kids formed bands, whereas black kids were singers or in singing groups. Then the Jackson 5 came along.

Camelle Hinds, bass player with the early jazz/funk outfit TFB (Typical Funk Band) and later Central Line, explains the Jacksons' impact:

'The Jackson 5 totally changed everything around. Here, for the first time in my life, I see these young kids that look like me, that had the most talent and they're *in a band*. They're creating music that is so beautiful … for example Jermaine Jackson, the way he was playing bass made me want to play the bass, and those bubblegum basslines were pretty adventurous for a young musician. Maybe he wasn't playing bass on all of the songs, or playing it at all, but that didn't matter. The important thing was the idea that we could see them doing the music as well as the singing. Then when we had their cartoon show it gave us a bit of an insight into what it must've been like to be in a band – OK, so it was a cartoon show and probably complete fiction, but it showed us how much fun it could be. It was an amazing inspiration for so many of my generation of musicians – most of them will cite the Jackson 5 as the reason why they wanted to form a band.'

David agrees, reckoning that the group was the watershed between old-school soul and new wave funk, and that it was as much the Jacksons' look and attitude as their music that inspired his peers. Indeed the Jackson 5 made such an impression on him it still resonates nearly forty years later. In

TFB Mk II in Superfly mode after playing at an upscale Hampstead house party. Left to right: Lipson Francis, Henry Defoe, Steve Salvari, Errol Kennedy, Camelle Hinds.

1976, Hi Tension were playing at the *Q Club*, in Praed Street, Paddington, then London's most upmarket black-owned club, and a favourite of visiting African-American celebrities. In their audience was Johnny Jackson, drummer for and cousin of the brothers, who were here on tour. Johnnie was so knocked out with their set that he invited the young band to a soundcheck, and introduced them to four of the Five – it was the painfully shy Michael who chose to hang back. That blew the Londoners away:

'We were invited to their hotel in Mayfair, had drinks with them, then went to soundcheck. We were chatting with them, they gave us advice – all except Michael, who would only talk to his brothers in this little voice. Can you imagine how much that meant to us as a young black band? This was the biggest young black band on the planet and *they're talking to us!*'

Camelle goes on to describe how their wave of bands separated from what had gone before – the F.B.I.s and the Gonzaleses:

'That time was the cusp of two generations of soul bands. Those earlier funk bands were mature soul bands whose tradition went back to the fifties and who knew the sixties. They came out of a line that went back to rhythm and blues and bands like the Rolling Stones, and who were playing Otis Redding with artists like Geno Washington. We didn't know any of that, we were kids – we started with the Jackson 5! Even if they were playing funk, their way of looking at things was different to ours.

'Then there was the generation we were in this country. The previous scene was very much the *Afro* UK soul scene, because there were so many Ghanaians involved. Our generation were essentially young Caribbeans so we didn't necessarily know that Afro UK scene. We had different influences.

'Not that we didn't cross with those guys or they weren't inspirational to us as musicians. Henry [*Defoe, TFB/Central Line's guitarist*] was tutored by one of the guitarists in the Breakfast Band, and we had Max Middleton out of that band playing on our first single. They used to play at Scorpio

Sound Studios, behind Capital Radio in Euston Road, where the engineer was a guy who played with that jazz/funk band Pleasure in America, he produced the Breakfast Band and then he produced Central Line's first single. That's how I got my first session. I went down there and I watched them play: Richard Bailey would be on drums, Kuma Harada on bass, Max Middleton ...

'All those guys, they were like prime musicians for us. A complete inspiration, but theirs was a West End scene, that didn't really disperse until the clubs got rid of the groups and started putting discos in. At that time we weren't even old enough to go out, let alone get into those clubs – some of us were fourteen or fifteen when we started the groups.'

The new bands like TFB, Hott Waxx (the precursor to Hi Tension) and Midnight Express (Errol Kennedy's pre-Imagination group) developed locally, where they could always find an audience. They started out at schools, universities, youth clubs, fetes, local carnivals, community centres and the house parties of, according to Camelle, 'well-off kids who'd seen us at their colleges'. Later they graduated to discos and pubs like the *Three Horseshoes* in Hampstead (currently stripped of two, to become *The Horseshoe*), the *Green Man* in Romford Road or the *King's Arms* in Wood Green, premises that were better known for the notorious reggae club *Bluesville*, and now the site of a police station.

It didn't really matter what the setting was, as long as there was a crowd. David reckons all they wanted to do was play music:

'We all had jobs – I worked for London Transport – we lived at home with our mums and dads and used to rehearse and play anywhere we could. In the beginning we were all at school, Aylestone High and Willesden High, and our first gigs were at schools. We had no real thoughts that we could make money out of it.'

Some did, however, make forays into the big league, with results that weren't always as successful as Hi Tension's. Kenny recalls TFB's *Q Club* debut:

TFB Mk III prepare themselves for the big time. Left to right: Camelle Hinds, Norman Walker, David Walker, Lipson Francis.

'The night we were down there, Muhammad Ali and his people were in the house, so it was really buzzing. We were raw, and we knew it, but we were up for anything. I'm sure a couple of us were fifteen and shouldn't even have been *in* the club, but we were manning up. We started playing the first number and we were really excited. We got to the second number and noticed people moving from the dancefloor to the bar, third number and there's only a few people on the dancefloor. On the fourth number, we're on stage and Count Suckle [*the Jamaican former sound-system operator who owned the club*] walked right across the stage and whispered "One more, just one more!"

'Imagine how we felt – in front of Muhammad Ali! And Suckle, it seemed, had a long memory, because for years any club we turned up at that he had something to do with he'd say to us, "Not tonight, guys!" Even if we hadn't been booked to play!'

Camelle remembers their first brush with the proper music business, and how little had changed since Teddy Osei's generation in terms of deliberate artist misrepresentation:

'This was in 1973, and we'd won this talent competition at the *Roundhouse*, put on by *West Indian World* newspaper. The judges should never have given it to us, because this reggae group, the Equators, were far better than us, but we had all this exciting gear on and we were jumping about, wanting to put on a show, so they gave it to us. We won five hundred quid and a publishing deal with these two guys who had an office up in Savile Row, real cigar-smoking, boardroom types.

'This was our first taste of the record companies and we were so excited – I think I was only seventeen – and they told us they had got us an out-of-town gig. Brilliant, except it wasn't as TFB! They had another band, the Chequers [*a largely white pop/soul group*] who had a hit at the time [*the stringsed-up reggae "Rudi's In Love"*] and they'd been booked for a gig in Carlisle but they couldn't do it. So we had to go up and pretend to be the Chequers, we didn't even know their hit and had to busk it!'

All of this allowed this wave of young players to find their musical feet well removed from outside interference. Plugging in to the music coming in through *Contempo* and *One Stop*, they switched from pop-soul and reggae to focus on funk, jazz and jazz/funk, using American models of astonishing sophistication, lyrical intelligence and downright funkiness. By now the US scene was such that 1974 alone produced *Keep On Steppin'*, *The Payback*, *Change Up The Groove*, *Breakin' Bread*, *Stepping Into Tomorrow*, *Skin Tight*, *Love From the Sun*, *Light Of Worlds*, *Winter In America*, *Sweet Exorcist*, *Sun Goddess* and *Do It 'Til You're Satisfied*. Camelle recalls the effort they put in as they soaked this music up:

'We'd go and see *any* funk or jazz/funk act that came over from America ... the Bros Johnson: we'd be there ... War: we'd be there ... Crown Heights Affair, the Blackbyrds, Stevie

Wonder … we were there. Of course we bought records at
Contempo, but also *Cheapo's*, where we knew from word of
mouth we could get the rare records coming over from the
States – Philip Catherine and Larry Coryell or Lenny White.

'Dez Parkes was crucial because he was so authoritative on
that stuff, we used to go round his house to sift out all these
rare musics, Michel Colombier … people that nobody would
know of. We'd be looking at the musicians on there and we'd
start tracking them on other albums. Somebody like Ted
Taylor performing a cover version of Earth, Wind & Fire's
"Be Ever Wonderful". We were studying all the different
connections – who's the engineer on that record? Oh, George
Massenburg who put out his own gear and he engineered
for Earth, Wind & Fire and also Ramsey Lewis. And who is
that drummer playing on there? Oh he used to play with …
I'm sure we knew more about them than they knew about
themselves! But that was our study, and it pushed us to try
and get better as musicians.'

Kenny believes the music's lineage was important to the
formation of their sound:

'We were connected with the previous generation, but in
doing so we were connected to stuff that went back much
further than that. Take a guy like Joe Harriott, the sax player
who came over from Jamaica in the 1950s, he was bebop but
he had the Caribbean in his playing – it wasn't pure Charlie
Parker. Then you look at who's playing with him and you see
percussionist Frank Holder, whose brother, Herschell Holder
was in Root Jackson's F.B.I., who we knew. Then musicians he
used to associate with were involved, in the early days, with
the bands we were in – sax player Lloyd Smith, a trombone
player called Pat Daniels, and Freddie Wall, the trumpet
player who gave me my first lessons. These guys were
connected with the jazz and the Caribbean, both of which
they loved, and they loved funk, so they were passing that
on to us.

'In the same way it's like listening to Kool & The Gang
and their trumpeter Spike Mickens, and you're listening to
Clifford Brown who was a big influence on Spike. OK, so

it's one stage removed, but it sends you in search of Clifford Brown – a bit back to front, but it becomes an interesting way of learning. I was lucky to have met Donald Byrd and he said we should listen to Stravinsky as well what we were already listening to and it became like a quest for me – *Stravinsky, he's the one!* But when you realise when you're listening to Donald Byrd you're listening to Stravinsky in a roundabout way, it opens up your mind.

'Plus we're Londoners, so we're adding all of what we know from London. We were adding all sort of bits we're hearing from the radio or the lovers' rock dances, we've got bits of calypso in there. Although there was a lot of jazz, it wasn't with

Central Line in the early 1980s. Danny Cummings, Camelle Hinds, Jake LeMesurier, Henry Defoe, Linton Beckles, Lipson Francis. Amazingly, nobody has any idea who the cheerful-looking bearded chap second from the right is, but he was not a member of the group!

the same musical syntax as the originals, and when we'd learn our things off records it was always our own interpretation. We weren't aiming to have anything to do with the charts – our ambition was to be on the cover of *Blues & Soul* and to play at Hammersmith Odeon, because that was our circle. So we didn't feel under pressure to do things a certain way. We'd be in a room and Breeze (*McKrieth, guitarist*) or Tubbs (*Williams, bass*) would play a riff, somebody would say "OK then, what goes with that?" and I'd come up with something [*he plays a couple of runs on his trumpet*], then they'd say "I can work with that." And we'd get going.

'A lot of people liked the energy that doing it like that brought about, but really all we wanted to say was "We are going to sound like us, however that might turn out."'

By the second half of the 1970s, a tidal wave of talent was about to break on London. Best friends Camelle and Kenny, together with Henry Defoe, Lipson Francis, and Norman and David Walker, were part of an east London scene that produced TFB, then Central Line and Light Of The World, Imagination, Incognito and Beggar & Co. Roy Carter, who became bass player with multi-million selling disco-soul band Heatwave, was from this east London pool. So too was Errol Kennedy, Imagination's drummer, who joined the posse from Woolwich after Camelle and Kenny crossed the river to practice Jackson 5 songs with his sister Grace, who would go on to win *Opportunity Knocks* and star in her own BBC TV series. Up from Balham to play drums on Central Line's first album was Mel Gaynor, later of Simple Minds. Singing background vocals on this set was one Diane Sealey, who had yet to reinvent herself as D.C. Lee and sing with Wham! and the Style Council before going solo. Light Of The World's first drummer, Everton McCalla, was also a founder member of Freeez in 1981, the group that had LOTW/Incognito guitarist Bluey playing on their first single. Steve's Headquarters were from north London, and so was Linx, David Grant's first band, which included bassist Sketch Martin, formerly in Headquarters and later of 23 Skidoo, as well as Junior Giscombe as a backing singer. The Harlesden/Willesden/

TFB at the *Sands* disco in Luton, mid-1970s. Left to right: Henry Defoe, Errol Kennedy, Camelle Hinds, Lipson Francis; Steve Salvari is out of shot.

Cricklewood axis, centred on Aylestone High and Harlesden High schools, gave us Hott Waxx, Hi Tension, Kandidate, Atmosfear and Phil Fearon, who became the mainstay of disco-soul band Galaxy.

As the decade progressed, it became standard for the London groups to open for US acts on tour in the UK. Steve Salvari, keyboard player with Headquarters and later with TFB and Central Line, remembers this as proving the bands had a future:

'We'd get gigs opening for the Players Association or the Ohio Players, because promoters were expected to put another act on but weren't going to pay for two separate bands to come over. Sometimes we'd get *picked up* to back a singer that came over on tour too. Although those gigs didn't happen all the time, they were always good because it meant we'd be on a big stage in front of big crowds who were always very good to us – their own. There was hardly any snobbishness about being local boys, and crowds connected with the music we were playing. Then the more they got to know us we started getting bigger followings *because* we were British.'

The music business didn't seem to get this last point, as Steve continues:

'Between about 1974 and 1978, any black artists in Britain were being moulded on the notion that all anybody wanted from a soul act was Tamla Motown. Acts like Billy Ocean and Hot Chocolate, really brilliant artists, being forced into that template. Music business managements at that time had been in place for donkeys' years, and they had no notion of a black act representing something British – if they weren't singing reggae then it had to sound American, which meant Tamla Motown. Which, in turn, was pushed to the record companies, as it was the reference they understood.

'These managers that were effectively running the British music business were people like the Delfonts [*legendary theatrical impresario Bernard Delfont and his brothers Lew and Leslie Grade*], theatre managers who needed acts to put on in them. Even if that circuit was gradually dying out, that was how show business still seemed to work – television too. But it also meant the groups were being marketed as pop acts and had to conform to that when they got a record deal, because that's what the companies wanted. Listen to Sweet Sensation, who had a hit with "Sad Sweet Dreamer" in 1974, they were produced by Tony Hatch, who's best known for the *Crossroads* theme tune [*creaky British 1960s/1970s daytime soap*].

'When the BritFunk guys came along we wanted to go our own way. We were younger and hadn't been listening to Tamla Motown – our bands were Earth, Wind & Fire, Herbie Hancock and Ramsey Lewis. Then because we were British and we had our own outlook on stuff, they didn't know what to do with us. Take Kandidate, for example, their management signed them to RAK Records, which was Mickie Most's company, and he'd had a load of success as a producer with pop and rock records. He'd produced Hot Chocolate a few years earlier, but things had moved on and Kandidate had much more of an edge to them. Take their hit, "I Don't Wanna Lose You". It was a good tune, but they were manipulated into being what Mickie Most's idea of what soul music should be. It was a sign of what would surely happen to the music if it carried on that traditional industry route.'

Just as frustration was starting to set in, a funk revolution happened in the UK. More in spite of the music industry than because of it.

IT'S A COMMON MISCONCEPTION that *Saturday Night Fever*, released in the UK in 1978, marked the beginning of disco. In reality, it was the beginning of the end. The roots of disco lay in the decade's early years, when an explosion of soul music was triggered by the massive increase in black-owned radio stations in the US in the late 1960s. To feed this beast, the black music industry had to produce not just more soul music but more *types* of soul music, as it coincided with advertisers chasing a burgeoning black middle class. The self-explanatory radio format Quiet Storm was born at this point; orchestrators such as Gamble & Huff, Gene Page and Barry White made symphonic funk; and jazz/funk bubbled through. The *Soul Train* TV show, first aired in 1971, showed everyone just how sexy this new soul could be, and it proved its commercial power with Earth, Wind & Fire and Parliament/Funkadelic rocking stage shows on a previously unheard-of scale (for black acts, anyway). Suddenly the American record business was all over it, spending real money on black acts as large quantities of their music found its way into the record collections of Middle America. Once that happened, disco was never far away.

Naturally there was a knock-on effect in the UK, where glam rock was on the wane and the industry was quick to offer up this post-Motown soul as a new Saturday-night soundtrack. That was a shrewd move; with its booming, relatively uncomplicated rhythms, abundant top end, melodic hooks and sentiments either breathtakingly optimistic or dedicated to the dance, this evolved funk found fulsome favour over here. Tunes like "Ain't No Stopping Us Now", "We've Got The Funk", and "Oops Upside Your Head", along with more or less anything by Maze, were universal floor-fillers. It even became bona fide pop music: Barry White was the fourth-biggest-selling album artist in Britain in 1975, above David Essex and below Perry Como; while the only male artists to sell more singles than George McRae that year were the Davids Bowie and Essex.

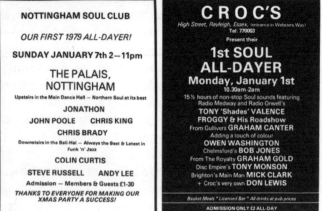

'Where it's At' was to be found in the back pages of *Blues and Soul*.

As a youth demographic, funkateers more than held their own against punks, revivalist mods and nascent New Romantics, albeit with far less media attention. Nowhere was this more visible than in the southeast, where, under the stewardship of a cabal of larger-than-life deejays who dubbed themselves The Soul Mafia – Chris Hill, Steve Walsh, Jeff Young, Robbie Vincent and so on – previously unremarkable nightclubs like *Cheeky Pete's* in Richmond, *Flick's* in Dartford, *Scamps* in Hemel Hempstead, the *California Ballroom* in Dunstable, and *Maison Royale* in Bournemouth were reinvented as cathedrals of groove.

At the same time, a wave of land-based jazz/funk-dedicated pirate radio stations emerged in the southeast. This was before the 1984 Telecommunications Act gave the Department of Trade and Industry draconian powers to use against radio pirates, and dozens of stations sprang up, some boasting tens of thousands of listeners and many broadcasting around the clock. The earliest, Invicta, broadcast from 1970 onwards under the slogan 'Soul over London', and petitioned the Home Office for a legal all-soul station. JFM, the first on FM, grew out of the 1960s' illegal community station Radio Jackie. Switching to an FM frequency in 1980, it shortened its name to JFM, and opted for so funky a schedule that many listeners believed the initials stood for Jazz Funk Music. Horizon Radio took on club deejays, but expected them to pay to present their shows as they were plugging their big-money club gigs. Not surprisingly, a dozen of them quit to start their own station, Solar, the Sound Of London's Alternative Radio. The iconic and well-reggaefied black London station DBC (Dread Broadcasting Company), established in 1981, brought a sound-system vibe to the party with Dark Star & Lady Di's Friday-night funk extravaganza.

The UK edition of *Blues & Soul* became jazz/funk's house journal, covering clubs and shows, and employing a few dee-jays as columnists – a teenage Pete Tong was their advertising executive, building a name as a deejay after work. The maga-zine's role in establishing jazz/funk as a movement across a

wide region cannot be under-estimated, as it facilitated a growing sense of community among groups of fans – or 'tribes' as they called them-selves – spread across the southeast (and in Man-chester). That gave the magazine a unique role – beyond listing US record releases – in marshalling the scene, and doing a great deal to set its tone. In turn, *B&S* was massively rejuvenated by increased advertising spend by record companies, club promoters and the deejays themselves.

THEN THE JAZZ/FUNK ALL-DAYERS moved things up a level. Daytime raving had long been a feature of Northern Soul, a scene which because it was more about dancing than drinking remained unhampered by the 1970s' restric-tive licensing laws. Now clubs ran charabancs to take over larger (and probably softer) southern venues on the oc-casional Sunday. In 1976, enterprising promoters started seeking to hoover up local ticket sales by featuring sec-ondary jazz/funk rooms at the events. These were so over-subscribed that by the next year jazz/funk entrepreneurs were running their own all-dayers at venues like *Reading Top Rank*, *Tiffany's* in Purley and Alexandra Palace. Pub-licised on the pages of *B&S*, these 11am-to-11pm events attracted crowds of six or seven thousand (twice the size of a seated *Hammersmith Odeon*). Tribes from around the re-gion would fetch up carrying banners and wearing match-ing teeshirts bearing such legends as Merton Soul Patrol, Herts Steppers, SAS Crew (Soulful & Sexy) or Benfleet Funkateers.

The high point of their calendar was the Caister Soul Weekender. Starting in 1979, the above-mentioned deejays would hire an out-of season holiday camp at Caister-on-Sea, near Great Yarmouth, to put on two days and nights of non-stop dancing, drinking and tomfoolery – human pyramids, toga parties, beachwear, whistles, klaxons as regulation accessories … It assumed the sort of eminence that Glastonbury enjoys in the rock world, and continues today – the same music, mostly the same deejays and punters, with the only noticeable difference being that the tribal tee shirts are two or three sizes larger.

By the start of the twenty-first century, the jazz/funk weekender had spawned its own nostalgia industry among south-of-England forty-somethings.

Perhaps understandably, all this prompted a degree of resentment among London funk's first wave. Some weren't happy that the scene they felt they had worked hard to set up was being taken over by a group of white deejays who, they believed, took it straight into the mainstream to line their own pockets. The bands however, as Steve explains, didn't see it that way:

'By the middle of the decade there was a good live scene in London – the *Greyhound*, the *Nashville Rooms*, places like that – but it was primarily for rock bands. We were struggling to break out of the smaller venues because the bookers at the bigger rooms didn't know about the funk scene and didn't believe we could pull a crowd – they were just getting into reggae and because we were black but plainly weren't reggae it baffled them. So although we were gigging, we weren't being pushed to develop or build careers. Sometimes gigs were so low-key they felt like rehearsals. What saved us was those funk deejays, they had their own scene and could bring us up into it.

'There were people who were unhappy about the way the scene changed, and that's going to be the case with anything that shifts like that. Everything needs to grow to survive, and those guys were instrumental in pushing it to what it became. Whoever or whatever they were, Chris Hill, Robbie Vincent, Steve Walsh and those guys had a deep love of the music, and as they promoted it they brought the bands along with them. This was absolutely crucial for us in our development as artists, because *every* band wants to play to the biggest audiences they can. The all-dayers gave us the chance to headline proper shows in front of an audience that *really* appreciated us. Although they'd go mad for the Americans, because we were theirs and were embedded in that scene we were like family to that crowd – you'd see the same faces at every gig. But although they loved us, they weren't going to accept any old thing, and that pushed us on to get better and try new things. Because those gigs were a dancehall environment we saw what they wanted and could react to it immediately. We all grew as artists on that scene.'

Kenny maintains it was a more mutually beneficial state of affairs:

'The biggest audiences were the all-dayers and the week-enders. The Funk Mafia had a big audience, and although they were going with or without us we added something to the crowd that was already there. They worked out they needed the bands to make the all-dayers and weekenders properly work, because the combination of bands and those deejays would be a potent force. They realised it more than the bands, who for the most part were just happy to go along and play. It was something that worked for us at the time, because we were playing big gigs and getting much better at what we did, but with hindsight we probably could have made more of it in terms of building for ourselves.'

Using that same hindsight, it's easy to see why these young musicians didn't build for themselves – they didn't really need to. The record industry had embraced the Soul Mafia deejays, taking them on as A&R men or consultants, and thereby opening the door for the London bands. In a flurry of activity, Hi Tension signed to Island; Light Of The World, Incognito and Phil Fearon & Galaxy to Ensign, a Phonogram subsidiary, in which Chris Hill was influential; Central Line and Junior Giscombe to Mercury, where Jeff Young was in A&R; Atmosfear to MCA; First Light (Paul 'N-n-n-n-nineteen' Hardcastle was half of this duo) and Total Contrast to London Records; Second Image (managed by Robbie Vincent), Shakatak and Level 42 to Polydor; and Imagination to R&B, Pye's disco subsidiary, to whom Freeez were also signed. All of which was a long way removed from the self-sufficiency of lovers' rock; one of the few parallels to that ethos was Linx's first single "You're Lying", which came out on their own Aves label, but as soon as it started selling well it was picked up by Chrysalis.

In the by-now disco-crazy mainstream, BritFunk was holding its own. Steve maintains that was because they'd had ample time to get ready:

'We'd been learning our craft for years, and were fortunate in that we could try things out and refine how we did things away from a very big spotlight. Our crowds encouraged us all the way, and we could really develop according to our own instincts and what we could see was working, rather than as the result of marketing meetings in which some blokes who'd never been to a club tell you what they think will make people dance.

'The all-dayers put us in front of the sort of crowds a lot of rock groups would dream about, so we learned stagecraft and how to put on a show. When bands like us or Hi Tension went on *Top of the Pops* and could look as exciting as any American funk band, people were amazed, but it was what we'd been doing for ages.'

What was remarkable was that, in the beginning, this subculture was more or less left to itself. Most record companies didn't profess to understand jazz/funk, so they left it to the deejaying A&R men/consultants who knew *precisely* what was required. When the bands did get a major label push, the impact was immediate and impressive.

Hi Tension were up first when, in 1978, their singles "Hi Tension" and "British Hustle" went top twenty and top ten respectively, each selling over 200,000. The following year Light Of The World hit the lower reaches of the charts with "Midnight Groovin'", the first of a series of top forty appearances that stretched into 1982. In 1981, the LOTW off-shoot Beggar & Co – Kenny, David Baptiste and Breeze McKrieth – proved immediately successful, scoring three big chart hits, albeit one of them with Spandau Ballet. Central Line's "Walking Into Sunshine" was a hit on both sides of the Atlantic, as was "You've Said Enough" the following year. Freeez were chart regulars during the first few years of the 1980s, with "Southern Freeez" and "IOU" going top ten, and the latter doing very well in the US. Linx hit the charts five times between 1980 and 1982, with "Intuition", the follow-up to "You're Lying", -up being the most successful, and then David Grant's solo career kept him in the top twenty until 1985. Imagination were Top Of The Pops regulars between 1981 and 1984, and also had hits in Europe and the US. Phil Fearon, with or without Galaxy, was virtually a top twenty resident during 1983 and 1986; Junior Giscombe enjoyed success in the UK and the US in 1982 with "Mama Used To Say" and continued to be found in the British charts for a couple of years; snf David Joseph, post-Hi Tension, had a chart hit with "You Can't Hide (Your Love Forever)" in 1983. Incognito's 1981 album, *Jazz/Funk*, did very well in Switzerland, even if their single "North London Boy" was all but ignored in north London. Second Image's records were big in the clubs, and regularly troubled the lower reaches of the charts. Shakatak broke through in 1982 with the single "Easier Said Than Done", triggering a succession of hit singles and gold albums that saw the group build a huge audience in Japan. And Level 42 forged an international career on a string of top twenty hits that lasted from 1980 until they broke up in 1994.

The bands showed off their musicianship, and exulted in the sheer breadth of the genre. Hi Tension were sophisticated party time, produced by Osibisa's percussionist Kofi Ayivor, and effortlessly tore it up on *Top of the Pops*. Light Of The World's self-titled first album is a true genre classic, a spiky, mostly instrumental masterpiece of horn play, infectious rhythms and clever musical layering. Central Line's embryonic-electro "Walking Into Sunshine" was as clever as it was restrained as it was a massive hit, but they surpassed it with the not-so-obvious choice of Nat King Cole's "Nature Boy" inna jazz/funk style. Freeez's "IOU" and accompanying video completely captures the moment when British funk osmosed into hip hop; Linx showed how easy it was to be smooove without sacrificing funkiness by building tunes like "You're Lying" and "So This Is Romance" around Sketch's bass guitar. Mirage's "Summer Groove", Junior's "Mama Used To Say" and David Joseph's "You Can't Hide (Your Love Forever)" were irresistible.

While still playing to their 'home' crowds in the suburban clubs, the groups were now getting regular TV exposure. Their records were all over daytime radio, their music was evolving as they cut albums in proper studios, and most were selling singles by the truckload. What could possibly go wrong?

THE SUBURBAN SOUL SCENE was never going to be as black as its West End counterpart had been, but that needn't have been an issue – for years convoys of Escorts and Cortinas had set off from Wood Green or White City, heading for soul nights in places like Welwyn Garden City or Bognor. These were specialist events where kindred spirits were made welcome; indeed being black and from London was usually a plus point. Many of the later wave of clubs, though, were more mainstream-oriented, which meant less commitment to the music and all that went with it. All too often, locals would resent the urban interlopers who were habitually better dancers, generally cooler dressed and usually a big hit with the ladies. Confrontation was frequently on the cards.

Although there was never a massive problem, it was easy for club managements to see the black guys as trouble, and the best way to prevent that was to stop them coming in. 'Sorry lads, it's full in there' was how bouncers with more developed people skills would greet black faces, while 'Oh, they've been in earlier' was the glib explanation when half a dozen white guys who clearly hadn't were ushered in moments later.

Steve, who played at these clubs with Central Line, remembers the group being stopped at doors and having to patiently explain 'We're on stage in an hour!' He endorses the notion that nothing inflamed a certain element more than seeing white girls fraternising with black guys. Grinning and spreading his hands in a gesture of apparent blamelessness, he recalls:

'That's what used to set them off, us getting amongst their women … And there was nothing we could do about it – so many of them were *so* keen.'

This sort of door policy spread, as venue managers who had been nervous about black music looked to justify a ban on black people. Kenny believes there was more to it:

'It was like that scene in that Michael Douglas film *Falling Down*, with the black guy outside the bank who was *uneconomically viable*. That was their attitude towards us at those out-of-town clubs – uneconomically viable. We came there to dance, we weren't going to buy round after round of beer and then scampi and chips. They thought we'd buy one blackcurrant and lemonade that would last all night, and they wanted an excuse to ban us because they said we didn't buy enough drinks.'

It must be stressed that there was no noticeable collusion from the majority of the punters, most of whom would have been horrified if they'd been aware of why their soul scene was so bereft of soul brothers. It was a vivid illustration of how easy it was to fall out of step with what was happening in the world beyond what you thought you knew. The London jazz/funk scene was the first manifestation of black and white youngsters being comfortable with each other, in an English-created black milieu that appeared to embrace its wider situation. Kenny likens this nightlife apartheid to the *Cotton Club* in 1920s' Harlem – a white audience with black performers – and suggests it had much greater social consequences than might at first seem apparent.

While these suburban white kids would not have been bothered by a multi-culti dancefloor, they had little day-to-day contact with black people. This is at a time when Trevor McDonald was still a sports reporter and Diane Abbott a local councillor, and black people were only visible in a very narrow spectrum. To remove the option for white kids to socialise with their black peers further skews worldviews. On a scene where they're offering little more than entertainment – 'We were the turn', as Steve puts it – Kenny's *Cotton Club* analogy holds water. Then if suburban funk fans regularly see black guys turned away at club doors because they are 'trouble', it leaves them to imagine how intrinsically dangerous ordinary black people must be.

It would also be ludicrous to assume that the deejays who controlled this scene endorsed such policies. When the scene was still low-key, many had rocked healthily mixed houses in urban environments, genuinely putting the fun into funk. Kenny backs this up:

'Many of the Soul Mafia were concerned about it – a couple were willing, if things weren't right, not to play certain clubs or to even pack up their equipment and walk out.'

Steve is slightly more stoic about what might be perceived as tolerance of a particularly nasty state of affairs:

'It was due to club owners and promoters. The deejays were making a living and they were all there because they loved the music. One thing's for certain, though, if it hadn't been them it would have been somebody else. It was always the same, in the Motown era in London there were enough clubs that played pure soul and wouldn't let black guys in. I can remember clubs that played pure reggae – all that Trojan stuff – and it was all skinheads in there with no black guys getting through the door. It's why the blues dance scene flourished.

'I can remember a lot of places where we were playing to an all-white audience with our bredren outside, couldn't get in, but you can't really expect us to take responsibility for that. We were young guys making music and trying to make a living out of what we loved to do – it wasn't a game. I would suspect that a lot of those deejays weren't strong enough to have done anything about the situation, because then they just wouldn't have worked.'

Kenny expands on the bands' position: 'For us, we were glad of any audience, as those people come and see you because they like your music – they are always welcome. The realisation that there are certain other people who aren't allowed in or don't feel comfortable in different areas is hurtful, and you want to play to those people. Sadly, we found that wasn't always possible. We wanted to play in black areas or venues where we could find a multi-racial crowd, but because not a lot of the promoters of funk and soul were black, they weren't interested. In certain areas where there were black promoters they would be more interested in

bringing over Gregory Isaacs or somebody like that. So it was never that the bands didn't want to play other gigs there, but those promoters that would take you into those areas weren't necessarily into the music.

'There was a big jazz/funk scene in Manchester and Liverpool, and we all found that was where you could get that more multi-racial, cosmopolitan audience. It was up there that everybody could get into your gigs and there was never any trouble.'

Dez Parkes remains highly critical: 'When that scene started, we were very unassuming – we had our scene and we just wanted to go out and enjoy ourselves. It wasn't about making a load of money. It was very like the tradition that had been going on since we came from the Caribbean, that here was somewhere to remind ourselves of who we were after a week of trials and tribulations. Like the blues dances, that soul scene was for us that had a passion for that music.

'What happened when it went so mainstream was people got to see what we took for granted, and saw that there was money to be made. And to make that money, it had to change. Although it was the promoters and the club managements that fixed policies, and I don't doubt that the deejays loved the music, you have to ask yourself this: In that whole Mafia thing, the only black deejay was Greg Edwards, and he had the *Soul Spectrum* show on Capital Radio so he had more pull than any of the others. But you have to ask yourself was he the *only* black deejay in London that was good enough?'

It's easy to understand how jazz/funk's suburban demographic affected the scene. What's less comprehensible is the shift that happened in town. By the end of the 1970s, the underground London funk clubs had disappeared, and the new wave of venues weren't coming at it from that specialist point of view. Looking for the more recently established higher-spending set, they imported suburban door policies. Suddenly West End clubs were adopting a quota system. To stay on the right side of the Commission for Racial Equality (now the Equality and Human Rights Commission), and to promote a *soupçon* of cool, door staff would count off the handful of black guys to be allowed in, and after that it was 'Sorry lads ...' The most notorious culprits were the *Lyceum* and the *WAG Club*; the latter had such a severe approach that BBC soul stalwart Trevor Nelson recalls:

'The *WAG* was a classic – the first time I was ever allowed in the place was when they phoned me up and asked me to deejay – they'd never ever let me in as a punter. Still makes me laugh.'

While this hurt prospective ravers, the bands' problems were with the record companies. Although the initial British funk hits looked like the perfect launching pad, big record company wisdom dictated that further progression could only come about by following big record company guidelines. Hi Tension were the first band to get a deal, and the first to be affected. David explains:

'How we got a deal was Kofi [*Ayivor, Osibisa's percussionist*] came to our rehearsals, liked what he heard and took us into a studio. We did a demo with him, "Hi Tension" by Hi Tension, which he took direct to Chris Blackwell at Island, who signed us on the strength of that track. Kofi understood what we were doing, because he understood how the drums and percussion should work on songs like that. It's that recording that was released, and it was good enough for over 250,000 people to go out and buy. Then when we did our next track, "British Hustle", we've been given this guy to produce us, this Alex Sadkin – we'd never heard of him. He was completely different and he didn't get it – he took so long to set up the sound in the studio he almost killed the track! But we knew how to play it and keep the excitement up, and it was another 250,000-seller. Because it was a hit he got to do the album.

'That was *so* bad. He killed the vibe of the album, totally killed it. We'd been playing live for years, we knew how to get a vibe going and keep it from sounding like it was done in a studio, but this Alex Sadkin would spend all day setting up a drum sound. He'd be in the studio going "dum ... dum ... dum" [*mimes playing a drum*], which was costing *us* money! That studio was £1000 a day, which we couldn't afford but it was billed to us because that was the system. After that we weren't going to make any royalties off that album, and to make things worse it just about did sixty thousand. We'd had two singles do a quarter of a million each, but the album wasn't what people who already liked us wanted.

'It opened my eyes to how things worked. I would have assumed, naively, if you're a record company and you saw the style or the sound we were trying to achieve, wouldn't you go and get some brother from somewhere that understands it? *No!* We weren't nurtured at all. Everybody acted like we were going to learn something from this guy, but I learned nothing, other than I was very disappointed with Island Records.'

This 'we know best' approach became a template. Central Line had a sympathetic and capable producer in Heatwave's Roy Carter, and after their debut album *Breaking Point* established healthy sales in the UK and the US, they wanted to flex their musical muscles. Fully aware of how the jazzier end of things went down, their record of choice was fifty-year-old jazz'n'soul standard "Nature Boy". Camelle is still smarting:

'Because I was born in 1957, I remember the Nat King Cole version playing around the house. It was one of my dad's favourites and he told us "If you can't make any money

off that song, you might as well give up!" Then I heard the version with Jorge Dalto and Ronnie Foster playing keys, and George Benson playing guitar and singing [*from George Benson's* In Flight *album*] and it completely blew me away. By that time then I was listening to Yazoo and Culture Club, looking at the level of the vocals and production, and I wanted to do something with that sensibility but with this jazz record. The record company didn't see it that way. Acting as gatekeepers, they sat on it for a year because they wanted us to continue as we had been.

'When it did come out, "Nature Boy" was the biggest hit we ever had – by a long way. It got to number 21, but the one after it barely scraped in to the top fifty. That was because it took so long for "Nature Boy" to come out, the band had lost faith in that particular path, and we reverted to what we'd done before, but our audience had moved on. The record company didn't seem to care and wouldn't listen to what we were saying about what we knew would go down well. We were becoming increasingly frustrated because we weren't being allowed to make that leap. In 1984 we decided it just wasn't working and we just wanted them to let us go, because we felt they didn't have a clue what the music was or what to do with us.'

Light Of The World's first album, *Light Of The World*, was essentially the stage show they'd been refining for years, and communicated that excitement through the storming semi-instrumental singles "Swingin'" and "Midnight Groovin'". When it was a big hit, Ensign Records responded by sending this successful London funk band to Los Angeles to record the follow-up, *Round Trip*, with Californian soft soul producer Augie Johnson, best known for the studio group Side Effect. Also on record company advice, they had acquired a lead vocalist, with the plan being to broaden their appeal. Good as the album was, there was an underlying feeling that by shifting away from their jazz bloodline they were flattening out what had made them special in the first place. The single "London Town" summed this up. The chorus *'I wanna party in London town!'* became an anthemic badge of identification on dancefloors across the southeast, and it reached number 41 in the charts, but while it was *about* London, it somehow wasn't *of* London. It sounded like an American's take on the city, which, according to Kenny, is pretty much what it was:

'The idea came from Augie. He said that we hadn't got a song about London on the album, and he had this idea kicking around in his head. He said to Tubbs 'Play this' and [*Kenny sings a slowed-down "London Town" bassline*] and we built the track from that. The rest of us had about half an hour in another room to come up with the lyrics. There's nothing wrong with it – we loved it – but I've got all the parts transferred to audio files and there's all sorts of alternate brass parts to it. [*He plays a brass-heavy remix that sound a lot more like Light Of The World.*]

'The thing is, Light Of The World was supposed to be a blend of sounds, and with all respect to those guys, it was never about having a band where one or two people stand out there and sing. It was a *collective*, like, say, Earth, Wind & Fire, where those guys can sing but most of the time they're not and they're another part of the band. The record company didn't understand that. Going to LA with Augie Johnson was an opportunity and we loved the idea of the sophistication – like "Pete's Crusade" – but some of us weren't happy getting into the ballads and the singing. It was fine to have a couple of tracks like that on an album, but we were being asked to do more and more. That was the whole thing about Beggar & Co, we wanted to remain true to what our vision ever was, which was "Somebody Help Me Out", with all the chanting and the *woah-woahs*.

'Myself, Baps and Breeze had written that song for the whole of Light Of The World as what we should be doing, but some of the guys didn't want to do it because we'd been getting in the charts with the other stuff. The record company didn't want to do it either, they said we shouldn't be going back to that after doing *Round Trip*. So we recorded it anyway, and put it out as Beggar & Co, the three of us. It sold twice as many as any Light Of The World record, and should've been the biggest record Light Of The World ever had.'

Once again, the group themselves were right about what ought to be required of them. "Somebody Help Me Out" was in the charts for over two months, peaking at number 15; their follow-up, the equally raucous "Mule (Chant No. 2)" also outsold every LOTW single; and in between the trio provided the horns and chant vocals for Spandau Ballet's top-five hit "Chant No. 1 (I Don't Need This Pressure On)".

Much of this record-company interference was with one eye on American success. As Camelle remembers, that missed the point of their music being Made in Britain:

'They thought the best way to sell us in America was to turn us into Americans – they tried to turn us into Cameo, Light Of The World they saw as Kool & The Gang, Hi Tension were Earth, Wind & Fire … But the irony was we'd actually done well there as ourselves, as the American black radio and club crowds really appreciated the fact that we took a different stance from American funk. They saw it as unique, and would go mad for the occasional thing – Junior's "Mama Used To Say", Light Of The World's first album … our first album and "Walking Into Sunshine" and "You've Said Enough" were big hits.

'What Americans didn't want was us sounding American – they already had enough Americans, they wanted something different. The record companies didn't see that or didn't have the confidence to go with it.'

What finished the bands off was being squeezed by the legacy they had done much to create. Former jazz/funk scenesters were by now forming their own bands – Haircut One Hundred, Wham!, Animal Nightlife, Spandau Ballet, ABC, the Style Council and so on – often helped out by jazz/funk players. With these developments, the record companies' repositioning of jazz/funk as just another pop style was complete, effectively slamming the door on the original bands. Camelle explains:

'Look at the bands that came after the first wave of new romantics – Duran Duran, Haircut One Hundred, Spandau. They were all soul boys, but they were mostly white and *they were mainstream.* The record companies recognised them – they saw them as part of pop music, but they just saw us as black bands [*he makes quote marks with his fingers*]. That's where the real frustration set in, because same as those other bands we were influenced by everything that was going on around us and in the charts. *Of course* we wanted to be in the limelight and played on Radio One. What happened was we started appearing on *Top of the Pops* as musicians or backing vocalists to white groups, which was just a hundred-quid session fee. There was no stability in it for us.'

Steve is less equitable about what he saw happening at record companies:

'It all seemed to be progressing nicely, then Level 42 got signed to Polydor and the whole dynamic changed. I can remember around 1980 when they were supporting Light Of The World, and Camelle and Tubbs [*LOTW's bass player*] were slapping long time before Mark [*King, Level 42's bass player*] and doing it very well. But while our groups might have got ten grand for an advance, suddenly Level 42 were getting two or three times that because they were a white band. It's been going on as long as the music business: as soon as you got white bands that could make black music, they got the priority and had more money spent on them. We had to deal with that on a daily basis. It was dispiriting, to say the least.'

This allusion to such apparently institutionalised racism in London's record companies is not without foundation. As Dennis Bovell touched on in the preceding chapter, there was little corporate empathy with any black music that wasn't Bob Marley or Bob Marley-ish. After the Tuff Gong died in 1981, and before rap took over, black acts were viewed as either The New Bob Marley – songs of sufferation, dreadlocks, promotable to the rock audience – or *Not* The New Bob Marley – fairly cheerful, Jheri-curled, lacking 'credibility', and thus commercially worthless, not economically viable.

Black audiences weren't even subdivided to that degree, but looked on as one homogenous downtrodden mass, partial to any black act that gave voice to their wretchedness.

These lazy stereotypes were afforded so much traction because so few black people were employed in any aspect of the mainstream soul music industry. which obscured just how diverse black tastes could be. More worrying still was the extent to which casually racist language was used in offices when discussing black bands. While it was probably no more than in life in general, it would often shock music journalists as it coming from the people responsible for a significant part of black British culture.

Steve maintains it was impossible to do anything about it:

'When white groups stood up for themselves, they were being strong-minded and were admired for it. When we stood up for ourselves, it was because we had chips on our shoulders. And that would affect how other black groups got treated, because according to them we were all the same.

Beggar & Co at BritFunk's 30th Anniversary in 2011, Kenny is second from the left.

'That attitude was one of the big contributors to the Brit-Funk scene not lasting that long. The peak was between '79 and '83; it was all over by '84, which is too short a space of time for a music like that to be able to develop and establish itself properly.'

It's a great shame that BritFunk, one of the slickest, most musically stylish movements to come out of black London, doesn't believe it fulfilled itself either creatively or commercially. When you compare it to lovers' rock, however, it's not hard to see why that happened. The reggae genre developed as completely self-sufficient, and was controlled all through the process by the same people who had thought it up, nurtured it and developed a production/promotion/distribution set-up that was quite happy to turn its back on the mainstream. It wasn't perfect, and as we've seen some residual frustration remains, but the industry always called its own shots. BritFunk, on the other hand, put itself at the mercy of those who not only did not actually make the music, but in some cases did not even like or understand the music. Camelle is aware of the differences:

'In the reggae field, they were much more astute about how they could actually take their stuff to market, therefore how they could nurture what they were doing and make sure it always stayed viable. They kept hold of it. We, on the other hand, came into it from a world that was all about the major labels, and to us it was really exciting to be with a major record company. We didn't have that sound-system mentality, where you take care of your own business. The reggae side of things had much more business acumen than we ever did, and that was to our detriment. With us it was all about sign on the dotted line come what may! Then once we bought into all that, we started coming up against gatekeepers who didn't have the good of the music at heart, and that fucked it up totally.'

ALTHOUGH THESE GUYS ARE UNDERSTANDABLY dis-appointed, as Steve points out their influences weren't limited to setting up potential pop stars:

'Quite apart from that whole generation of London soul boy bands that wouldn't have stood a chance if it hadn't been for our scene – Kenny and the horns worked with Heaven 17 as well as Spandau, and did stuff for bands like the Jam... Baps toured with George Michael, Kenny did TV work with him... Camelle played bass in the Style Council ... Bluey's Incognito was at the start of that whole acid jazz movement. Then there was the generation that came after them – Omar, the Brand New Heavies, Jamiroquai... they all used to be at the gigs watching us and were encouraged to do their own thing.'

Their influence continues beyond even that, as Kenny, Camelle and Steve all teach music, music theory and music business at various London colleges, Steve produces and manages young soul talent, and it's not unheard of for any them to pop up on stage somewhere with different funky jazz-type projects. Or even as Light Of The World, Central Line or Hi Tension. In April 2011, Steve organised a Thirty Years of BritFunk concert at London's O2. With a stellar line-up including Beggar & Co, Central Line, David Joseph Junior and Incognito playing to a packed house, it proved more than simply a nostalgia fest for the mostly-middle-aged-would-regret-it-in-the-morning audience. The bands got a great deal out of it, too, as Kenny recalls:

'There must have been about 250 people walking about backstage, some of us who haven't seen each other for twenty years. Some of us had fallen out or had disagreements, but seeing the crowd that turned up – and *stayed*, because it went on until about two in the morning – it made us realise what we'd achieved and what an effect it could still have. Hopefully it happens again, and everybody will turn up and go on stage.'

CHAPTER EIGHT

'If You're Not Dancing, Fuck Off'

|||||||||||||||||||||||||||||||||||||||||||||||||||||||||||||||||||||||||||||||||||||||||||||||

The new sound systems
rewrite raving

'THERE WAS A WHOLE LOAD OF KIDS OUT THERE – in London – that by the end of the seventies fitted between a lot of the different styles that were prescribed by the media. As a result, we were falling into the cracks – not really finding what we wanted in anything that was being put in front of us, so we had to start making something up. What that turned out to be were warehouse parties … it was pirate radio … it was genuine street fashion …

'The brilliant thing was we were making it for *ourselves* so it reflected us and where we lived – it was particular to *London*. I'm not saying what we made was perfect, probably it wasn't, but at least we weren't making it according to some marketing executive's idea of what we ought to be wanting.'

Sitting in the appropriately multi-culti *Café Oto*, behind Dalston Junction, Derek Yates is describing the clubland revolution in 1980s' London. These days he's Course Director of Design and Illustration at Camberwell College of Art; back then he was straight outta art school, and in demand designing flyers for dances. Derek created the most iconic London motif of that era: the Soul ɪɪ Soul Funki Dred head.

His visuals played a vital role in finally propelling the scene overground, after years of being more or less unnoticed by the established media or entertainment industry.

'It was a bunch of people who weren't really *Soul Train* and weren't really Bob Marley, but at they same time they were all of that. Just none of it exclusively. It was how mixed up people's tastes *really* were in London – you could be into a bit of electro and a bit of Run D.M.C., but also into Yellowman *and* lovers rock *and* Parliament. We took bits from a load of movements: I was *sort of* into breakdancing and I was *sort of* into graffiti, but I wasn't into *New York* breakdancing, graffiti or hip hop. London had such a strong cultural feel of its own, what so many kids were really into was how things became something else when they came to London. That was what became Mastermind, became Good Times, became Soul II Soul ... all those new London-based sound systems, that were very different from traditional reggae sound systems.

'The best thing was that we almost sold it back to the media, but they never quite got it. Still don't. Although, looking back, perhaps that was a good thing, as it allowed the scene to carry on defining itself.'

This sound-system-led scene developed into a genuine social 'movement', precipitating significant cultural and commercial shifts. During the next twenty or so years it would prove to be every bit as game-changing as punk ever was, in effectively repositioning black music as part of the fabric of British pop. That said, apart from one spectacular exception, the scene produced almost none of its own music, so this is the only chapter of *Sounds Like London* not to be driven by musicians. Instead, the movement was all about how you presented music that somebody else had made.

HOW TO DEAL WITH THE SUBURBAN club-door policies described in the previous chapter was hardly rocket science: the inner-city convoys just stopped making the trips. It was when the West End began to operate the same sort of entrance apartheid that things became more complex. Cour-

Jazzie B of Soul II Soul; his sound system rewrote the rules of raving.

tesy of a generation of kids who had been all through school together, the capital's soul scene had been quietly and organically building its own internal multiculturalism. Derek Yates's experiences as a white native north Londoner would have been commonplace:

'We couldn't all go to a club together, not the mixture of friends I had at that time – there were Greek kids and black kids and Asian kids and white kids … We went out on a Saturday night, and we couldn't get in to the same club. We went to a black club, which would be a reggae club and more likely to be local, then me and the other white guys are going to feel like we're the only white kids in there. Then if we went to a mainstream soul club in the West End, the majority of them weren't going to let the black kids in.'

Most remarkable, as Derek puts it, was 'the mainstream totally missing a trick – there was a whole load of inner-London kids just like us, who wanted to go out.' That state of affairs was perfect for sound systems: business opportunity meets social exclusion meets musical potential. Forced to forget about West End clubs or plush suburban discos, London's black soul scene became self-contained, vaguely outlaw, community-based, ever-innovative, and in complete empathy with its crowds.

To get there, however, the very concept of a sound system had to evolve from the big funk outfits, still run like reggae outfits, that had flourished in London since the mid-1970s – TWJ, Black Caesar and that stalwart of the Notting Hill Carnival, 6X6. While the internal dynamics, micro-economics and ghetto sensibilities of the blues dances remained important, the new sound systems needed to recognise how sophisticated and cosmopolitan young black London had become. Such a generation of operators was falling into place: British-born; grown up around local sound systems at weddings, christenings and funerals; and seduced by the glamour while living in a wider world. One such new kid on the block, Trevor Nelson, was by the early 1980s already running his own Madhatter sound system:

'Even though I saw myself as a soul boy, I still wanted to be part of a sound system, I saw it as my protection. And while we weren't the biggest sound system, we were a *proper* sound system – we had box boys, we built our own speaker boxes … We had to have the credentials otherwise nobody would have accepted us as being true to what we were trying to do.

'My sister was part of that earlier [*jazz/funk*] scene, she'd tell me about those nights like Chris Hill and the Southgate *Royalty*, so when I was at school I subscribed to all of that. We had tee shirts calling ourselves the Dalston Funk Force because I thought this is what you do, you get a little tribe! But when I got to be eighteen or nineteen, I realised it was about individualism. Then by the time I got to deejaying, that British jazz/funk scene was more or less dead. The London crowd didn't want that Caister-ish "wooh wooh!" thing, we were looking for anything that sounded fresh and new. It had to be on a local level because the West End ostracised us – we knew that, everybody knew that – so there was an almost anti-West-End vibe. My scene was in Hackney and

Derek Yates's graphic evolution of the Funki Dred head.

there were plenty of people who would only rave in Hackney, then there were the people who were outgoing enough to go raving all the way across London – they'd travel eight miles to Brixton or Streatham or wherever to rave in a like-minded situation. So you got this hardcore travelling all over the city, but they wouldn't go down the road into the West End, they'd say "Well it's not for us, they don't want us there." and in most cases they'd be right.

'Although we were staying local we didn't want to rave with the local reggae scene, because those guys weren't moving on. That blues-dance scene went on a lot longer than people realise, the *whole* of the eighties, creeping into the nineties, so while the scene had to go back to house parties, now there was a new set of deejays cutting their teeth and things were changing. In the beginning in my scene there were only about twenty like-minded people and the core of them were my friends from college [*Trevor went to Westminster Kingsway*], but then there got to be more of them. Just people from Hackney who wanted to stand out and be different from the usual Gabicci-wearing, Farah slacks-wearing, skins-wearing crew. Then once people got into the parties, and saw people dressed a bit different and dancing to all this different music, it started to get them away from that whole tribal identity thing.'

Another such deejay, Norman Jay, was cutting his teeth on his brother Joey's sound system, Great Tribulation. We meet in upmarket Brixton Village – formerly Granville Arcade – in a bakery/coffee shop so cutting-edge that they have Duralit toasters on the table for customer use, and you collect little pots of spreads from the counter. Of course Norman is wearing a hat, and, just as inevitably, he is cheerful and charming, even if his early sound-system memories aren't all positive:

'The sound system started in 1974, it was purely a reggae sound system with Joey playing lovers' rock and Nina Simone's "My Baby Just Cares For Me", that kind of thing. I didn't join initially, although I used to go to lend some brotherly support at sound clashes [*two sound systems playing in the same venue in competition*]. But there was so much about that culture I was totally opposed to – particularly, rather ironically, the sound clash. To me, the sound clash was never about your audience, it was about *you*, and beating the other sound. I hated that. All I wanted to do was play continuous music and see people in front of us going "Wicked tune!". Not blasting it at another deejay, and he's making noise over your music, and you can't play because he's spinning back or his people are pulling out your cables. That, for me, epitomised the sound-system culture that was so introverted.

'As a self-sufficient business model, though, you can't beat a sound system, and I thought "What if I extricate a sound system and put it in front of a different audience and change the soundtrack?" [*He claps his hands*] Then *bingo*! We're on a winner. I was always a soul boy who had grown up in a reggae sound, and to my way of thinking there was no reason why we couldn't run a parallel universe of playing different music.

'What really motivated us was going into the clubs where the deejays played continuous music and they were breaking *our* music, but there was never going to be any way in for us. I was very conscious then, a lot of guys my age were – not just the reggae men, all of us. I was young and angry and all the time thinking that black deejays were conspicuous by their absence. When I read magazines like *Blues & Soul* and read about those deejays in my mind I assumed they were black and there was an accepted status quo there, but that couldn't have been further from the case. There was only Alex Pascal, Tony Williams and Greg Edwards and even they were from overseas, not homegrown. We weren't working in the record companies or in the media, so our only entry level was the sound systems. Like it always has been with sound-system culture, it was born out of necessity and we needed to do this for ourselves.

'But the good thing about not being able to break through then, was that perhaps it might have been the wrong time. It meant that we were allowed to nurture and learn our craft, and by the time we broke through we were ready. I believe the whole sound-system ethic of being self-sufficient and not relying on a promoter or a club owner to dictate policy was what allowed us to succeed. I never played in a club as a deejay, so I learned all my skills outside of that environment – MC-ing, selection, turntable skills, rudimentary electronics … we never had the platform for anything like that until we started our own sound systems.'

Significantly, when Norman did join Joey's sound, and it started to change direction, one of the first things he did was change the name:

'I didn't feel right playing under the name "Great Tribulation". I knew the meaning of it, but wanted to deejay under a name that was more upbeat, more optimistic. When I moved away from playing purely reggae, I had an epiphany moment on hearing the Chic track "Good Times". I'd always loved the group, and this name was perfect for what I was looking for.'

At the same time as Norman was reinventing this West London sound system, across town Hornsey/Archway sound system Jah Rico was renaming itself Soul ɪɪ Soul, and, quite literally, turning itself around. Over thirty years later, Jazzie B sits on the terrace of his comfortable Regents Park home, and remembers how sound systems had been changing for a while, and how that was altering the audiences:

'It was the breakthrough of the lovers' rock sounds that opened everybody's eyes to the real entertainment prospects of the sound system, and things started to get more refined. Lloydie Coxsone was on the cusp of that new generation, because sounds of that era had a whole different energy to the ones that went before. They weren't like yardie-style sounds, they were more about *us* in London – more fish and chips than rice and peas! Then we wanted to take it up a bit more. Lovers' rock made the dance more sophisticated and we, Norman, Paul Anderson *[Trouble Funk sound system]* and Mastermind took it on from there. We acted like reggae sound systems, so we had all of that heritage and attention to detail, but we were banging James Brown.

'The crowds were changing at that point. Now there was young white boys and girls from working-class backgrounds, who were far more integrated. They'd been young kids growing up when there was three sound systems in every street, and they knew all about them. In our area [*Holloway*] it was Greek kids or English kids like Yatesy [*Derek Yates*], and as we got older we got into music together, just like we'd be playing football together. But the cool thing about them was they weren't trying to be black or anything like that, they were just *there*.

'There wasn't a master plan, we were just reflecting what was going on around us as kids growing up in London. We wanted to define street culture as it really was, too. It wasn't all about sufferation or being dowdy or downtrodden. It was about being optimistic, doing quite well for yourself and having a bit of a swagger. We wanted to say "We're here, and we're enjoying ourselves." Kids in London, across the board, could relate to that.

'We wanted to create an atmosphere that was edgy enough, through the sound-system vibe, but nobody was going to feel threatened. I think most significant is when we turned the decks around. All reggae sounds will work with their decks against the wall, usually in a corner, so they've got to play the sound with their backs to their crowd, to protect their equipment and so nobody can see the records they're playing. That, to me, was *ex*clusive, more about them than their crowd. We started off like that because that was what we knew, then we turned them around so we faced the crowd and we could all be part of the same experience – *in*clusive.

'What we were doing wasn't a black thing or a white thing. Everybody was welcome provided they'd just come to dance and enjoy themselves We knew the only real difference between us and the white kids from our area that hung out with us was they didn't have to cream their skin.'

Considerably more important than inclusiveness in itself was the fact that it was being driven from a black perspective. For the first time since the days of the Soho jazz clubs, black people were running a black music scene that was intentionally open to all comers. That represented a significant step forward from lovers' rock, which while it undeniably made a huge advance in establishing a British black music style, kept it to itself. Jazz/funk went too far in the other direction, and lost out after handing the reins to the mainstream music industry. Norman has no doubt that what they were doing went way beyond simply playing records:

'For me it was always more than a music thing, I had a pro-black agenda, make no mistake. Because I was a bit older than my peer group and I'd been through all that jazz/funk *Blues & Soul* thing, I was very conscious of them not appropriating what we created here, assimilating it for themselves and taking the credit for it. That was what had been holding down the progress of black deejays in this country. We had our own sound-system culture in this country, where we could do our own thing, and because we kept it as a subculture for so long we could keep hold of it. Then when it went above ground it was because the social climate was right. It happened naturally.

'The greatest thing is that my generation made *us* visible. We were actively part of the creative process of the youth culture we all love and everybody takes for granted today. We were always bubbling away, and I always knew that were we to get a foothold, we would make a difference that would change the course of history. That's why I was so driven, so they couldn't rewrite history without us. I think we all knew that.'

Trevor explains:

'The key thing was the variety of music. Because it's local you'd have to play across the board – however hip these parties ended up, all of them had a basis of local people in there, otherwise it would never be a success, and that meant people with all sorts of tastes. But having to play that sort of variety meant you could play *everything*. I'd do a party in Hackney and I'd try to play an Ayrton Moreira tune as well as a brand-new hip-hop tune next to a soulful tune. I would try to educate the local crowd on what I liked so I could be a bit more specialised. I did that by doing "drinks for free" parties. [*Trevor laughs heartily*] We'd make our money on the door, but the people just opened their minds and started dancing to everything! That was my way of doing it, and they'd go home at the end of the night

knowing they'd had a good time, they'd want to come again and they'd tell their friends.

'The scene caught on so quickly because of the quality of the music. If you were a music fan and wanted to expand your experience, you *had* to go to those parties, because that was the only place you were going to hear that music. It wasn't like today, when you've got access to eight million radio stations and *every* kind of music over the internet. Back then it was purely down to the sound systems and their selectors. You had to work at it, and in that era, on a sound system you had to be known for your tunes – not your personality or the clubs you played in, just your tunes. Which meant you had to stand out, so we would play things just because we wanted to be different – tunes nobody would expect – but at the same time you had to do it with quality. You wanted people to say "That guy's got tunes!".

'That was when we started exploring what came to be called rare groove. For instance we started looking at Afrobeat, discovering Fela, starting in on Hugh Masekela, buying Manu Dibango, and I found Hamilton Bohannon and South African music. To me it was nearer to jazz/funk because it was all very percussive, but it was taking off in another direction. Norman was into his Philly thing, but much more than the Philly that most people knew about, and he had an appreciation for Northern Soul too, in a way that nobody else down here did. Soul II Soul would play anything they felt would work, and most of it did.

'We'd have to hunt for the American records – I knew what time every secondhand record shop in London got deliveries … I would drive to Norfolk, a shop called the *Soul Bowl, in a Mini*. I was scared shitless because I didn't usually drive on a motorway, but I would for music. I flew on a plane for the first time, to New York, and gone in warehouses full of rats just to look for grooves. I would do anything for music, and I wouldn't even think twice. I've spent my bus fare and walked home from Seven Kings, wherever that is – in Essex somewhere – *walked* back to Hackney because I'd spent my last penny on a record. I didn't have to, either. I could have come back the next day, I didn't have a party or anything to do that night, but I just wanted that record *now*. Just having it under my arm it was good.

'The crowds at those parties in the early days appreciated that you were taking the music more seriously than if you'd just gone up the High Street. Admittedly with some tunes you had no idea what the crowd's reaction was gonna be! It was all down to your gut feeling, so your own instincts were very important. Usually, the crowd went with it because they were every bit as dedicated as we were – it was *their* scene and they knew it.

'You look back at the really good deejays from that era, the ones that have survived – the Norman Jays, Jazzie, me, whatever – and that was because firstly we were different, but importantly we had a quality control to what we played. I think we all pushed at each other to play different music, unlike today which is a little bit more safe. I think we were always in that kind of soundman competition, so we were trying to bully each other with our selections. Of course there were guys who were playing stuff just to be cool and trendy and faking it, and a lot of them got into the best clubs in London while we were still playing the sound systems. We used to get very frustrated, but the point is we're still here.'

FOR NORMAN, WHAT THE NEW SOUND SYSTEMS were able to achieve with their music serves as yet another denunciation of the status quo that then prevailed.

'I was losing interest in the jazz/funk that was being pushed at deejays by the record companies – record companies they were all involved with. I wasn't interested in what the soul mainstream was doing. I'd been to that as a punter and got bored with it then, I didn't feel part of it any more. But I wanted to deejay, and I thought the way in was through the Funk Mafia thing. I thought what I could bring to it would be of value and broaden the base. But that isn't really what anybody wanted. I can remember I approached those deejays like Tom Holland or George Power [Soul Mafia deejays], going to their nights and badgering them ... "Can I do a warm up? Can I do a warm up?" I was always told "Yes", but then waiting patiently for hours and hours, getting fobbed off with "Not just yet" until they'd say "Not tonight". To them I was that annoying anorak kid, but with a bag full of records they would have died for. I'm not joking, because I was a record buyer anyway, I'd come straight from Contempo and my bag was brand new. It was another reggae tradition – when I come I'm breaking seals. I used to love that, a reggae tradition, they did it with dub plates, I did it with the cellophane! [US import twelve-inch singles and albums arrived shrink-wrapped.] Brand new! You ain't even heard this music yet! Crisp biscuit! Not just new music either, but different music. That was when I realised that it was us who had the knowledge, not them.

'I used to hold them in such deference, but if you judged a deejay on his music we were streets ahead at our house parties. And I think they knew it too, because, after all those knockbacks, when I did get a chance, I can remember being told not to play certain records ... you can't do this and you

Norman Jay on the Good Times sound system, rocking Powis Square at the Notting Hill Carnival.

can't do that. That's when I knew I should be on my own sound system, where there ain't *no one* fucking telling me what I can and can't do. Sure, it's risky, the crowd will instantly relate or let you know you've fucked up. It's the greatest baptism of fire anybody could endure, *[He laughs long and hard]* but it made us and the audiences grow. That's why that scene moved forward so quickly, and we had that whole subculture going on for years and years and years – we were ramming dances that you'd never read about in *Blues & Soul*.'

To progress beyond local house parties and to turn things from a scene into a subculture, Norman figured, organisation was required:

'I used to wonder how come these people are running our scene, running our music, and we're almost invisible? But what I learned from the Funk Mafia people was they were fucking organised – it had nothing to do with music. Once I understood that, it took the chains off and I knew we had to do it too.

'It had dawned on me that I didn't know Funkadelic *[the London sound system, not the band]*, I didn't know Madhatters, I didn't know Soul II Soul ... I'd heard through the vine that these sounds are out there, but I ain't got their phone numbers, I don't know who they are. All the Mafia deejays knew each other, all the club owners knew each other, and it's jobs for the boys. We're on the outside and we *still don't know each other*. So some time in eighty-two me and my brother organised the first meeting of all the prominent soul sound systems operating in London.

'It was at my mum's house, in our bedroom, and I got all the emerging black music deejays and sound systems to turn up. It was at that meeting I first met Derek Boland *[Derek B]* properly, or Rapattack, or Mastermind, or Funkadelic, or Madhatters; I can't remember if Jazzie was there or not. All those sounds, and that was the first time that we all actually knew each other. Me and Joe made sure everybody exchanged numbers, 'cause in my head I'm thinking "This is the only way we're ever going to move forward, now we know each other." We tried to do gigs together and everything, but it was the culture then that gave this perception that black people can't work together – some of the deejays themselves believed it! – and in no time at all the coalition we'd formed fell apart.

'What it did, though, was it showed who was really serious and who had just come along for the ride. There were a few of us that were motivated and had a clear vision of what they wanted. This focussed us. I guess out of that group came people like Jazzie, myself, Derek Boland, God rest him, Trevor and a couple of others.'

This is a crucial issue. To move things on, the new wave of sound systems needed to grow. While lovers' rock had represented black Britain, it didn't represent black Britain within Britain at large. It never really wanted to; indeed in many ways that was the reason it flourished. Now, a few years later, here was a generation of soundmen who never thought for a moment that what they were doing couldn't be part of the mainstream – 'some open-minded brothers' as Trevor puts it. It was vital to reach a wider crowd, to present black music in a purer form. Trevor continues:

'The race thing was massive for us, but that never meant what we did was *ex*clusive. My mentality was I did it with black people in mind, but white people were welcome. The key to unlocking black music in this country was tapping into that white crowd, but from our point of view. We knew we had to make an environment that was genuine and would be what our crowds wanted, but at the same time was comfortable and not intimidating for white people. That's been the key to black music ever since.'

AS THE 1980s PROGRESSED, London's house-party land-scape was changing. Both the New Cross Fire in 1981, in which thirteen black youngsters died when fire swept through a packed sixteenth birthday party, and the collapse of a floor at a Clapham party a couple of years later – it was in a flat above an empty shop and no one was seriously hurt – pushed local councils and the police to work harder to shut them down. New powers enabled the authorities to seize equipment rather than simply request for the volume to be turned down. With black parties being disproportionately targeted, this was widely seen as routine racist harassment, but many of the deejays themselves had become concerned. Trevor explains:

'We'd do them in empty properties, running power in from outside, or if anybody we heard about was buying a flat we'd say "Have you put a deposit on it yet? When you moving in? I'll buy the keys off you for fifty quid for a weekend." Then we'd keep a rave in there. Or if somebody had a flat but hadn't moved in yet, we'd ask "Are you going to decorate?" You'd rinse it out, then when you couldn't hold no more raves in there, you'd decorate it for them! Or sometimes, if you knew somebody in an estate agents', you could buy the keys to an empty place off them for fifty quid. As long as you made sure it was left how you found it, nobody would be any the wiser.

'Totally unregulated, and these parties could be rammed – "Health and safety? What's that?" Then environmental health got wise and started shutting them down, and more than that they said "We'll more than shut you down, we'll take your gear and then we'll lock you up!" It changed things.'

Like Trevor, Norman enjoyed the necessarily risky beginnings. He relates the changes more directly to New Cross, as he had family living in the area at the time who knew people at the party.

'All those kids getting killed in that house in New Cross really changed the house-party thing, not immediately but it got people thinking about looking for other options. I can remember house parties where you could feel the floor bouncing up and down about four or five inches – I can't understand why more didn't collapse! Some of my earliest parties ... *boy*! ... I'd be locked up by now for health and safety reasons! *[He laughs loudly]* Some were in the most scary places. I can remember going into places where there'd be huge areas of the floor *missing*, a space where you could literally fall down to the floor underneath. We were so popular, our dances were *rammed*, we'd fill three storeys of a Victorian house, put our boxes in every available area, deejaying from an alcove on the first floor, and New Cross made me realise how bad it could be if a fire did happen ...'

The solution was simple: bigger venues with easier access and exits, and fewer nooks and crannies; environments that would also allow bigger, broader-based crowds. At that time, there were a great deal of empty industrial buildings in London, in pre-development areas like Goods Way in King's Cross; where Westfield stands just north of the Shepherds Bush roundabout; Curtain Road, by Old Street; Tooley Street, in between the southern ends of London and Tower bridges; or what became the Olympic Park, just south of Hackney Wick. To the resourceful soundmen, these disused offices and warehouses were dancehalls waiting to happen.

It's a common misconception that warehouse parties were cavalier affairs – find a disused space, kick the doors in, run power from a lamp post, and you're away. The reality of the successful ones was far more mundane, and drew on Norman's flair for organisation:

'The idea for a warehouse party manifested itself when, in '82 or '83, I read about a big event in Australia where twenty-odd-thousand people turned up to a disused warehouse – Grace Jones was there. I pictured it in my mind ... *Amazing*! At that point I'm doing house parties for a hundred or a hundred and fifty people, and I always wanted to do something bigger or grander, to take the next step. It had been in my head for a while and this thing I read about helped it germinate, gave me that flash of inspiration.

'It helped that we were already doing the Carnival, so I knew all the rudimentary things to keep us self-sufficient: you need a generator, 'cause there ain't gonna be no power in the factory, and we had a van – power and mobility. So we knew we could bring the sound system in and hook it up to the generator to play records. Then once I'd scouted the place we are going to use, all we need is some way of securing the building so people don't bunk in. Remember, this is a sound system, *it's a collective* – we roped in a few friends, but there's enough of us in the sound to run the dance, we've got the driver, box boys, selector, security ... and I took care of the promotion and the media.

'Then you have to have the debrief afterwards – "What went wrong? How can we improve? How come all these people got in for free? How can we get people in quicker? How do we deal with the Old Bill? What are we going to do if they try to take the speakers?" *All* of these things, we used to sit down and discuss, because we knew we had to deal with them. Nobody was doing that kind of thing then.

'You had to have your wits about you, too. We were able to get away with it when Old Bill was shutting parties down, because I used their prejudices against them and put white guys up front. I knew that if I was seen as the face of it, we wouldn't have got off the ground, so I teamed up with my middle-class white mates, instructed them on the mantra of what to say when the Old Bill came – even wrote it down for them!'

It helped in this respect that one of Norman's sound-system partners was Judge Jules. A white former law student – hence the nickname – he would regularly confound constabulary with rapid-fire legal jargon. On plenty of occasions, suited-and-booted young white guys convinced police that commandeered premises belonged to their fathers, who must have forgotten to inform the local nick that there would be a birthday party here that weekend.

Trevor was always confident they could bring an audience into the warehouses, as their ingrained sound-system

A rare view from behind the Soul ɪɪ Soul rig at the Africa Centre.

mentality was all about pleasing the punters. The time-honoured principle described with regard to the *Paramount Ballroom* in chapter one, and that was also the cornerstone of the West Kingston lawn dances of the 1950s, remained the same – 'undersell and over-deliver'. Things were no different in the 1980s: your crowd had still stumped up hard-earned cash to come in, and they were still expecting to forget the week at work and all that went with it. If they've paid a tenner to get in, you'd better give them a twelve-pound dance. This, Trevor reckons, was more about music than environment:

'The warehouses were perfect for us. Our crowd wanted cover, they didn't mind the odd mice running around, but they wanted a roof, a hard floor to dance on, and a good sound system – music was the key, not drugs or anything else. That was why there was never a black crowd at those big raves in fields, where chancers were making all that money and selling drugs and Es and stuff.

'It might sound weird, but we've always been hard people to impress yet very easy to please. Really, we were unfussy people, still happy if things were simple – remember our original nightclubs and dances didn't have flashing lights and t'ing, we had a red bulb in the corner and one bouncer that *nobody* fucked with. It was simple, you had electricity and that was all you needed. Unless you're not playing the right tunes – you could put me in the best club in the world, but if I'm not playing the right tunes then the black crowd aren't having it. They'll just stand there looking at you [*he strikes an arms-folded, glaring pose*]. We'd cut our teeth knowing how hard we'd need to work, so that was like second nature.

'We knew it was all about the tunes, how to play them and how to react instantly to the crowd to keep them dancing. That was all that ever mattered when we did the house parties, and we took that into the warehouses and the wider situations. It's just the job we did, but compared with most mainstream clubs or discos, it was on a whole other level.'

BETWEEN 1983 AND 1986, this was London's hottest underground scene. Promotions like Family Funktion, Shake'n'Fingerpop, Dance Wicked, High On Hope, Soul II Soul and Too Damn Funky featured deejays including

SOUNDS LIKE LONDON

Paul 'Trouble' Anderson, Judge Jules, CJ Mackintosh, Derek Boland, Gordon Mac and Dan the Man. Venues ranged from the totally illegal and broken-into to the semi-legal – it was not unusual for youthful commercial estate agents to 'loan out' premises just to be able to hang out with a sound system – and the fully legit, with the warehouse vibe recreated in spots like the *Arches* in Vauxhall, the *Fridge* in Brixton and *HQ* in Camden Town.

Publicity was handled in standard sound-system style – flyers were handed out around a venue, outside other dances, or left in cafes, shops, barbers or colleges. At this point the club flyer was far from ubiquitous, and blues-dance handouts were never in any case the most imaginative of documents. Once again, traditions were adapted to address a new market that was becoming increasingly aware of design and expected

a visual connection. *The Face* launched in 1980; 'designer' became a buzzword in the elaborate post-punk fashions; and even the reggae world, in which images had always been optional extras, caught on. On Greensleeves' Disco 45 sleeves, a bunch of hand-drawn characters, many of whom would only be found on London's streets, showed the music's progression from Jamaica to a Westway sound system. Derek Yates remembers Jazzie asking him to design a flyer for Soul ɪɪ Soul's Serious Shit sessions at *Portlands* in Great Portland Street.

'That generation really understood the importance of visuals – Jazzie certainly did – because it was an obvious way of instantly identifying with your desired market as doing something different. We did flyers that looked interesting and exciting, and let people know that it was a sound system, but it was a sound system that was open to them ... as long as they were cool! That was the great thing about illustrating the flyers, you could show people at the dance that looked like the people you were handing them out to. It worked, because it really opened things up, and it probably paved the way for the club-flyers-as-art-in-themselves thing.'

Norman talks of the personal touch:

'I never used to use the words "soul" or "funk" or "dance" or "club" on our flyers, I just used the word "party". Everybody will come to a party, but the moment you start putting tags on it you're excluding people ... the rock'n'roller or the punk who goes "I can't stand that soul boy shit!" They're not coming! So I just used to put on my flyers "Shake'n'Fingerpop *Party* BYOB' – bring your own beer. We wanted people to turn up with open minds, after that it was up to us.

'I'd get my mate who was a burgeoning graphics student to scrawl something, then I'd go up to the photocopier place in King's Cross because they were open on Saturdays. Ten thousand copies, cut them up, then go down to all the trendy bars down the King's Road and all the fashion shops and the hairdressers. A completely different way of promoting than through the magazines, because there you pay for an advert, then your gig will get written up, but who the fuck are you reaching? My hairdresser friends, my student friends don't read *Blues & Soul*! So we had to find another way of reaching them.

'It was how it's been done in sound systems for about forty years, and it gives you the personal touch that always works. "Oh, this flyer looks wicked!" Yeah? Give me a call, and I'll put you on the guest list if you bring half a dozen mates. Person to person to person contact is how we did it – built up networks, and our parties were always infinitely better.'

Their efforts to attract broad-based crowds paid off in two influential areas: London's student population and the fashion crowd. Norman remembers the former as open-minded kids who wanted to enjoy the music and be part of a scene that felt rebellious but was relatively safe. On top of that, being from out of town, they weren't party to London's internal prejudices:

'These were white kids, mainly, who were just coming to London. I always knew they were there, but I didn't know where, as at that time I didn't know about the halls of residence like at LSE or Goldsmiths or wherever. I lived in inner-city London, and I only really knew black kids who lived on council estates – I don't remember any kid from my school ever going to university while I was there. But here were these kids who were young like me, they're dressed like me, they liked fresh sounds and they liked attitude. Then we realised what the crowd we tapped into was, and we went for it. For a lot of them, that was their introduction to our music culture, properly, and they appreciated what they were getting. They were very good to us, because they spread the word among other students and other colleges, then when they went home they told other people about us, which helped it get all over the country. It was a properly multicultural crowd too, and evolved into more a class thing than a race thing. Kids that had a certain attitude towards life, a way of thinking ... liberals, I guess.'

Flyers distributed around hip clothes shops, and colleges like Central Saint Martins and the London College of Fashion, attracted fashion students and the fashion-conscious, so it wasn't long before the fashion business caught on. Soul II Soul and Good Times were regularly invited to set up at large-scale parties in designers' own warehouses, even when they weren't required to play music. Über-stylist Ray Petri, for example, was famously obsessed with sound systems and the reggae aesthetic, as Jazzie recalls:

'Those weren't the crowds that were truly following us, but such was our kudos that we ended up in there – everybody from the Ray Petris of this world to cool designers such as Christopher Nemeth and John Moore. Then there was the Katharine Hamnetts and the Vivienne Westwoods. I remember the first ones really had nothing to do with the music, because they just hired the sound system. They were fashion people who had this whole fixation on reggae sound systems as a fashion thing – they liked the idea of big speaker boxes and black guys with locks just standing around. I think

The Soul ıı Soul sound system was a sonic work of art; Derek Yates made it literally so.

they had a whole sexual thing going on with it, and definitely it had something to do with Ray Petri.

'It was important for us because this was our whole philosophy of being a dread, our blackness, and taking it uptown. We did start properly playing these events, when one of them hired the system for a hundred quid and whoever was supposed to play the music – quietly – didn't turn up, so I went and got my records and played it like a normal dance. They started to vibe off it, and it went on from there. That was important to us, to show what we really about. Our aim was to break the expectation of what people had of us, to break that glass ceiling. Even at that time we [*black guys*] were all tarred with the same brush, but we weren't just muggers and stroppy kids – it hasn't changed much today, every kid carries a knife and everybody's in a gang.

'It was this crowd that got us into the media, so the style press started writing about us, not the music press. So it was very important for us to be saying to this influential crowd that we had had enough of sufferation, that we were here and we're enjoying ourselves, and that you will too if you come along with an open mind.'

Norman saw the connection between what they were doing and the fashion crowd as vital to the scene's growth:

'The whole soul boy thing flirted with the mainstream, but it ran out of steam because it never addressed the idea that youth culture isn't just about music. It's lifestyle, fashion, art … it never addressed that, and the music lost out to the New Romantics, which was the mainstream and all about dressing up. Until then the only press we'd got was appearing in papers like *The Sun,* in a negative way – *All-night, black, drug-taking party in Brixton* … But the new magazines, who had come to us through the fashion world, they put it in a way that the new, enlightened, working-class and middle-class youth in Britain could find palatable. They did the same with hip hop, which is why the youth took to hip-hop culture so eagerly.

'They were lifestyle magazines, *not* music magazines, and the new wave of sound systems – me and Jazzie particularly – understood that it was about a whole lifestyle.'

Jazzie addressed the lifestyle aspect with gusto. During the late 1980s it seemed as if half of London was wearing clothing emblazoned with the Funki Dred logo, which was marketed through a series of Soul II Soul shops and market stalls in Camden Town, Tottenham Court Road, Dalston and the Angel. By that time his sound-system crew had achieved a look that both acknowledged and set them aside from London's other black tribes – ripped peg-leg jeans, bomber jackets, bandana, topped off with dreadlocks shaved at the back and sides. This hairstyle became the defining Funki Dred statement. While it appeared to be acknowledging Rastafari in a very modern, London-centric manner, Jazzie has admitted it was because the guys didn't want their very proper West Indian mothers to know they were locks-ing up, and could hide the growth on top by perpetually wearing hats.

Derek Yates, who was hugely significant in Soul ɪɪ Soul's evolving look, even created and drew their own comic book, *The Adventures Of The Funki Dreds*:

'At that time, especially in London, there was a visualisation of street culture, the first time it had happened on that scale. It was a weird mixture of the fine-art influences of the time,

Never one to limit his ambition, Jazzie, with of course the Funki Dreds, conquered the planet Arg.

of the Harlem Renaissance, mixed with graffiti, mixed with people like Tony McDermott *[Greensleeves' graphic artist]*, mixed with fanzines, mixed with people drawing their own record covers. The major influences on my work are a collection of covers on reggae records I've bought, and Pedro Bell. All were done by untrained artists, so they have a sort of crudeness to them, but also a real direct visual strength I found really exciting. It showed a direct relationship between producer and consumer that was just somebody thinking "Fuck me this is a good idea, I'm going to do it!" Importantly it wasn't *owned* by the mainstream, you felt you owned it. That made people like me associate with it more, because it did feel like you could do it too – it was, sort of, democratic.

'It was a very sound-system relationship between the artists and the public. Jazzie picked up on this and understood from very early on that a strong visual identity would be vital for Soul ɪɪ Soul. There was already the Funki Dred look which he'd figured out as a way of giving the dreadlocks thing a London twist, and Jazzie said to me one day "We need a tee shirt!", I think it was for the Carnival, What set off my thinking about that logo was the DBC tee shirt, a really classic piece of artwork that really told the story of that time. I remember seeing that and thinking "Wow! This is the first image I've seen anybody wearing that is *mine*. That is my culture that is my people … that is my music." Ironically it was a black geezer smoking a spliff, but it was what I lived every day in 1981 or whenever it was. It was *ours*, it felt *ours* in a way that nothing else I'd ever seen felt *ours*.

'With the Soul ɪɪ Soul logo I took that DBC idea, which was still related to some sort of cliché of dreads with spliffs, and made it a bit more London. I wanted to make him look a bit more like the people that I go to clubs with, so I've given him the short dreadlocks shaved at the sides and I've given him the round glasses. Some people thought it made him a bit whiter, but at that time and around that culture, black and white are funny terms – at that time white people had their hair cut like that, black people had their hair cut like that, white people wore round glasses, black people wore

round glasses ... I wanted it to look like all of us, to look more *London*. The DBC tee shirt looked London enough to stop me at the time, but it wasn't the London of Soul II Soul.'

Jazzie, however, is far more pragmatic, positioning his retail empire as the acceptable face of Thatcherism:

'All those things came about as a result of the size of the parties we were doing, where people really needed to see who was who. We had our look with the locks shaved at the sides, and we all wore red bomber jackets and tore-up denim jeans, then when we started to screenprint our own tee shirt we wore that with it. It was so we stood apart from the crowd at our dances, but when we started with the tee shirts people were "Aaw, let me get one of them, let me get one of them ..." So we started to sell them in the dance, just stuck one up on the wall where we had our sound, and we were selling the tee shirt as much as we were getting people coming in the door. Our dances were like a pound or two quid to get in, which weren't nothing then, but the shirts might have been five or seven quid.

'But people really started to link with it as being part of the whole collective thing, and it just escalated from there. We already had four or five market stalls, and the shop in Camden High Street, later we got on in Tottenham Court Road, selling secondhand clothes and remaking clothes. It was an underground thing and that's what people wanted. Everything was related to us, but because we were in the

High Street, we were a sort of version of Vivienne Westwood and all of that sort of punk thing. We'd sell Troop and Kangols and flight jackets and all that b-boy aesthetic, and because we were who we are people accepted it as authentic. In Camden we had a ninety percent white clientele, mostly tourists, and, because it wasn't so different to what we were wearing, they knew we were selling them authentic London street culture.

'It was about being entrepreneurial. People were surprised that we did all that, but people coming over from the West Indies when our parents came over were always trying to do a little t'ing, and we were no different. At the time, Maggie Thatcher coming up had legitimised the moves we were making, although I don't think we were what she had in mind. But as it turned out we were practically selling a lifestyle in the shops before we had the Soul ⅠⅠ Soul clothing and the other merchandising, This was before we'd released any records, so with the tee shirts and the clothing going all over the country and all over the world thanks to people visiting Camden Market, we were already in people's minds.'

This, Derek believes, played a major part in establishing Soul ⅠⅠ Soul so deeply in youth culture at the time. In a post-punk, post-Bob-Marley world where many people were far more socially open-minded, that logo became a beacon of multicultural-ness – even if you didn't know its origins:

'Soul ⅠⅠ Soul went mainstream because it was a complete product. It had merchandising, it had a visual element. They were a brand, built by Jazzie. Although I designed the logo, Jazzie defined the identity of Soul ⅠⅠ Soul, and by the time the mainstream got interested that identity was total: they had sound applications; they had visual applications; they had punchlines, catchphrases … a *philosophy*! It would be really interesting to go back and define the Soul ⅠⅠ Soul brand according to those corporate branding guidelines that I have to look at all the time, because it's all there – every aspect of what's needed to build a successful brand is there.

'It all began with that tee shirt, because it meant Jazzie's sound system was about more than playing a record. Anybody could buy into it and feel part of something. They could see people in Camden Town wearing it, and think 'Fuck me, that's a good tee shirt', buy it, and they might get into the music that way. Or you could identify yourself as being a Soul II Soul fan, which then became a metaphor for "I am cool because I'm wearing this tee shirt – I go to the Africa Centre, I go to London warehouse parties, it doesn't matter I'm only fourteen and my mum won't let me out."

'The Soul II Soul logo worked on a broader level, and Jazzie completely understood its power because he totally got that thing that people like about teeshirts – you buy a piece of clothing that you put on your chest and you immediately give out fifty messages about yourself. You walk around in a Soul II Soul tee shirt, you're saying "I'm not racist, I believe in multiculturalism", "I have good taste, I like black music" … all of which would make you attractive to the opposite sex! You were defining your attitude as a person. I can remember thinking that was the point at which it changed, for somebody young and white such as myself … Or maybe it didn't change, but there was a point at which I realised that the coolest, the most contemporary, the most cutting-edge thing that I could do was to hang out at a sound system, to associate with people like Jazzie B.'

Appropriately enough, when Jazzie's crew tried to get the first batch of commercially printed tee shirts from a print shop in Essex Road, the Greek proprietor wasn't at all keen on dealing with these large black men with the radical-looking logo. He directed them to Tyrone Whyte, a black tee-shirt printer and UK Karate Champion, who was only too glad to help. Such was the value of subsequent orders, Tyrone was able to expand and re-equip his operation with state-of-the-art electronic equipment in new factory premises.

AT MUCH THE SAME TIME, two hugely significant, black-owned, London pirate radio stations were set up. Kiss FM, launched by club deejays Gordon Mac and George Power in 1985, involved Norman Jay from the beginning, while Derek Boland's WBLS, first on air in 1986, featured Jazzie B on a deejay roster that also included a young Tim Westwood. These operations stepped into the gap left by the enthusiastic official crackdown on the jazz/funk pirates described in chapter seven. WBLS in particular shifted the approach away from a kind of borderline cheesy '*radio presenter*' mode to a sound-system-centric vibe. Whereas the previous generation had aped legitimate radio as a prelude to applying for their own licences, these stations accepted their illegality, and used it to represent an audience that was already happy to rave at illegal parties in unoccupied buildings. Norman believes it was the evolved spirit of DBC:

'You have to remember this is pre-internet days, pre-global networking days, so 'new media' was the coming of the pirate stations – we could start pirate stations that gave people like me and Jazzie access to the media for the first time. It was one more sound-system way of doing things. I remember radio stations which again perpetuated the whole suburban white soul boy thing – we could never get on them! – whereas DBC was so wicked because it was like a blues dance on the air. That was the culture then, that the kids or the audience understood, because it was of the black council estate, which is what Kiss did but from the warehouse perspective – which was not just about the black experience, it was everyone's experience in London. Kiss was the all-important voice, it accurately reflected what was really going on on the street.'

Repeated DTI raids ensured that WBLS lasted only a matter of months. Its shutting down simply served to strengthen Kiss, which hoovered up deejays including Jazzie and Trevor. The station was so in tune with what young London had become that it soon had half a million listeners. Even though it was illegal, Kiss was voted the city's second-best radio station in 1987 – behind Capital Radio and in front of Radio One – by readers of the London *Evening Standard*.

Kiss FM was, maintains Trevor, 'the tap in for a lot of kids to get into the scene and the music'. Despite its popularity, canny business sense in terms of advertising sales and promotions, and more or less perpetual petitioning of the

Home Office for a licence, however, the station was raided so frequently that it scaled back to weekends only:

'We were taken off air *a lot*, it was like fifty percent of the time Kiss FM wasn't on the air – I'd be surprised if I did more than fifty percent of my shows. Sometimes we'd be on on Friday night and taken off on Saturday. My show was on Sunday, so I was always fingers-crossed all through the weekend … please … *pleeease* … or if we were going to get busted, then at least let us get busted on Friday so we can get back on by Sunday. If it was busted Saturday night I had no chance! I actually think that added to our popularity, added to the whole desire to get grooves, the fact that your favourite station – and Kiss beyond any dispute was the best station – was barely on air.'

The Soul ıı Soul merchandise laid the foundations for their global triumph before they'd ever made a record. Here (from the left) Jazzie, Aitch B and Daddae lounge outside their first shop, in Camden Town.

Kiss FM did a massive job of publicising the new sound systems, and the quintessence of their impact on London youth culture was Soul II Soul's Sunday night sessions at the Africa Centre in Covent Garden. Running from 1986 until practically the end of the decade, it was the perfect club environment: legal, regular, and possibly the most appropriately named venue in town, as the Funki Dreds renamed it 'Africa Centre of the World'.

THE SOUND SYSTEMS EASED OUT of the warehouse scene during the middle of the decade, believing that it had become out of control. The druggier end of acid house was taking over, bringing with it, as Jazzie puts it, 'chancers and violence'. He was determined not to lose the scene's impro-vised vibe, however. The Africa Centre's unadorned hall was suitably low-key, and perfect for the soundsystem's ban-ners and streamers. Trevor and Norman were regulars on the decks, as were Judge Jules and CJ Mackintosh, as well as long-time Soul II Soul associates Nellee Hooper and his Wild Bunch sound system from Bristol. Live vocalists included Bobby Byrd, Vicki Anderson, Darryl Pandy, Rose Windross and N'Dea Davenport.

The location of the Africa Centre was important, too. The sound system was playing so many gigs around town in its bid to become the biggest that the operators felt they were spreading themselves too thin, sometimes having to divide equipment and records to be in two places at once. As with the funk clubs described in chapter seven, a central site attracted kids from all parts of town, and thus effectively spread the word of Soul II Soul. And the crowd they attracted to these nights validated everything for which these sound systems had been striving. Here was a multi-culti, multi-racial, wide-age-ranged assortment of ravers, dreads, b-boys, soul boys, suburbanites, sticksmen, students, tourists and the merely curious, all of whom completely bought in to the situation. The reason those Africa Centre parties are still talked about as the capital's best-ever club night is that the sense of community between hosts and crowd was on a par with the first sound-system lawn dances in 1950s' Jamaica. It was the ultimate collective, epitomising the Soul ɪɪ Soul motto 'A happy face, a thumping bass for a lovin' race'. Jazzie remembers having five or six hundred people packed in there:

'There was a balcony, too, but that got closed off because it became unsafe – so many people up there feeling the groove you could see it bouncing up and down. We'd respond to how the crowd was feeling that night by getting different vibes going, we'd break new tunes in there so they'd be getting stuff they could only get there – like the old-time Jamaican sound systems – and if we'd pressed up too many of a tune we'd bang it about four times during a session to get a load of people coming up wanting to buy it!

'We had all sorts in there, and because the vibe of the place was so full on, if you couldn't get into it, you just didn't go – if you hadn't come to dance people would let you know! The whole thing was so inclusive, which was how we came up with the "Happy face ..." motto. We used to get a crew of black guys in there who came up from south London who were a little bit edgy, more like wide boys, but because it was such a unique thing we were doing, we were able to turn the lights on and say "You, you, you, you and you ... look, we know who you fucking are, but *this* is what's going on in this place. Join in or fuck off!" Those hardcore elements understood and ended up being our security.

'There was such a sense of community and purpose in there that one bank holiday we were rammed in there with a queue of about four hundred outside who couldn't get in, I went on the mic and said "Look, you've been in here for four hours now and there's as many people outside want the same experience, how about you do them a favour?" And they actually fucking left! No complaints, just "Fair enough, see you next week." We swept the floor and let the late shift in.'

Trevor remembers the Africa Centre crowd as being *in* the West End but not *of* the West End:

'I used to look at that crowd and say "My God, this is London," because they were from all corners – *locals* from all corners of London. We had a core of dancers, which you had to have, we had a few fashionistas, a few musicians, usually, and we'd see deejays from other circles standing at the back to hear what's going down – that used to make me and Jazzie laugh! But really it was about real people. We knew that, and so did the people who came there.'

It wasn't completely without problems, but even they were suitably self-regulated:

'There was a famous occasion when somebody had gone to the police to report a Walkman stolen, and the police came in to the Africa Centre adamant the perpetrator was inside. They said they were going to shut the place down if they didn't find him and the guy sacrificed himself. He came out of the crowd and said "Yeah, I nicked a Walkman" and they took him away. That's how much people loved that club.'

Jazzie backs that up:

'If anybody *'lost'* anything [*he makes quote marks in the air*], like a Walkman or a bag, we'd get on the mic and ask if anybody had found it. Without fail, within ten minutes it would be handed in. Really, we didn't have a lot of trouble until we really started to blow up and I'm convinced that the *WAG Club* and this other club round the corner were the ones that kept sending the Old Bill down. Up until that point, there were no broken shops or anything going off, and as soon as the police started getting heavy with us everyone started to get more frustrated and some things, not much, went off.

'That went against the grain, and showed other people reacting to us in a way that hadn't moved on. The point in us evolving into what we became was that it really wasn't a black-and-white thing, it was the content of people's characters that carried us through.'

THE LOGICAL NEXT STEP was to start making music. The hippest club, interest from the new generation of media, six-figure radio audiences and a slick merchandising operation already in place ... if lovers' rock had had that kind of support system, it would probably rule the world by now.

At first, the sound-system scene attached huge kudos to new or rare records, and appeared to have very little interest in making its own music. No one's really sure why that was, other than it was never part of the soul scenes in which it grew up. Trevor agrees that their way of thinking was far closer to the jazz/funk guys than to reggae's entrepreneurs:

'The feeling was that it would never work, because it just wasn't set up for people like us. We were thinking about the established record companies and they weren't exactly biting our hands off. I can't speak for the others, but I was always scared to make music. I was always "Awww … in case I fail", that sort of attitude, and I think that a lot of people were like me. I remember Jazzie having this conversation about getting into music, and Norman saying it will never work. I remember us having a meeting, and Jazzie making this announcement about "I'm gonna make some tunes", and Norman, Joey and me just sitting there looking at him. We were sceptical. Until "Fairplay". That tune changed everything.'

"Fairplay", the first release by Soul ɪɪ Soul as recording artists in 1988, was the result of continuing experiments by Jazzie and the collective. In true soundman style, he'd cut specials for his dances on dubplate and see how they went down, honing the music with each attempt, then give the well-received cuts a push on the radio.

It made perfect sense for Jazzie to make records; he had a day job working as a sound engineer, in the studios owned and operated by the first British teen idol Tommy Steele, no less. Having recorded several of the jazz/funk acts mentioned in the previous chapter, he understood the process, and had access to a studio and dub-cutting facilities. He'd been doing unofficial remixes and mixtape-style acetates for the sound system for a long time, and had pressed up some of his own specials for sale in the Soul ɪɪ Soul shops.

Pretty much a template for what became the Soul ɪɪ Soul sound, "Fairplay" was one such special. Virgin A&R man and Africa Centre regular Mick Clarke was so impressed when its huge bassline and Rose Windross vocals boomed out of the Funki Dred's sound system that he signed them to a three-singles-and-one-album deal. It was the perfect way to get your demo to a record company: shudderingly bass-heavy reproduction and a reaction by the crowd to 'their tune' of cheering and singing along. Most important of all, Clarke appreciated Soul ɪɪ Soul's world, and figured it might not be the best idea to put them through conventional record-company channels. Jazzie still chuckles at the memory:

'Clarkie got it. The record business, and to whatever degree the media, didn't get what we were about – still don't, really – but Mick Clarke did. More than that, he understood how we did things, and knew it could only work if he let us do it our way.

'I'd always made records for the sound, but my thing about selling them turned around when the clubs were too full. The warehouses we were playing had reached capacity, and at the same time everyone was wanting mixtapes from us, as we were famous for the London beats we were making.

Somewhere along the line the two things connected, and my thinking was that if that allowed more people to get into our things, then we'd be the biggest sound system in the world. If you're listening to my records, then you're listening to my sound system. That was the genuine reason for it, and the commerce thing came further down the road, because we had the shops. Then it was like 'How many? We sold a thousand? Fucking *hell*!'"

Coincidentally, this is very similar to what happened to Coxsone Dodd, Jamaica's most famous soundman. Dodd needed to be convinced he could sell his specials, and was astounded to find that he actually could. He went on to found Studio One.

'So we knew all of that before we signed a record deal, so we could prove we knew what we were doing. We said "Right, our record's got to be on white label, and *we've* got to sell them." The record company said "What, like bootlegs?", and we just agreed with them, even though it showed that within the company they didn't really know what we were doing. They gave us the promos, so then we were like the distributors for our own records but with Virgin paying for it all! We were selling our records like imports, to all the little record shops, and it was really like a little hole in the market and we filled it. It taught us how to promote and distribute our own music.

'It helped because they didn't have a set-up like that yet, or if they did it was all based on Loose Ends and stuff like that, which was still pretty industry standard. When we came along we made everything much more street, and after initially fighting to get press we embraced the fact that the press didn't get it, and it really blew up for us.'

Even to say 'it really blew up' is something of an understatement. Neither "Fairplay" nor its follow-up "Feel Free" charted, but after that, during 1989, Soul ɪɪ Soul's "Keep On Movin'" and "Back To Life" could be heard floating out of virtually any open window. Tunes that were perfectly representative of the new wave of sound systems, and the crowds that they attracted – a bit of soul, a bit of reggae, a

Soul ɪɪ Soul's was one of the slickest, funkiest live shows on either side of the Atlantic.

bit of hip hop, a bit of pop, all wrapped up in a seductive, big bass beat – to become the Official Summer Soundtrack. This was contemporary London on vinyl, and the rest of the world immediately bought into it. Those tunes kicked off a six-year run of success that included top twenty singles all over the world, two UK number one albums and two Grammies. Soul ɪɪ Soul eventually sold almost seven million albums, making them Britain's most successful black act ever.

With hindsight, Trevor is certain that only Jazzie could have achieved this:

'It's to do with his determination as an individual – when he wanted to do something, he invariably did it.'

BY PROVIDING AN ALTERNATIVE, controllable outlet, the combination of the new sound systems and the success of Soul ɪɪ Soul changed how black music operated in this country. With intelligence and resolve, they took the self-help spirit of lovers' rock and the mainstream aspirations of jazz/funk, and expressed black Britishness in a way that contributed hugely to culture as a whole. While this was the first time this had happened on such a wide-reaching level, it was, given the timing, not too surprising. This generation of black Britons remained close enough to the Caribbean or Africa to have assumed the resourcefulness and work ethic of their immigrant parents, while being sufficiently well versed in London's machinations fully to understand the ways of their hosts. Forty years on from the *Windrush*, this was a significant turn of events.

During the 1990s, the audience for a much broader spectrum of British black acts was ready and waiting, and it became much easier for them to be taken seriously by the UK music industry. Artists like the Brand New Heavies, Beverley Knight, Young Disciples, Urban Species, Galliano, Massive Attack, Omar, Us3, Mica Paris and Roni Size all did well. Making direct nods to Soul ɪɪ Soul, black bands on both sides of the Atlantic adopted snappy, bite-sized philosophies, while hippie-fied hip hop became very fashionable. What didn't surprise Jazzie was that neither in the UK nor the US did record companies start knocking out Soul ɪɪ Soul clones:

'They couldn't. Because it wasn't a manufactured thing, they couldn't just put a few together. They only ever got about half of what we were about, and never got the idea that we were a *collective*, not a group in the accepted sense. We ran it as a sound system, whereas in the days of rock'n'roll or, say, Eddy Grant, they could understand that and fix it, so it was the guy with the guitar who could sing who'd be out front, and he was the one they could concentrate on. Then America tried to put their finger on it because we were so cool to them over there, and they missed the point, treating us as too black for certain situations and not black enough for others.

'We never stopped being a sound system and you can't just manufacture that. Also, there is no way this could have happened in any other part of the world.'

Jazzie now has an OBE, and Trevor and Norman an MBE each, but their most vital legacy today is on the streets of London, among the *next* generation of sound systems, who automatically plugged into how it all worked from a British rather than Jamaican point of view. Most importantly, they could see how far it could go.

The coming waves of London black music – latter-day 'collectives' like the So Solid Crew, Roll Deep and so on – benefited hugely from this template, using pirate radio, the internet, club nights and dances to operate as self-contained, self-supporting sound systems. As we'll see, this savvy outlaw mentality pushed itself into the mainstream to such an extent that London black music has become a cornerstone of the UK pop business. Without Soul ɪɪ Soul, Madhatter, Good Times and so on, there would be no Dizzee Rascal, there would be no Kano or N'Dubz, and not much Rita Ora. Trevor agrees:

'I don't think there would ... although you'll never tell them that.'

3

Maybe it's because I'm a Londoner

'We've been here for a long time now, so it's inevitable people are going to feel more comfortable around each other, and you don't need a firm knowledge of black culture to like Chipmunk or Dizzee Rascal.'

Ruby Mulraine, Radio 1Xtra executive producer

CHAPTER NINE

Who Needs a Record Company?

London bass in the digital age

ON FRIDAY JUNE 25, 2010, just as the build-up to the England vs Germany World Cup quarter final was gripping the entire nation, Dizzee Rascal exploded onto Glastonbury's main stage. Wearing an England football shirt with DIZZEE 10 on the back, and proclaiming a frankly superfluous 'I'm Dizzee Rascal from London city', he was instantly one of the weekend's biggest hits. Not there for any kind of novelty or camp value, or even as one of that year's multi-culti quota fillers, he was there in his own right. As much a part of the audience's musical landscape as anyone else on a bill that included Snoop Dogg, Slash and Gorillaz. It was Dizzee's third consecutive Glastonbury, each met by an escalating reaction, and this time he was eclipsed only by Stevie Wonder and the solidly Glasto-friendly Muse.

That he could rock this particular house was hardly surprising. Here was a man who had grown up on east London sound systems, MC-ing raves in which there was literally nothing separating those on the mic from those who had paid good money to get in – nimble, crowd-pleasing skills were a basic survival tool. This set was significant as an unequivocal, live-televised marker of quite how much a mainstream rock crowd had accepted a sound that, a decade previously, was all but unknown outside certain parts of London. And that the scene itself was happy to be there made the point that everybody had more in common than they did keeping them apart – indeed Dizzee's England shirt was never the 'PR masterstroke' that a couple of stupidly cynical reviewers claimed it to be.

Of equal consequence was that this had come about with minimal encouragement from the industry. By remaining true to itself, grime and its immediate family of jungle, UK garage, dubstep and so on had taken up where Soul ɪɪ Soul left off, and plugged in to how many youngsters *really* thought about their lives and their music. As a result, it had built an impressive fanbase, which the establishment actually seemed at pains to deny. Dizzee's first Glastonbury – 2008 on the Park stage – came in the year that a spectacularly boneheaded rant from Noel Gallagher served to encapsulate the industry viewpoint that popular music meant white men with guitars, and little else. Reacting to the announcement that Jay-Z would be closing the event, the former Oasis guitarist fumed: 'Sorry, but Jay-Z? Fucking no chance. I'm not having hip hop at Glastonbury, it's wrong.' Thankfully no one who mattered took any notice.

Dizzee Rascal didn't scale the heights of Glastonbury's Pyramid Stage unaided, however. By that time he had become the poster boy for a subterranean London black music movement that had been simmering on pirate radio, in raves, on sound systems and in specialist record shops for the best part of twenty years. It had been progressing creatively, expanding commercially, and learning from its own past to become, by the middle of the noughties, everything the previous chapters in this story would have wanted to be. It all began with a deliberately forbidding style that had enough of a sense of irony to call itself 'jungle'.

'WHAT HAPPENS WITH PRETTY MUCH any sound that comes along and black people feel it, if it's not black they're going to put black on it. That's kind of what we do. If it's rock, and a black man gets into rock, and we put some black on

Dizzee Rascal at Glastonbury, 2010, where he stole the show so comprehensively it amounted to grand larceny.

that, then Jimi Hendrix comes along and starts putting loose-ness and groove into it. I think that's what happened – house music came along and it was Chicago and stuff like that, which was all cool but we wanted to put some black into it. And some London.'

Marc Williams is explaining how jungle came about, when London sound systems appropriated hardcore from the rave scene to spice it up with breakbeats and dancehall reggae. We're sitting in a corner of *Mosaica*, a very swish restaurant on the ground floor of the Chocolate Factory, an arts-centric complex of studios and offices in the shadow of the Alexandra Palace, in Wood Green. Marc is a part owner of the upmarket eating place; he bought it because he has studios upstairs and it was going to close down, which would have left Marc and the artists he works with with nowhere to eat. Marc is the manager of Labrinth – *Mosaica*'s other owner – and they're one of the most successful partnerships in modern British

music. More of that later, though. Right now he's back in the late 1980s, on his Archway-based sound system, Lifeline, mixing hip hop and reggae as the capital's musical perspective shifted once more:

'Jungle came about because there were so many of us out there who loved reggae, loved hip hop and were on the edges of the rave scene and liked a lot of it. But moving forward into what became jungle and drum'n'bass, it was a sound-system thing, because in that situation what separates you from the next man is your beats and how you lay them down – you've got to know when to shift.

'The good soundmen are always trying something new. You've got your sure shots, but you can't get anywhere if you just lean on records they've heard a million times. You are always in that position where you're treading new ground and you don't know if it's going to break underneath you. That's the only way to stay fresh. It's like "You ain't heard this one", but even as you're playing it you know it's a risk, they might not like it and then you've got to know when to move: "Yo yo, make a move, man, pull that tune off *quick*! Talk to the people ... keep them running ... get the next tune on!" Then it's calm, like "Don't worry, I got you! OK so I caught you out on that, now let's go ..."

'That's the sort of thing that led to experimentation, even with a small sound like Lifeline. We all looked up to Soul ɪɪ Soul, we were from the same area in north London and they were like the main boys in the block, they inspired everybody to move forward. I remember playing in Elthorne Park [*in Hornsey Rise*] with Soul ɪɪ Soul – I won't say battling them, just at the same gig! – I was about sixteen and I blended "Computer Love" with a reggae tune [*warming to the memory, Marc sings the chorus of the Zapp hit and mimes manipulating a turntable to bring in a dubwise bassline – it sounds deeply funky.*] They had never heard anything like that before. Then I put on "Holding Back The Years" by Simply Red and mixed that with a reggae tune as well – everyone went absolutely nuts over it. So we had that feel back then, and once we knew how it could work we were blending reggae and hip hop all the time:

'It was with that same mindset, later, when we were doing a remix of something that somebody played me a break beat and I put it on a house track – *chkachkachaka* – and from there it was easy to add a dubwise bassline on it because that was my thing. I think I was one of the first people to take a breakbeat and do that, and from there you could feel there was a load of us – the Rebel MC and guys like that – who clearly loved their reggae but also loved hip hop and dance music. ... It was all of us thinking "How do we put our black influence on that?"'

THESE MID-1980s DEVELOPMENTS were happening at street level, away from a record business that had never quite grasped reggae and had yet to come to proper terms with hip hop. All through the 1980s and well into the 1990s,

despite the story told in chapter eight, the mainstream remained largely untroubled by the evolution of British black
music. With the record companies and music media actively
resisting black appointments to positions of real responsibility, the same clichés as twenty years earlier remained the
default setting. That's not to say there weren't underground
developments elsewhere; for some time a new breed of club
promoter had taken over the warehouse party scene, making
the most of sound-system technology to blow it up into massive outdoor events. Originally straight outta Manchester, it
was becoming so widespread as to be the default setting for
what seemed like an entire generation of British pop kids.
As a side effect, it even instigated a massive cultural change
from drink to drugs – the vast majority of raves didn't have
liquor licences – to the extent that the UK drinks industry
went into something of a panic, and developed alcopops in
a bid to lure kids back on to the bottle. Stoked by tabloid
outrage, the authorities grew so concerned about acid house,
and these usually illegal events that were attracting five-fig-
ure audiences, that there were questions in the House. It all
led, eventually, to the Criminal Justice and Public Order Act
1994, which specifically targeted outdoor raves and went so
far as to criminalise 'two or more persons making prepara-
tions' for such an event.

Naturally this scene produced its own music. Faced with
serious sales figures and acres of style-press coverage,
the industry claimed hip hop/house hybrids of its own,
courtesy of warehouse party deejays and producers like the
Beatmasters, Coldcut and Bomb the Bass. For about twenty
minutes, the term 'hip house' was bandied about as if it
was a bona fide genre. Add to that the techno-centric tidal
wave from Northern Europe crested by Black Box, Snap!
and Technotronic, and pretty soon there was a new addition
to rock's rich tapestry – the genre now officially known as
'dance music'.

A great deal of the tunes were pretty good. With music subdivided into so many splinter genres, it was impossible for
there not to be something for everybody, and the scene was

so huge it allowed a significant cross-section of deejays to cut their teeth – Fabio & Grooverider were good examples. However, coming on the heels of the warehouse parties, it had a different complexion. Literally. Unlike the parochial social engineering of Jazzie and Norman, the rave scene was so widespread that in effect it created its own mainstream. Despite its apparent outlaw status, it functioned much like the regular industry, never really bothering to think beyond the largest obvious consumer group. Not that there's anything inherently wrong with that – it simply meant that as this movement boomed across the UK, it was no more a black scene than, say, punk or Two Tone.

Under such circumstances, it's easy to understand what Marc meant when he spoke about putting some black and some London into the proceedings. And for many youngsters, this would have applied to more than just the music.

AS THE 1980s ROLLED INTO THE 1990s, the notion of black Britishness became more delicately balanced. A large proportion of those coming of age had parents who were born here, and multi-national backgrounds that could include two or three Caribbean islands and more than one continent. Add to that African/Caribbean-Caucasian mixed race as London's fastest growing ethnic group, and for many youngsters 'back home' was what they saw out of the window; anything else was just an interesting holiday. The capital's constantly evolving street slang provides the best illustration: Jamaican patois remained its foundation, but it included at least as many hip-hop reference points and a grab bag of longstanding Londonisms – you could visit three different time zones within the space of a sentence. That this vernacular was in use by kids of all races further muddied the cultural waters.

That kind of linguistic mash-up, of course, was nothing new to the capital's sound-system underground. Since the start of the 1980s, as dancehall had taken over London's reggae, deejaying styles had shifted up the gears. The first Kingston sound system to tour the UK was particularly influential. Jamaican champions Ray Symbolic came over at the beginning of the decade, and the ultra-fast chatting style of their top deejay, Ranking Joe, left a deep impression. Especially with Saxon Sound, a Lewisham-based operation that was one of the capital's biggest, and probably the most innovative and visionary – alongside its singers Maxi Priest and Peter Hunnigale, the deejays included Smiley Culture, Asher Senator, Tippa Irie and Papa Levi. They immediately put the new style on their home turf with crisp, semi-cockney patter atop spring-loaded dancehall riddims, incorporating their local environment into the lyrics – Papa Levi is (in) famous for rhyming 'Sugar Minott' with 'Kenny Everett' in a righteous toast about Jah Rastafari. Smiley Culture hit the pop charts twice in 1984, with "Cockney Translation" and "Police Officer", and was closely followed by Tippa Irie's "Hello Darlin'" – the tunes have since been accredited with kick-starting the Jamaican/London jargon crossover. Particularly the former, which, as the name implies, was a kind of ital Berlitz, translating such terms as 'Old Bill' into 'dutty Babylon' and delivered in appropriately bilingual fashion.

Crucially, this Londonised a Caribbean tradition of story telling and use of language that had previously been the preserve of reggae. While that was to prove pivotal in the evolution of jungle, more immediately it was an important step for young black London in general.

General Levy, who made the switch from ragga to jungle in the early 1990s, enlarges:

'In the early '80s, there were a lot of Jamaican sound system cassettes coming over here [*the forerunners of today's mixtapes, recorded off sound-system control towers*] ... Stereograph, Jammy's, Kilamanjaro ... with deejays Charlie Chaplin, Johnny Ringo, Brigadier Jerry and Josey Wales. This was when the MCs was beginning to become predominant in a lot of reggae music, and it brought a lot of togetherness to black music because it brought back the street slang. With the singers there was like a conscious vibe there all the time, but with the MCs there always was a conscious vibe but it

346

brought more communication thing on the street slang. Like all the latest talk, all the latest shoes to wear – Clarks bootee [*toasts*] *I have a pair of Clarks bootee / I have a beaver hat …* All the latest styles, so people across the world were kept locked in on this or that.

'The sound systems over here, like [*Lloydie*] Coxsone, Saxon and Java, were breaking it down to us, kind of like an English interpretation of Jamaican culture, or they could chat about what was going on around us in a way we could basically relate to. It was rebellious, too, because reggae music is rebellious, and when we were in school we used it that way. We'd get into school with our headphones on, it's brought the [*sound*] clash with you, and these schoolteachers telling us "Don't do this, don't do that" and we're looking at them,

Dizzee takes five in the studio.

with their boring selves, like they don't even know what's going on. I'd bring words into school that I got off the tapes, sometimes words that I didn't even know what they meant, and when things got really messed up I'd use these words like I was swearing, but I wasn't swearing! They'd have me in the headmaster's room and my mum had to come up the school and they'd ask her what these words mean!

'It's important kids have that sort of language, because we were all living at home with our parents and when you're young you feel like your parents they're on your case for every little thing, getting in your head and trying to understand every little thing which is going on. So kids like to have a secret language that only their crew will know – if you're on the same level then you will understand the language. Not just for their parents either, sometimes you need to keep something for yourselves that the rest of the world, that's been giving you stress, can't understand. Music, the reggae music we listened to, was that way of communicating.'

This dancehall-style MC-ing, with the sort of London twang pioneered by Saxon, became the defining factor of jungle as a stylistic development. It was perhaps inevitable that the new black British style came from the reggae world. Jamaican music had always turned over genres faster than any other form, as sound-system operators were perpetually seeking to gain an edge. Now a significant change was required as, post-Soul II Soul and Saxon, crowds expected more open-mindedness, and for their music to speak clearly to them as Londoners. No route to broader appeal could ignore the house music boom, yet this had to be balanced with core audiences who didn't want to lose touch with their basic blackness or their own undergrounds. That meant sticking with an underlying reggae vibe, because although hip hop was making a deep impact, there was no chance of it becoming as self-defining as its Jamaican counterpart. Which is another language-related issue. Hip hop was then so firmly established as American, it was virtually impossible to rap in English with any other accent. There was always something deeply suspect about London rappers who did so.

Jamaican patois, however, was part of life here, and so many kids grew up with their parents or grandparents speaking it that it seldom sounded fake. Reggae in the capital was due for a musical shift too, as since the end of the 1980s dancehall had been losing traction over here. Since "Sleng Teng" in 1985, the style had become darker and, with a few notable exceptions, less welcoming to women. Many blamed this on a combination of the sudden American interest in the music and the shift from strictly ganja to significantly cocaine and crack. Whatever it was, the playful sexiness and bawdy humour of the slackness era was being replaced with tales of violence and mayhem from artists who would rather be fighters than lovers. It wasn't reflecting life in London a great deal either – and that had now become even more important, as this audience was so culturally mixed and well aware of the likes of Smiley Culture. Ever the pragmatists, soundmen started to search for something that would address these issues.

The hardcore end of house music, which in terms of tempo was not too far removed from ragga, made reasonable musical sense to a lot of the disenchanted dancehall crowd and the generation coming up under them. Although it wasn't unusual to find black kids at hardcore raves, however, this had more to do with increased multi-culti socialising than their being genuinely engaged with the scene. That said, enterprising souls soon began to retool the hardcore sound, and take it from a rave to a dancehall environment. Not a great leap, really; forward-thinking deejays like Marc Williams were already messing about with hip-hop loops, and were not afraid to use funk and rap samples. Creating new soundscapes to define London's youthful street culture, they were open to influences from all quarters, apparently colourblind, as inventive and innovative as they were unconventional, and not remotely beholden to the establishment. It might be wishful thinking, but the very name 'jungle' seemed to reflect a wry left-field humour. Ask half a dozen people how the name came about, though, and you'll get six different answers – and they'll all be true.

Wookie works that Malcolm X vibe on a London rooftop.

WHAT'S ACKNOWLEDGED to be the earliest jungle tune, despite its lack of toasting, dates from 1988. Built on a ragga bassline, "We Are I.E." by young Londoner Lennie De-Ice ruled dancefloors. It was punctuated by the Amen break – an almost regulation breakbeat, sampled from the Winstons' 1969 soul song "Amen, Brother" – as well as sampled gun-shots, and topped off with eerie vocals from "N'Sel Fik" by Algerian husband-and-wife duo Cheba Fadela and Cheb Sahraoui, which in 1983, fact fans, was the first internation-ally successful *rai* music song.

In reality, "We Are I.E." was the first high-profile manifestation of a distinct scene that had been building steadily, as a crowd that would have been raggamuffins now called themselves 'junglists'. Sound systems had been gradually shifting, as women seemed to love jungle, and flocked to it, bringing everything the guys could ask for – a dancehall dress sense and the sort of moves that would have earned a XXX rating anywhere else. Jungle also appealed to the hip-hop set looking for something genuinely homegrown, as the tunes owed a fair bit to that style, using breakbeats as well as many of the same samples and sounds. The toasting itself may have been ragga in delivery, but the hybrid accent was just as familiar to the hip-hop crowd, giving it that degree of instant communication General Levy was talking about. Also, UK hip hop had, likewise, been moving in a direction that acknowledged rave sounds, corrupting them into a pretty unique uptempo hybrid. One of Marc Williams' old groups, A Homeboy, A Hippie & A Funky Dredd – I think he was the Hippie – had a couple of massive club tunes in 1990, "Freedom" and "Total Confusion", with that kind of running-man hip-hop vibe that seemed to owe a debt to hardcore.

The establishment of jungle as the capital's main home-grown black sound also marked the beginning of east London's dominance. Garage producer and deejay Wookie, Hackney born and bred, remembers how the area's Unity sound system was central.

'My earliest memories of that music was from east London at the very end of the 1980s, and Shut Up And Dance. I was sixteen or seventeen. They were jungle before the name even came in, they had a tune called "Ten Pounds To Get In" which came from a hardcore edge but it had a different sound to it – they were probably the first ones to come with a little tinge of sound-system reggae. That tune was *massive*, later they did a remix called "Twenty Pounds To Get In"! Then there was [DJ] Hype, who made this big tune "The Bee" with a guy called The Scientist, I was at school when that came out, and the intro was just a bee going *zzzzz zzzzz*, then the beat started and it was that hardcore sound, but it had a breakbeat and bassline.

'The switch had started from hardcore and it was out of that sound jungle was born. It happened because of the samples they used – these guys would have grown up listening to soul and reggae and hip hop and playing it on their sound systems, so that was the samples they were using, and it changed the way hardcore was sounding. They started playing with *breaks* like a James Brown loop and chop it up and make this groove out of it, then they might have a vocal sample from a sound system to put on top. That was how the jungle stuff was developing, and more and more it became, essentially, reggae on a fast beat.

'You could say that was when London took it back from the north, because the hardcore scene was predominantly Manchester – A Guy Called Gerald and all of them up there. When it came into the jungle thing it was developed down south, in London, and the east London sound system scene was central to it. Hype used to be in a sound system with PJ of Shut Up And Dance from the Pembury estate at the bottom of Sandringham Road, and there was Unity Sound – my dad used to be in Unity. It had been going since the seventies, and had a link up with Jammy's in Jamaica so they were at the forefront of the new digital reggae sounds. Now people coming off that sound them were carrying into this new scene. Peter Bouncer used to sing on that sound system, he did Shut Up And Dance's "Raving I'm Raving" and "Junglist" for Congo Natty; and the Ragga Twins were the Unity MCs Flinty Badman and Deman Rockers. East London had a massive part to play in that dance music scene, because as well as the sound systems and the early jungle raves there was the pirate station Kool FM, which was probably the first to really start playing the music.'

Wookie makes a good point when it comes to the importance of east London. SUAD launched their own record label, which quickly became the benchmark for early jungle with their own cuts, tunes from singer Nicolette, and genre classics from the Ragga Twins including "Hooligan 69" and "Spliffhead", both of which made it into the lower reaches of the charts. SL2 were from Loughton, The Scientist from

Basildon, and both the influential DJ Zinc, and Leviticus, of "The Burial" fame, hailed from Hackney. Northeast London played its part too, with the grim warehouse-dominated landscape of Edmonton's Lea Valley Trading estate playing unlikely host to London's hottest early jungle rave at the roller disco *Roller Express*. But it was far from strictly parochial. In south London, the pirate stations Phaze One and Passion FM pumped jungle out across that side of the Thames, while Streatham boys Fabio & Grooverider were developing their own take on the sound at a club called *Rage*. Jumpin' Jack Frost, producer of that seminal track "Burial", was from the south side. In north London 4Hero and LTJ Bukem were flying the flag, while the Tottenham-raised Rebel MC was reinventing himself as Congo Natty and making serious waves as a born-again junglist.

As the style progressed and became increasingly sure of itself, the reggae connection became more pronounced. As well as sampled vocals from singles and Jamaican sound-system mixtapes, many producers built their tunes on classic reggae riddims, just as JA producers had been doing from the days of rock steady onwards. Of particular note were the Ed Solo tunes "When I Was A Yout'" and "Top Rankin'", constructed around, respectively, Pablo Gad's "Hard Times Style" and the riddim that began life as "I'm Still In Love With You" by Alton Ellis. Likewise the Ragga Twins' "Shine Eye" brought Black Uhuru's "Shine Eye Gal" to a new audience, billing one-time Uhuru vocalist Junior Reid in a 'featuring' spot. Not that the ex-sound system twosome were unconditionally enamoured with Jamaican music; they titled their 1991 jungle album *Reggae*

The Artist Formerly Known as Rebel MC, now the righteously Rasta Congo Natty..

Owes Me Money. SL2 pulled off a memorable skank when they put Wayne Smith's "Under Mi Sleng Teng" and Jah Screechy's "Walk And Skank" into the top twenty as the foundations of jungle hits "Way In My Brain" and "On A Ragga Tip". Somewhat ironically, "Walk And Skank" is a take on Slim Smith's Studio One classic "Never Let Go", one of reggae's most versioned riddims.

Special mention in this area must go to the former Rebel MC, who had turned his back on pop rap after chart success had earned him the undying scorn of the credibility-obsessed mainstream music press – as well, curiously, as sections of the UK hip-hop scene. Now as the righteously Rasta Congo Natty (aka Conquering Lion, Ras Project or Tribe of Issachar), he praised Jah inna jungle style and used the lyrics on his albums *Black Meaning Good* and *Word Sound And Power* to delve into blackness from a London perspective. He was musically clever enough to pull it off for a broader-based audience, and his ragga/jungle brought in such talented JA guests as Dennis Brown, Barrington Levy, Super Cat and Capleton, but it was never short of a sense of fun – his take on John Holt's "Police In Helicopter" starts off *'To all the jungle-ists … To all the 'erbalists …'*

JUNGLE DIDN'T MERELY BORROW RIDDIMS from reggae. As its producers moved away from the rave-y, sometimes open-ended grooves favoured by house deejays, towards more conventionally timed twelve-inch singles, once again the soundman's dubplate was the be-all and end-all of his sessions. The demand from junglists for one-off specials caused a revolution in London's smaller disc-cutting operations. Wookie watched it happen:

'I'll guarantee you that everybody that's in this music scene, their dad was in a sound system or around one and they were influenced by that. As I said, my dad was in Unity, and I can remember him coming home at seven in the morning, bringing back his Tannoy speakers and I can hear them all outside, with the van and that, the sun's coming up and I'm looking out of the window. [*He laughs warmly at the memory*]. Because of these sound-system backgrounds, when jungle and drum'n'bass came in they started cutting dubplates because they'd taken on the whole reggae persona – record a tune on a Thursday night, mix it on Friday and you're cutting the dubplate on Saturday for the rave that night.

'The place to go was *Music House* in Finsbury Park, in that parade of shops that's opposite the park in Seven Sisters Road, by the *Kentucky*, there's a chemist shop that's been there for ages and *Music House* was above that, on the top floor. It was owned by Chris Hanson, who used to be in the reggae group Black Slate – I think he bought John Hessle's lathe when he retired. My dad and my brother used to work there, so Chris is literally like an uncle to me, and I used to hang out there. When I made my first tunes I used to take my keyboard into *Music House* and he'd put them on DAT for me.

'It was a hub for the London sound-system business back then [*late 1980s*]. They had practically all the reggae sound systems going there, Saxon used to go there, although I think Unity used JTS in Tottenham Hale. Jazzie used to get his dubs cut there, Chris was the first one to cut a dubplate of "Fairplay", "Keep On Movin'" and "Back To Life", in fact he might have been the first one to master that stuff, as he was doing all their Africa Centre stuff. This was before it really took off for them, because Jazzie was still driving his white convertible Golf – that was where I first met him in that car, parked outside *Music House*. [*Wookie used to be an in-house producer at Jazzie's Camden Town studios.*] As jungle got big it really boosted Chris's business, then it got so big it completely took over *Music House* to the point at which the old soundmen couldn't even go there no more.

'They'd moved to Eden Grove in Holloway, and it's when they went there that jungle exploded. You'd go in there and there'd be a big queue, like eight or nine people waiting and he's cutting five tunes, he's cutting ten – these are all jungle guys, and the reggae man's like "*Blood claat!*" and he's walking out of there *vex*! These young bloods stolen not their bread and butter, but their whole way of doing things, the whole way of cutting their dubs. It was the same when garage came in, at first when they tried to get in there for cutting their dubs there wasn't enough of it to make a difference, but when it got big they prevailed and that's definitely where *Music House* made their money.'

As a natural progression from this, jungle producers started pressing and selling their own records to independent shops, like *Black Market Records* in Soho, this scene's answer to *Contempo* or *Groove*. That moved things away from being almost exclusively in-the-dancehall, and, as Wookie describes, turned jungle into quite a lucrative business:

'This is where the dubplate comes in to play, because now you've got raves that are playing *tunes*, as in six-minute tunes – twelve-inch singles. Although there were a lot of white labels, a load of jungle was getting released. All those guys had their own labels. As well as Shut Up And Dance, Hype had Ganja Records, Jumpin' Jack Frost had V Records, with this guy Brian Gee from Bristol – they signed Roni Size and Dillinja … Records were selling *massively*. You had the masters, get it pressed yourself and then go up and down the place to the shops yourself, or use one of the street-level distributors that were springing up. All twelve-inch vinyl. Back in the day Hype was selling fifteen, twenty thousand of one record, and he's just one man doing his thing, they were all doing it.

'It was like lovers' rock in that respect, except that the people that bought the records weren't necessarily "Ooh, I like that record, I'm going to buy it and play it at home", this was more about wannabe deejays. By that point in the nineties, the whole deejay craze had gone … crazy! You'd see all those big superstar deejays in all different types of music so everyone wanted to be a deejay, but in jungle and drum'n'bass more than most.'

OF ALL LONDON'S POST-EIGHTIES black-music genres, jungle is probably the most underappreciated, and the least understood. While this may have played a positive role in its development, it's particularly unfair. Jungle was so important.

By building on the foundations described in the previous chapter, it succeeded where other styles had fallen short, and by providing a bridge between large-scale rave culture and the specialised sound-system world it created a sustained black-music scene that was open to everyone. It went nationwide relatively speedily. The Midlands became something of a jungle heartland, with Milton Keynes as its focal point. Local boy Dave Jones, who later made a dubstep name for himself as Zed Bias, Maddslinky and Phuturistix, explains that particular whereabouts:

The birthplace of large-scale raving in a club, legally, was the *Sanctuary* in Milton Keynes, the biggest club in the Midlands. It had a capacity of three thousand, and if they wanted they could spread into the venue next door, *Rollers*, which would make it six or seven thousand. They'd put a funfair and everything in there. This happened because after the Castlemorton rave in '92 [*a five-day free festival, so*

Zed Bias rocks the house at Club FWD>>.

*well attended by an estimated forty thousand ravers that the
authorities were unable to shut it down*] they weren't going
to let that happen again, so they fixed it so they could just
come in and confiscate your gear. Then there was the Act [*the
Criminal Justice and Public Order Act*] in about '94, and all of
that basically made it so the superclubs had to exist, because
nobody was going to risk their money putting on these big
illegal raves any more. Jungle Fever, Fantazia, Helter Skelter
and Dreamscape, they were all put on at the *Sanctuary*.

'Milton Keynes made sense because it is right in the centre
of England – if you drew a dot on the centre of a map that
would be it. It was the meeting place for all the romance and all
the trouble between London, Nottingham, Manchester, Leeds,
Wales, Bristol ... This was the same sort of thing as the jazz/
funk and soul weekenders and all-dayers, it was before 1Xtra
and with no involvement by the mainstream record business,
it was people, enthusiasts, who wanted to go somewhere to
celebrate their love of this particular music, more than just
going to *listen* to it. They put on their best clothes and go down
there with all their boys and *they are raving*.

'I worked as a doorman there, walking around inside –
herding sheep we used to call it, because all the kids that
were in there were goggle-eyed, didn't know where they
were and needed herding around. It was amazing for me,
witnessing these early jungle raves – there was happy
hardcore upstairs, but you wouldn't catch me there – the big
people at the time were Zinc and Hype and Rocky and a very
young Shy FX. I can remember when he played "Bambaata"
for the very first time in a rave, and that is still one of the most
honest reactions I've ever seen. You talk about marketing all
you want, but I saw three thousand people stop and stand
still, they didn't know what they were listening to, then all
of a sudden the drop came in and there was like a delayed
reaction. It seemed to go on forever, a good six or seven
seconds, then the place went *absolutely mental*. I've never
seen anything like it, as everybody in the place realised what
was happening to them. That's when you know something
massive's happening.'

In the middle of all this, jungle had set an easily accessible template of profitable, mainstream-accessible self-sufficiency for everything that came after it. Jungle bypassed the record companies, trusted its own instincts and audiences, swapped conventional music media for flyers, and replaced Radio One with tower-block pirates. Nothing that hadn't been done before, but enough to elevate jungle to a point at which, during its 1994/1995 peak, it was a pop-chart regular, had spread far beyond London into huge venues with multi-racial crowds, and yet seemed to maintain its outlaw status. Check "Incredible", General Levy's 1994 collaboration with M Beat – pure dancehall on top of speedy drum'n'bass, with a video showing a crowd of mostly black kids dropping dancehall-style moves, it's on the independent Renk Records and went top ten in the pop charts.

BY THIS POINT OLD-SCHOOL JUNGLE was mutating, thanks in part to its fiercely unregulated nature. While the lack of regulation may have been creatively stimulating, this free-for-all entailed inevitable copyright problems. An early high-profile case should have served as a warning. In 1992 Shut Up And Dance put out "Raving I'm Raving", a pop-friendly, bassline-loaded, house-y number that rocketed to number two. Almost as quickly, it was banned from the airwaves. The tune was built on a rock song called "Walking In Memphis" by Marc Cohn, SUAD hadn't cleared

the sample, were tied up with m'learned friends for months, monies earned from the record were ordered to be given to charity, and the label was left more or less bankrupt. Lessons weren't learned, however and Wookie reckons the cavalier attitude to sampling hastened the demise of jungle:

'Why jungle changed is because they could no longer sample the reggae stuff they'd been using for ages. The reggae artists and producers have all got connections in London – through the sound systems – and they had started catching on. Whereas things might have been let slide, now they were looking at it thinking "This music's getting big, they're sampling my voice and they ain't paying me no royalties!" They wanted *money*! For instance when they sampled Top Cat on a certain tune he took them for a lot of money. That was the beginning of the downfall of jungle, because they could sample less things and the artists hadn't developed that could recreate the energy of that sound in the studio over here.'

That shift took jungle away from its ragga connections, with producers moving into drum'n'bass – shorthand for 'socially acceptable jungle'. Drum'n'bass had been around for a while, a by-proxy pop music, which was, as Wookie describes it:

'More that rave-y kind of vibe, it went back into the university crowds – predominantly white. Drum'n'bass is a predominantly white scene, whereas jungle was a predominantly black scene. In essence, there's no difference between jungle and drum'n'bass, but with it no longer using that reggae sampling I think it lost that Caribbean influence. Once you took that out, because the vocals defined it they were kind of forced to go back into the rave scene as such. It got harder and definitely more rave-y, because there was no vocals and it was just all atmospherics.'

For jungle producers, the crossover was straightforward. DJs Zinc and Hype and Dillinja quickly started bossing things, likewise Fabio & Grooverider and Ed Rush & Optical; Shy FX managed to keep the ragga vibe going for years with tunes like "Bambaata"; and Jumpin' Jack Frost signed Bristol-based Roni Size and Krush to his V Records label. Around the same time, a wave of influential newcomers brought a spectrum of black backgrounds into drum'n'bass: Goldie, the jungle-influenced graffiti artist whose Metalheadz brand would become the scene's most recognisable creation; Neasden radio pirates 4Hero brought a reggae vibe; LTJ Bukem, who is a classically trained pianist, once had a jazz/funk band. It now became an 'in concert' proposition – vital for grown-up rock-world success – as acts performed with instruments and bands rather than just decks. With the style's name readily accepted across the pop and rock worlds, it put these guys right into the mainstream mix, producing music that won acco-

lades, sales figures and credibility in equal amounts. Annie Nightingale and John Peel championed the sound on Radio One; Roni Size's Reprazent posse won the 1997 Mercury Music Prize with their *New Forms* album; and in what must be some sort of mark of distinction, David Bowie messed about with drum'n'bass on his *Earthling* album of that year. At the same time, drum'n'bass remained a huge influence on black music yet to develop – later in these pages, for example, Dizzee Rascal will cite it as being his pre-grime background.

This was London, or at least a meaningful part of it. Jungle represented the world of which it was part with very few filters: a situation that was largely black but totally accepted the 'white kids who didn't mind a bit of argy-bargy when they went out', as Dave puts it. As the music crossed into drum'n'bass it did so with exactly that approach – this is what we do, and of course you (white kids) will be able to get into it because it reflects you as part of our world as black Britons. As it seemed to happen too fast for the record industry to get a grip on it, before the artists and producers had set themselves up in business, it was able to continue largely unhindered. Despite its sociological relevance and musical appeal, however, jungle/drum'n'bass was being eclipsed on the London underground.

That wasn't so much to do with any apparent commercialisation; it was the natural order of things. Just as it seemed to be going legit, UK garage staked its claim as the street's rhythms of choice.

Roll Deep redefine chillin' out. This most influential grime collective numbers among its alumni Jammer, Skepta, Dizzee Rascal, Wiley, Tinchy Stryder, Flowdon, and Target.

'AS FAR AS I KNOW, OUR UK GARAGE was born out of the B-sides of house records, the dubs. Where they'd be all musical, house music or whatever, on the A-side, the B-side was a stripped-down dub which might have had a heavier bassline – or just *had* a bassline. We took that, with our West Indian backgrounds, and our reggae backgrounds, and out of that UK garage was born.'

The 'As far as I know' that prefixes Wookie's explanation of how UK garage got started is significant. It's a tale that has, over time, grown increasingly overcomplicated in the telling, and he's entirely right to qualify it like this. The origins of the garage sound lay in New York's *Paradise Garage* club in the early 1980s, where legendary deejay Larry Levan span original house music blended with soul, funk, salsa and disco.

Coming at the tail-end of disco, the place was a revelation, in becoming the first big, high-profile nightclub dedicated to dance and music rather than socialising or showing off – an aspect that would be echoed in Britain's rave culture. By the second half of the decade, that kind of soul-infused house was making a considerable splash on the dance scene over here, attracting the attention of the underground who sought to retool it for sound-system consumption. The first thing to do to better attract the, er, junglist massive was to speed up the 4/4 disco-ish tempo – which meant the vocals either had to come off or be stretched – and then start building on the bassline. A good starting point would be the 1997 sound-system classics "RIPgroove" by Double 99 and "Spirit of the Sun" by Lenny Fontana, each one UK garage before the name was coined.

Such was the dominance of jungle by the end of the 1990s, that this new sound was relegated to the secondary room at big clubs, and small local clubs or rooms behind pubs in London – the *Arches* in Vauxhall was probably UK garage's biggest early adopter. Indeed at one point, in the capital, fledgling garage was known as the 'Sunday Sound', because promoters or venue owners that would put it on wouldn't take a chance on it for a Thursday, Friday or Saturday night, leaving Sundays as the only nights available. Not that UK garage's secondary status lasted too long, as Dave Jones explains:

'What started out as UK garage was, essentially, a load of guys in their mid-twenties who *loved* US house, the sexiness of that music, but weren't playing it in the way US house parties intended it. They changed it up and MCs were chatting over it, bringing in the sound-system way of doing things – different music but the same vehicle. Around the same time, the jungle/drum'n'bass metamorphosis was happening via acts like Ed Rush & Optical – I don't want to name just them, because there was a lot of others, but they were the biggest purveyors of what I call the 'motorbike sounds', where the bass goes *weearrrr*! *weearrrr*! like a motorbike's being revved up. Basically, it scared all the girls away. They wanted to go elsewhere to get their sexy little groove on, and the garage raves was where that was.'

It was when London producers like Tuff Jam and Dreem Teem (one of whom was DJ Spoony) or the Heartless Crew sound system started making tunes which totally related to the scene that things really took off. The rush of music fuelled a rush of dedicated radio pirates and clubs: original stations London Underground and Freek FM were supplemented by ICE and Magic FM, while the seminal nights were Twice as Nice, Cookies & Cream and Sun City. It was at this point that the media and the record industry caught onto it, and it was briefly called 'speed garage', to differentiate it from US garage. Suddenly record shops and review sections were awash with fast, skittering tunes that didn't really acknowledge a black London heritage, weren't looking to develop the music, and, as Wookie puts it, 'sounded all the same'. It's hard to find anyone who was making the music on street level who has anything good to say about 'speed garage'. To the relief of many, it didn't last too long, and was replaced by 2step, the underground's answer. Wookie runs down the differences:

'House music is four to the floor, and what they called speed garage was four to the floor but with those fast, skippy beats in there. The garage we were making *wasn't* four to the floor. We changed it when all those skippy kicks came in and ended up with something irregular – *boom … te-te … boom*. That's where it must've got the name 2step from because you could probably do the side-to-side step to it!' [*Wookie laughs hugely at this.*]

This new, unique pattern fed into a cauldron along with hip hop, rap, soul, reggae, dancehall and of course drum'n'bass/ jungle to create what became UK garage, a London style that was strong enough to support a wide range of differing strands. Between about 1998 and 2000, it was all over the place. Almost literally – Ayia Napa, a resort on the south coast of Cyprus, became the party town for young black Londoners between May and September, turning its nightlife over to UK garage, with big-name deejays, artists and clubs taking up residences.

ONE OF THE MOST SIGNIFICANT effects of 2step's freeing-up rhythm patterns was to allow enormous potential for variation. The music's ability to sprout in all directions was illustrated by Wookie's "Scrappy" and "Down On Me". The former was positive and cheerful, the latter dark and edgy, but both became huge hits and enduring garage anthems. Dave's first big hit as Zed Bias, "Neighbourhood", was very nearly pure dancehall that brought the jungle vibe up to date with garage beats:

'When I started I'm loving this new sound [*garage*], but the only thing wrong with it is the beat is too rigid. Then somebody played me this 2step remix of "Spirit Of The Sun" on Labello Blanco. I was one of the first people to hear it. I was like "You know what, I've come home. I know what I'm doing now." It was jungle, but it was so not jungle! It was *swinging*! Jungle of that time had become all about the extrem- ities, but back in the day there was always other things going on. This got into that gap for people who like the aesthetics of how jungle was, but wanted to play to this audience.'

ZED BIAS
FAIRPLAY / PHONELINE

This swing became a big part of 2step. Introducing a degree of soul and melody to proceedings, it encouraged a conventional musicality in some areas – MJ Cole, who played the oboe and had studied at the Royal College of Music, gave garage an orchestral accent, while the Artful Dodger put a rock-group sound on it. All of which invited producers to put singers on top of the beats, and facilitated the arrival of UKG as a bona fide pop music. Echoing aspects of lover's rock, this was a street style that embraced the pop world within which it existed. Producers anticipated demand from their primary audiences, but were also identifying a way into the mainstream, which was obligingly receptive. As had also been true with jazz/funk, the industry believed it had a straightforward reference point. In the US, throughout the 1990s, the grafting of sweet vocals onto tuff hip-hop backing had turned the likes of Boyz II Men, Bobby Brown and Mary J Blige into household names, and allowed Sean Combs to reinvent himself as Puff Daddy/Puffy/P Diddy and so on. By the end of the decade, singers like Craig David, Mis-Teeq (Alesha Dixon's trio), Artful Dodger, Daniel Bedingfield (Natasha's older brother) and Kele La Roc were mainstream stars in the UK. According to Wookie, that affected how the music was developing at street level:

'The scene had established itself where there's a pool going on, everybody's self-sufficient and the street is making money, they're pressing their own records and they're selling loads – it's a sound-system mentality, nothing's changed. The major labels look at it and say "Ooh, there's a lot of revenue being made here" and start to pluck up all the top people, who now turn away from what they were doing before and start working for these people. They were facing this way, then [*he swivels in his chair*] they turn around that way and they're working on their albums. It's progress, don't get me wrong, but it neglects what they were starting to do before.

'So because there is only so many good people – a pool – the next level down start scrabbling [*he does a rodent-like mime with added scrabbling noise*], the music isn't the same quality *and* there's no vocals because all the singers have been snapped up. So the only people to do vocals on those kind of things is the MCs, meaning the music's getting tailored towards the MCs. It's getting faster and darker and there's less of a happy vibe, this is when the So Solids and the MC crews came along – they saw an opportunity and they jumped on it.'

It was around this time that the garage scene evolved into a state of apparent high bling, a clubland metaphor for conspicuous consumption: champagne and 'yack' (cognac), designer clothing, fancy cars and pole-dancer-style women. Little more than working-class kids have always done, perhaps – dressed up on a Saturday night and spent money getting wasted and impressing the opposite sex. Wookie agrees with many older guys when he says:

'That champagne-and-girls scene was the older rude boys who wanted to dress criss, but they didn't do it even half as much as the generation before then. Talk to my dad and he'll tell you he spent three or four hundred pounds on a shirt ... *what*!?!?! ... no wonder my mum's cussing you!'

The videos and lyrics that began to dominate the mainstream end of the genre came to define the image of UKG, and also reflected pressure from the record industry, which was using the more visible end of the US rap spectrum as its benchmark. A long way from Craig David's first hits, which nodded to the roots of garage by setting videos in pirate radio stations, this process spectacularly imploded when acts like So Solid Crew and Mark Morrison appeared to buy into the clichés, and spent more time in the dock than in the charts. 'They were,' maintains Wookie, 'just little kids who wrote their own downfall.' It also triggered a shut-out of UKG at many venues, giving club managers the excuse they seemed to have been waiting for to hang a sign reading 'trouble' around UKG's neck. And while sections of the press seized upon gunplay in nightclubs with worrying enthusiasm, the style itself was shooting itself in the foot.

'I WON'T NAME NAMES, BUT IN 1999, in London, there was a garage committee formed by deejays, producers and promoters, said to be in the top of the scene. It was done in a very Mafioso way, calling meetings, and if you weren't invited you weren't allowed in, that sort of thing.'

The perennially cheerful Dave Jones is almost spluttering:

'They used to tell people what they could play and what they couldn't play, who would get booked at whatever venue … trying to run it like the Illuminati. Then there's kids like me coming though from places like Milton Keynes, and I don't give a monkey's what you lot say! I'm still going to do what I'm going to do. You haven't let me in, but I've had, for a couple of years, some of the biggest tunes in the city. Full stop. I'm still going to see you down at Freddie Fresh's shop, I'll see you down at *Music House* and I know you're gonna want a cut of this tune that's coming out of the speakers … yet I wasn't part of this.

'I wasn't an advocate, I used to slag it off, and they couldn't keep me down. And I wasn't the only one that felt like this. So there was a revolt – the Garage Revolt of 1999, you could call it! – and I was probably at the head of it. This is the whole reason dubstep's here.'

As I sit talking to him over a full English with extra fried bread in a cabbie's caff by the side of Euston station, this is the first time his demeanour has wobbled. Even though he pulls it back with the crack about the Garage Revolt, this self-appointed legislature is clearly a sore point. And so it should be: it's an entirely similar restraint of trade as was exercised against Norman Jay and his sound-system counterparts by the Soul Mafia twenty years previously. The reaction was the same too: let's sort something out for ourselves.

Dubstep as a style had been bubbling under for a while, as a result of mainstream garage relishing its pop status and the established underground doing its best to get there too. Garage had stopped behaving like sound systems and driving itself forward with innovation. Even prior to the forming of the cartel you'd hear essentially the same tunes at raves all across town, with the big ones on heavy rotation on pirate radio. Dave believes that was because this self-appointed UKG aristocracy couldn't keep up with the evolution of the music:

'Their reason for doing all of this was their insecurities. They all thought it would all get out of their control. But they stitched themselves up because it's all very well being lord of all you can survey, but you're only lord of that. It's down here where all your potential audience is, but you don't see them because you don't appeal to them. The kids aren't coming to your shows because you're old and you're no longer relevant – that's just how things are – so at that point you move over and you become a support net and work with people that are relevant. That's how you get your longevity, you don't start closing people's opportunities down and trying to keep them for yourself. The control they tried to impose was a control they weren't due – they weren't allowed that control, so they never got it.'

A generation of young deejays and producers was coming up who drew on a different, wider set of influences and wanted to shift the music away from the limitations of proto-pop. They were relegated to the back rooms of raves like Garage Nation – if they got gigs at all – but being away from such main-hall pressure allowed for greater experimentation. The music forming was what became dubstep, a dub reggae approach to 2step, stripping it down to its bare bones, then building upwards from a big bassline, leaving enough space to incorporate other elements. It created music that could

be shaded in any way the producer fancied, but would always have a compulsive, heavy core. The music was, Dave reckons:

'More in the attitude, really, and that was an attitude I got from people like [*King*] Tubby's or even Congo Natty's jungle, leaving enough space for the elements you've got in there to breathe and work. To move speakers and move people.' In those early days, he admits, 'more didn't work than did.'

The major problem was that this scene lacked a focus. These contemporary soundmen didn't have their own lawns, or regular venues where they could feed off each other or build a crowd. That's where Club FWD, one of contemporary London music's most important establishments, comes into play. It was the brainchild of Sarah 'Soulja' Lockhart, who achieved at least as much for the scene as any deejay or producer.

East Londoner Lockhart had the organisational expertise to transform this fragmented scene into something more readily accessible. She used her skill set to provide situations in which artists, producers and deejays could develop in an environment that gave them the best opportunities. Her record label Tempa released an eclectic mix of music that was never less than quality, while her Ammunition Promotions was an umbrella organisation that gave real clout to individuals' tiny labels such as Dave's Sidestepper, Oris Jay's Texture, Artwork's Big Apple and DJ Zinc's Bingo Beats. She managed the likes of Skream, Benga and Geeneus, and negotiated deals for affiliated producers with EMI Publishing. She would take charge of London's premier pirate, Geeneus's Rinse FM, and it was her remorseless five-year campaign that won the station a licence to broadcast legally in 2010. Now her Club FWD>> was dedicated to new ideas and supporting dubstep as a concept. Dave, one of its original deejays, reckons that she was driven first and foremost by her deep love for the music, an affection that could frequently get the better of her:

'The night started off in the *Velvet Rooms* in Charing Cross Road, which had the deejay booth in the middle of the dancefloor, just off to one side. It was surrounded by this screen, and every time I dropped a big tune Soulja would run

Club FWD>>, a club night, quite literally, designed for the dubstep.

down and start slapping the Perspex until the needle jumped off the record and I'd have to start it again. She was proper rowdy, that one!'

FWD>> offered exactly the nurturing environment the new sound required, as it was small enough to set itself up as a *music* club, ensuring a crowd that was equally serious rather than simply out to rave. This forged a circle of musical evolution: producers would showcase concepts, audiences embraced their edginess as a genuinely alternative, and the enthusiasm of the producers grew. Dave is convinced it was vital:

'FWD>> needed to happen when it did, because there was a little gang of garage deejays ad producers – myself, El-B, Oris Jay and DJ Injector – who hated about eighty percent of the vocals that were going on, and were playing the dub mixes that were on the B-side of most garage twelves. Some of these were dubs of the pop hits – MJ Cole's "Crazy Love" had a *great* dub, "Crazy Dub". The way I would play them would be religiously breakdown to a big bass drop, so there's

Ravers have queued for five hours or more to get into that other cradle of dubstep, a DMZ club night in Brixton. Sharper-eyed readers of more advanced years will spot the irony of this line snaking its way past the Fridge, once the coolest club in town.

no beats, just a bit of atmosphere, then a big bass drop and everything else would come in minus the vocals, so what you were getting was the bassline and the beats. That little group gravitated towards each other, and thr darker tunes were, the more we would play them. We could see we were getting the better reactions off the dark stuff and the rolling breakbeats, and we were all digesting those reactions, so the scene was feeding off itself. FWD>> meant we could all see the same reactions.

'It didn't start off big at *Velvet Rooms*, a few dozen people used to turn up to hear the latest dubplates we were making and they were either refugees from the garage scene or they'd been coerced into being there [*he sniggers*]. And there'd be

Japanese tourists who wandered in off the streets because, it being that area, there was always tourists looking for cool clubs.

'It all started off very humble and only took off when we moved it to *Plastic People* on Curtain Road in Shoreditch. There I saw it go from the awkward fifty-people-through-the-door stage, to being too experimental and people not getting it, to really finding its feet. *Plastic People* had an incredible sound system, and we all grasped onto that as producers, because when you've got such a powerful system to play you can really fine-tune your mixdowns. A lot of us ended up making tunes specifically for FWD>>.

'This totally shaped how the music was sounding, because we knew what was heavy and what would work on the dancefloor, but it was also a listening place as well – it was quite a skunked-out crowd down at FWD>> so they'd go to listen as well. It set a trend for playing instrumentals and dub mixes because that sort of framework allows you to do pretty much anything. I, for instance, was making jazzy instrumentals that were still heavy enough to drop on the dancefloor, and others – Zinc, Horsepower, El-B, Oris Jay – were bringing a different vibe to the instrumentals.

'Once this scene found its feet it divided the garage scene. By making the statement with FWD>> we were saying "Look, a lot of this is cheesy bollocks, quite basically, we're not up for it, we want the beats, the basslines … put a few film samples over it and we're happy." It worked too, because as we grew, before FWD>> became trendy, it was leading the way with a generation of kids like Hatcha and Youngsta, who is Sarah Lockhart's younger brother, cutting their teeth there. Dubstep was spreading all over the place, but FWD>> was at the centre of it.'

It was certainly spreading south of the river, where, in the early 2000s, an unassuming record shop in the unassuming suburb of Croydon was kick-starting the genre's next generation. Big Apple Records had shifted from general dance music to specialising in dubstep, and had become a focal point for the music – where to buy it, where to get your records noticed, and where to hang out with other dubsteppers. Dave, El-B, Ben and Lev from Horsepower and Kode9 were regulars, Hatcha and Skream worked in there, and Artwork had his studio upstairs. It was also a hangout for two local lads, Mala and Coki, also known as dubstep duo Digital Mystikz, or DMZ for short. They were at the forefront of moving the music away from its garage roots with spacier, slower rhythms in their own records – "Haunted" – as well as tunes by the likes of Loefah and Kode9, all on their DMZ label. As significantly, they started the Brixton club night of the same name, which is talked about in hushed tones as being, with FWD>>. one of the two high churches of dubstep.

It's around now, the middle of the noughties, that dubstep became omnipresent. Championed on the wireless by John Peel, Mary Anne Hobbs and Gilles Peterson, the style was strong enough to build anything on top of it – artists from Eminem to Radiohead commissioned dubstep mixes of their work. It was sufficiently varied within itself to appeal to the underground through labels like Leofah's Swamp 81 or Ramadanman's Hessle Audio, and still get the mainstream moving with its more dance-music-ey end. And it went international with apparent ease.

The second time I meet up with Dave, he has just come back from a 21-city tour of the US, where the music has a longstanding fanbase that grew out of college radio and their garage scene. He tells me all the big London dubstep deejays tour the US, and Skrillex won a Grammy in 2013; Mala has recorded an album in Cuba; and the Europeans have taken to it as another branch of electronic pop. The 'Glastonbury of dubstep' is the Outlook Festival, which takes place every year in Croatia.

Even if dubstep is a massive global concern, with hardly any racial barriers between artists or crowds, it has been usurped in the UK by a style that was practically a carbon copy of the original immigrant sound-system way of doing things. While dubstep was wowing the world, the juggernaut that is grime was gearing up to redefine British pop music for the twenty-first century.

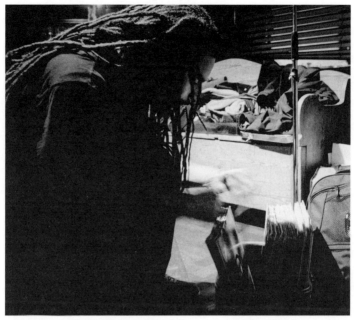

Mala, one half of DMZ, sorts through his records before going out to play a gig.

'WHEN I INITIALLY STARTED PRODUCING, I started grabbing reggae influences, hip-hop influences, mixing it with my own London flava, then you got the MCs on top of it and everything. I saw a vision. I thought 'Right, this is *it*! This something new, this is fresh! This can work.' Now, ten years down the line, you've got Dizzee Rascal selling millions of records, you've got people like Tinchy Stryder ... and you've got people like Chipmunk, who was growing up listening to people like myself and Dizzee, who has now come forward with an album and made a career. There's actually a scene.

'It's a scene that's wide open, because of the way we've changed the music and had a touch on everyone growing up. The people that I was performing to six or seven years ago ain't the people I'm performing to now. They still listen to us and they will still buy the albums, and still support the records, but now they might rave to us once or twice a year like when they go to Ibiza or a resort or somewhere –

because we're the headline acts on those type of bills. But everyone underneath that scale grew up with us, take the general raving culture from about 23 down and then from under-15 raves as well, all those people represent a new fanbase that wasn't there when we started but has grown up on this music and they're into it because that's all they know. So this is what London is.'

Grime producer, artist and entrepreneur Jammer is reflecting on the progress the genre has made since it first

Not your typical grime leisurewear, but then Jammer is not your typical grime producer.

bubbled up at the very end of the 1990s. In that time grime has turned characters like Dizzee Rascal and Tinie Tempah into superstars – the former won the 2003 Mercury Prize with his *Boy In Da Corner* album – and seen MCs such as Wretch 32 and Tinchy Stryder become regulars on TV quiz shows. Original grime collective Roll Deep were invited by the Tate Modern to write a track inspired by one of the gallery's sculptures – *Ishi's Light* by Anish Kapoor, since you ask – and found artists from P Diddy to Pixie Lott keen to collaborate.

Jammer's right about London, too, because in all this time the music as a creative force has seldom strayed far from the city, which has continued to drive it in a relatively narrow, self-serving direction. That parochialism has played a huge part in enabling grime to prioritise serving its original community without excluding the rest of the world. Thus in 2012 the MC JME, a member of Jammer's Boy Better Know collective, was able to have a top forty hit with a single with the no-nonsense title "96 Fuckries".

This generation, which includes Wiley, Kano and Skepta, pulled off such a coup not by adapting to the mainstream, but by dragging it along with them, and were able to do so because they virtually ignored it. When Jammer talks about changing music, it's as much about changing the *business of* music, because, thanks to the steady evolution of London's black underground, grime was able to rewrite those rules. Lovers' rock ... jazz/funk ... jungle ... funk ... each had a great deal going for it, but each fell short of achieving sustained impact for varying reasons. By the time grime rumbled out of the tower blocks of Bow and Stepney, it had learned from all that went before. These new players had business savvy, a thorough grasp of London's repositioned racial demographics, readily available recording technology, and the internet. As Marc Williams puts it, 'The industry had nothing to offer these boys, no carrot to dangle in front of them.' Jammer's early experiences are a case in point:

'Back in 1999 I produced a track named "Army", and in those days you couldn't really just phone a record label, so I put it on pirate [*radio*]. It was on Déjà, everyone's into it, really loving it. I got D Double E to do a vocal, we had a big set on there, and we were just smashing it, the tune was getting loads of love. I got a meeting with a label called Locked On Records [*a garage/dubstep-centric subsidiary of XL*]. I went there, played them the music and showed him the material and the guy was like "It's really good, man, it's interesting, but I don't how to market it or who to sell it to … I haven't got anywhere to fit this in." What he was really telling me was "We don't know the buying public". I was like, "Cool … Whatever." and left the meeting.

'I carried on striving, doing my own thing, still pressing up records, still putting them out, and I got a call a year later from Locked On. They were telling me about this really big tune that everyone's talking about and they want to sign it, but they don't know what it's called. They say they've got all the feedback from the pirates and they've got a tape of it. So I went in to see what it was, and they played me the same tune I took them a year before. Only now they want to offer me a deal for twenty grand! I'm like "I showed you this tune a year ago, and you didn't know if there was a buying public or where they were. Now you phone me back a year later telling me there's this great big buzz on the tune that I showed you a year ago, and you want to offer me *twenty grand*?" I just told them No, because I was sure somebody would come along and offer me triple that. And then that didn't happen, so I carried on selling that record for about three years.'

Jammer was seventeen at the time of that first meeting, but had grown up around his dad's sound system and roots reggae band, which explains his precocious behaviour. As we're sitting in the front room of his mum and dad's house in the leafy suburb of Leytonstone, where Jammer grew up but no longer lives, his dad drifts in and joins in the conversation, making some particularly pertinent comparisons between grime and the capital's vintage reggae scene. While it's true that the methodology and community service of grime is a throwback to the self-sufficiency of men like Dennis Bovell and Lloydie Coxsone, by this point that's become an entirely natural way to get things done – almost subconscious. What distinguishes grime from so much of what went before is that it's more the result of a micro-evolution that began with jungle. That style's relative success combined with London's street-level social integration to give the city's black music genuine respect, and it meant that the next wave saw chart success as a right rather than a privilege. The London underground of jungle and garage raves, radio stations and record shops was so pervasive that for many it *was* the mainstream, and the new kids coming up focussed on it exclusively. It's a mark of the speed at which styles turn over in the sound-system world that this next generation arrived so quickly. Grime grew up almost parallel to dubstep, and like that style was a reaction to where garage had gone, with the simple difference that it was a far more instinctive and anarchic reaction, with hardly any calming, sophisticating influences to separate it from its audience or make it more widely palatable. Which is why, presumably, Locked On Records didn't have the first clue.

IT WASN'T THAT GRIME had an open-door policy, it simply didn't have any doors to start off with. Or walls. Or constraints of any kind. Technology had put backing-track construction within reach of anyone who owned a rudimentary computer or Sony PlayStation, which seemed like everybody in east London under the age of twenty. Among them was Dylan Kwabena Mills, who introduced himself on the mic on pirate radio and at raves as Dizzee Rascal. A teenager who'd grown up in Bow, he'd raved to drum'n'bass before getting swept up in a youthful movement that, via pirate radio, was kicking against a status quo that was as much social as musical:

'Once upon a time, jungle and drum'n'bass was the dominant thing on pirate radio. Then garage came in, and that was closer to that whole suits-an-champagne thing. It became a scene, and I was the kid who couldn't get into those raves because I had my hat and my hood and my trainers.

There was a lot of kids shut out of those raves, especially the younger kids, but at the same time there wasn't really that much there they could relate to. I was of a generation that watched people like Heartless Crew, So Solid and Ms Dynamite, and we were coming up underneath them as kids.

'The scene separated as it started off a whole next side of things, it was much more street, *grimier* – that's why they called it grime! It was a lot rougher, a more hostile environment, but the younger kids preferred it because it was more about them. The big raves were the under-18-ers and the under-21 raves, and those garage people wanted to shut it out completely, but that's what grime was in the beginning: under-18 and under-21.'

A very young Tynchy Stryder gives substance to grime's claim that it's music 'by the kids for the kids'.

The garage/grime connection can be traced to the Pay As You Go Cartel, whose members included Wiley, Flowdan, Geeneus, Target and Slimzee. In their early days, they would play at Milton Keynes raves that also featured a fourteen-year-old Tinchy Stryder. Despite these links between grime and garage, the creative split grew up on east London's illegal airwaves, an initially unwitting creative cauldron, fired by the fact that these pirates had no desire whatsoever to become legal. In fact they revelled in a lack of Ofcom parental control:

'It was a situation that was *r-r-ruff*. No rules, really, kind of anything goes. People MCing on radio that can say what they want when they want, and as far as sound, people were just using what they've got. They used module basslines and whatever, simple products like Fruity Loops [*a rudimentary digital music system for Windows*], which has got beats and some bits of music on and you can put them together – people make some amazing stuff on that, I've made some stuff on that. People even use their PlayStations to make music ... they've found out there's no one clear way to make music.

'People were using a lot of different sounds – games-console sounds, lines from TV, traffic noises, sirens. Sounds which other people might not have considered to be music, but, like I said, there was no rules so there was no reason why those sounds shouldn't be used. People used to say we didn't know how music should be made, but it wasn't that we didn't *know*, we didn't *care*. We understood music more than just *sonically*, how it's about feeling any sound – if I can get that desired feeling out of any sound then I'll use it.

'When I first started off I started mixing drum'n'bass, that had a big influence on me. I couldn't quite get my head around the garage scene because I got into it late. I never really accepted it, so I had to just move on, and what I did then was make garage-tempo beats but *weren't* garage, were other things. I couldn't just sit there and try to make a drum'n'bass beat or a garage beat or a hip-hop beat, they were too limited with the sounds, so I had to work out a way to make *something*. That's the attitude I took into a proper studio with me, as I wasn't fussed about what sort of

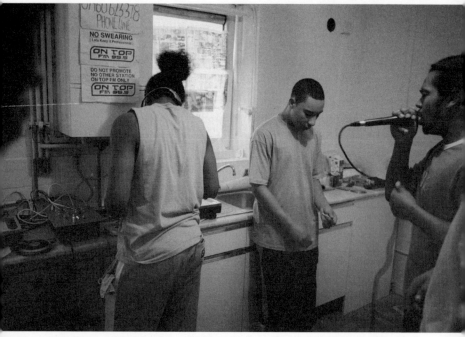

The glamour of the London pirate radio scene, where broadcasting might have to stop if there's washing-up to be done.

equipment I was using, it was "What was I going to do with that sound?" or "How am I going to make this into this, then spit on top of it?"

'That was how the scene worked – pirate radio was a scene in general, everybody did something slightly different, because on pirate radio you could do anything.'

That off-the-cuff approach didn't always meet with unconditional love from existing producers who were more finicky about sounds and musicality – Dave's reaction, for instance, sums up the dubstep party line:

'The kids making what they were calling *eight bar* or *sub-low* were using simple software where they wouldn't know what swing setting to give the beats, so it wouldn't have any shuffle, it would just have straight drum-machine programming – no groove. The sound was like galloping horses when you got it into the mix!'

But that was sort of the point – original grime was its own reward, and could afford to be entirely self-referential. It was under minimal commercial constraint, and taking part was the most important thing, especially if the only audience you were targeting was there with you in the pirate's studio, passing the mic.

Such immediacy had an evolutionary effect on the vocals, which moved on from jungle's essential, albeit heavily Londonised, Jamaicanisms to the capital's almost ubiquitous yoof-speak. So pan-racial were these tones that two generations on from the *Windrush* arrivals, it was now not only impossible to tell what a person's roots might be, but whether, unless you could actually see them, they were black or white. This really was the capital's first truly indigenous black population, a melting pot that was given a further stir when the Home Office did its best to shut the door on arrivals from Jamaica, while economic immigrants and refugees from sub-Saharan Africa increased proportionately. One of the most noticeable aspects of the grime wave was the number of participants who had African names – Dizzee's heritage is Ghanaian and Nigerian.

Inevitably, a new streetwise style attracted mainstream attention for mostly the wrong reasons. I was talking to Dizzee not long after he won the 2003 Mercury Prize for his *Boy In Da Corner* album, and he was frustrated and a little baffled about doing loads of press around the award, but seldom being asked about his music:

'Tell me about it! They're just looking for an angle … a story. But the story's the music.'

For much of the media, though, the story was an unfortunate incident that summer in which Dizzee was stabbed after being set upon in the rave hotspot of Ayia Napa. In some parts of the press, this came to define grime; to grime itself, this was an unwanted, if somewhat predictable by-product. Dizzee himself would palm it off with 'no point in talking about that when 50 Cent's been shot nine times!', but he still shows an understandable irritation at the lack of appreciation of what grime was really about:

'Really and truly, I was there to make music, I love to make music, but I was limited in my facilities, and pirate radio was an avenue to get my music heard. Because MCs on pirate radio could say what they like, they can be quite limited in what they say because, most of the time, everybody just goes with the flow of the week and often that could be raw. A lot of the time people on the outside didn't understand what we were doing, There's this little thing called clashing, where everybody starts writing lyrics for [about] each other, saying all sorts of things about each other. It's like the old sound-system thing, but it gets very raw over here and because people [MCs new to pirate radio] don't really get the nature of it, it can get stupid. Because it's pirate radio, it's a lot less controlled, it's much closer to the street where anything goes, so it could get self-destructive.

'It gave a bad impression, so then the clubs were always getting shut down, and you're hearing abut a shooting or a stabbing or a fighting – people just saw grime as pirate radio, raves, gun shootings … that lifestyle. It's all that as well, but there's a lot more talent out there. You've got to think about what people are doing independently, without record company involvement, without no one helping them, off the street, off their own back.'

What grime did, was invade the pop world in same way that hip hop did in the US. And this was as much about business acumen as it was about musical skills.

LIKE SO MUCH OF LONDON'S BLACK MUSIC, grime's driving force was a desire to overcome cultural colonisation and make music representative of the kids who would be listening to it. Jammer, who proudly admits to being a 'massive fan of Wookie and Shy FX', also talks about a lack of home-grown stimulus:

'When I was growing up we used to listen to a lot of Biggie Smalls, Tupac, Snoop, so they were the people who had a big influence on me looking at music as being something someone like myself could do. But I couldn't really relate to what they was talking about, because I'm not from America. I wanted something I could relate to, even if I wasn't aware of it. What made grime different is a lot of the things we're talking about were relevant to people that live here, and were living in the same situations and having the same experiences as us, because we all live here in London.'

A big factor in how tales of Harlesden rather than Harlem gained credibility is that they were told in the emergent black London dialect, and that worked because the music was completely new. As an MC-ed art form, grime – and the rougher end of UKG – had been designed, however subconsciously, for the composite cadence of the capital's youth, and this meant in turn that it was designed for the capital's composite youth. As a style, it organically represented so much about life within the M25 – at one point Jammer describes ten-year-old grime as 'mixed-race music'. Alongside its more cliched urban audience, grime also attracted a growing sub-section of middle-class fans, for whom it provided a suitably parent-upsetting, male-teenage-angsty alternative to the *X Factor* fodder and shoegazing indie rock that had been clogging up the music business since the turn of the century. That they accessed the music via word-of-mouth, often chaotic illegal broadcasters gave it a level of playground urban cool that money couldn't buy.

Perhaps most important of all was that grime was willing to embrace this expanded audience. While partly for pragmatic commercial reasons, this was largely because, like Soul II Soul before them, they saw themselves being as much a part of the United Kingdom as anybody else. What they had to offer – exactly as they wanted to offer it – was relevant to everybody else. This was the breakthrough in self-realisation that so many previous generations of London black music had not quite managed, and did a great deal to bolster grime's spirit of independence.

That kind of enabling self-confidence relied on financial security, which came from success, which brought greater self-confidence and led to increased success ... Pretty quickly, grime had achieved a self-sustaining upward spiral, rooted in a commercial system that was so incredibly straightforward it was about as close to a meritocracy as is possible in the music business. Dizzee explains how to get ahead in grime:

'When I first started off, I used to do pirate radio. Twenty quid a week you had to pay, because it was getting your name out there. At first I was at school, and then when I was out of school and making a little money, I'd do whatever to get it done and get on the radio ... I'd do MC-ing and a bit of deejaying, but with deejaying you have to pay for dubs all the time, so the thing is how many raves am I doing, and how big those raves are? You can get fifty or a hundred pounds, then, as you're out there, if you're good and you're known around the city, then they start giving you one-fifties and that. *Then* you get into the bit when you might start selling the records yourself, take them round to the shops. How many you sell is what money you get back – something like two pounds fifty a piece, if you've got sale or return. If you got a stand-up tune, you might take five hundred to a shop and they'll give you the cash because they know they can sell it, but that's at the very high level. Not everybody's at that level, you have to have a big tune on the underground, on the pirates and in the raves.'

Jammer stresses the importance of pirate radio in this equation:

'When we had Déjà Vu and we were doing the Nasty Crew and Roll Deep sets, the buzz that I had off the stuff that I made was really good. When I went into the shops, kids were already coming asking "Can I get this record?", "Can I get that record?" So I had the power of saying "You have to buy these records off me now". I wasn't going to give them to the shop, telling them I'll come back later to see what you've sold. It was the radio that created that buzz.'

Not just the radio, but the internet too. The first generation to grow up with the web, these guys were exploiting it mercilessly for showcasing, podcasting and streaming. When they got a grip on Facebook and YouTube, hilarious, rough'n'ready promo videos popped up, filmed on inexpensive digital cameras or sophisticated phones. That everything to do with these visual presentations seemed so random, including their uploadings, was always a plus point, and as artists appeared in the clothes they'd been wearing all day, they reinforced the notion of there being little difference between performer and public.

In the wake of such broad-based access to unadulterated grime, producers recognised the existence of an audience who couldn't take part in the rave scene or tune into the pirates, yet would clearly appreciate the excitement either situation offered. Grime mixtapes – live sets from the MCs and collectives released on CD or download – became massive-selling items, so much a staple of the scene that established artists like Dizzee and Wiley still put out mixtapes of their more cutting-edge stuff in between conventional album releases.

The gold standard for grime marketing went to Jammer with his *Lord Of The Mics* series of DVDs. Recorded on a digital movie camera, by himself, in the cellar studio at his mum and dad's house – grime's legendary Dungeon – these feature some of the biggest-name MCs in appropriately claustrophobic sound-clash action, live and ad libbed. The series – it's up to volume five at the time of writing – has proved so popular, they sell it off their own dedicated website, along with a recently added deejay series, *Lord Of The Decks*.

With such operations being run by teenagers out of back rooms all over London, it's not hard to see why grime not only went mass market so quickly and is still around twelve years later, but also has stayed true to how it started out. What do these characters need with a recording industry?

That said, grime as the first London black music style to genuinely cross over was far from finished with the mainstream.

CHAPTER TEN

From Pirates to Pop Stars

London's black music rules

'WHEN WE WENT INTO SYCO, we went in saying we wanted creative control – Lab's the artist, Lab's the producer … *we* started it and we do everything ourselves. I wanted to do it on our terms, to have control over the look, the feel, the sound… Everything.'

Marc Williams smiles as he remembers his negotiating technique when striking a deal between Labrinth, the artist he manages, and Simon Cowell's Syco Music. Far more significant than Marc's feeling confident enough to shout the odds at the 'most powerful man in pop', however, was the fact that he was there in the first place. At the company's behest, too. Until that point, in 2010, the record label had little raison d'être other than to sign up the winners of Cowell's TV talent shows – *X Factor*, *Pop Idol*, *Wherever's Got Talent*, that sort of thing. Labrinth was the first act to be recruited on an old-school A&R basis. In reality, this was no more music-business rocket science than releasing records by acts already enjoying huge TV exposure and established approval ratings: Labrinth had been producing and guesting on top twenty hits for a few years. The crucial difference was that these were by the likes of Tiny Tempah, Tinchy Stryder and Chipmunk – grime artists, streets away, literally, from

Labrinth, at the forefront of London's redefined musical mainstream –
young, black and in complete control.

Syco's regular roster of Gareth Gates, One Direction and
Susan Boyle. Marc continues:

'Simon's not stupid. He's a very clever man, and he knows
his TV empire will have a shelf life, so he's got to think two
steps ahead – he's playing chess, isn't he? What they got
when they saw us was access into a world that they didn't
understand. The guy who signed Lab, Simon Cowell's number
two Sonny Takhar, he *kind of* got it. As commercial-minded
as he is, he got the idea that it was cool and it was urban, and
then figured out it was best to be left alone. Fair play to him,
he just let Lab crack on with it.

'They won't ever *get* the urban [*music*] world, but with
Lab they don't *have* to get it – we understand that world and
he does it all himself. It's such an attractive proposition we
gave them, because they don't have to start hitting out for
producers and figure out the sound. We write the music up
here, we produce the music in here, we do the remixes …
Lab's whole album was done by us.'

That Cowell bought into this world in this manner was the most significant endorsement London's black music had ever received. Not that he was offering much more than other mainstream companies had over recent years in which grime persistently bothered the charts and the award ceremonies. Bidding to get some percentage of the music's turnover, they'd renamed it 'urban', and signed artists on what were essentially distribution deals with minimum effort or involvement. Cowell, however, so dominated the pop landscape that he'd assumed Svengali status, with far more muscle than any mere record company. Free of sentimentality and credibility-seeking alike, his wholehearted recognition of grime amounted to a royal warrant, because it was based strictly on commercial potential. And while it had little immediate effect on the scene – that was doing very well, thank you, without the nod from the man who gave us Jedward – it legitimized the genre in the wider world. If Simon Cowell was taking it seriously, then maybe everyone else should too.

One organisation that had been taking it seriously for ten years before Simon Cowell signed Labrinth was the BBC. In 2002 it launched Radio 1Xtra, a digital station devoted to black music.

SINCE THE DEMISE OF THE DANCE BANDS, frequent complaints about BBC radio had centred on its resolute lack of enthusiasm for black music, especially of the homegrown variety. From the music business side, record pluggers and radio promotions people would tell of dropping off singles at Radio One's reception, then returning the next week with a new batch to find the previous delivery alone in the box where they'd left it. Apart from personal favouritism by re-vered presenters like John Peel or Mary Anne Hobbs, the Beeb's acknowledgement of black music was limited to a few *specialist* slots, which although they may have given it reg-ular airtime, unthinkingly promoted the idea that it wasn't part of everyday rock and pop.

As we rolled into the twenty-first century, the modern internet- and pirate radio-powered black music business had reached a point where only grime was mounting a viable challenge to the domination of the BBC's own charts by *Pop Idol* contestants. And yet the very programming supposedly tied to those charts – Radio One's daytime shows – was treating grime as if it didn't exist. A favourite explanation among senior figures was that the music didn't 'fit' the daytime formula. Hardly a watertight excuse, given the organisation's charter to represent everybody in the country.

At the same time, Radio One's listenership was both declining and ageing, with surveys showing that more young people, particularly in London, were tuning in to pirates. In 2002 the average age of Radio One's audience was 31, which was flat-out embarrassing to a station whose original brief was to appeal to listeners between the ages of 15 and 29. That prompted the biggest shake-up in BBC radio since the station was launched in 1967.

Ruby Mulraine, who joined Radio One as a trainee in 1994, was instrumental in setting up 1Xtra in 2002. One of the new station's initial producers, she had become an executive there by the time she left in 2013. She recalls how the black music argument had been perennial, but by now nobody could ignore the evidence:

'They came to the conclusion there was an audience out there that was underserved, and that, literally, the BBC was seen as being quite old and quite white and quite middle class. They felt there was an audience they were missing out on, and the BBC's listeners were getting older and older. Really, we looked at the fact that we needed to make the audience portfolio a lot younger, and that there were certain portions of the UK demographic that didn't get served by the BBC at all.

'It had to be a really strong proposition, because to get the green light it had to go all the way up to government level – this *is* the BBC! So it has to be a reality, you have to have your facts and figures correct – somebody who is dealing with policy at the BBC is not going to understand the black music scene, and you can't tell them passionately.

Ruby Mulraine on the wheels of steel. In the background is Wilbur Wilbourforce, the other original driving force behind 1Xtra.

Previously, people would try to argue the case passionately: how this is popular music, it's fantastic, it's got potential ... all that kind of stuff. But that's meaningless to those in charge if there's no real kind of data there. However, when you're actually seeing that the top ten is being taken up by lots of black music, how 2-step garage was popular and people were getting record deals on the back of that. When you see that actually happening then you can give some facts and figures to people. That's what they actually understand.'

Radio One had in fact been compiling its own evidence, monitoring audience figures for the shows that it had been adding to its schedule since the mid-1990s. Then, in a move reminiscent of the 1960s' raid on popular pirate station Radio Caroline that filled their original deejay roster, the Beeb plundered London black music station Kiss FM. Fabio & Grooverider and Trevor Nelson, along with Judge Jules and Danny Rampling, were all brought over, while the Corporation's new *One In The Jungle* further boosted the black music quota. Even more meaningful were the internal changes, in which Radio One took on more black staff at senior levels – young innovators like Brian Belle-Fortune and Wilber Wilberforce, who was involved in establishing 1Xtra, and Ruby herself. She is hard pressed to remember any other black production staff when she joined, but maintains their recruitment made all the difference:

'It was important that they were there to fight the corner, but equally important that they knew how the BBC worked and people trusted them. That way they could really get things done.'

How they went about getting things done was very different to standard BBC procedures. The team understood that 1Xtra would be dealing with a genre of music that interfaced with its audience in a very unique way, rather than relying on conventional, record company-centred methodology. This was an instant, DIY culture, so the new station's staff had to be immersed in that world. Conventional BBC recruitment techniques were unlikely to reach the right people:

'We approached it in a completely different way from how the BBC normally would launch a station – we did it actively. Rather than just put an advert in the *Guardian Media* saying "Come and work for us", and only get a certain type of people applying, we went around the country to colleges, community centres and things. We would set up and announce "We would like some staff to work at the BBC, we are starting this new station and if you're into black music come and find us and we'll tell you more about it."

'That meant we were much more approachable. It was the case of people coming up to us in a community centre and saying "I'm a local deejay", or "I write a fanzine", or "I run a website", or "I do local community film work", or "I run a pirate radio station", and us saying that your skills are authentic skills that would be valued in our environment, you can come and work for us. If we started off by just getting a bunch of university kids in to run it, it just wouldn't have worked.

'It didn't matter that they didn't have conventional radio experience – that wasn't the point. I seriously believe you can teach radio quite easily, but you can't really teach the passion, and we just wanted people who had a real passion to make the station work. That's what the station was really based on, and that's what really drives it – they really believe we should have this station on a national platform.'

The actuality of making contemporary black music available across the whole country, 24 hours a day and presented in a sympathetic manner, became the turning point for this London-based industry. No longer did you have to be living on the Stepney estate from which Roll Deep was broadcasting to hear some authentic grime; suddenly kids as far removed as the Hebrides or Penzance could feel part of things. Similarly, if you were already a fan, you knew exactly where to find it on the dial – and it would always be there, with no need for retuning and without any chance of an Ofcom raid. The real value in the BBC's apparent legitimisation of a street style lay in how it subliminally changed perceptions among the mainstream industry and a wider audience alike. The former could no longer ignore it; the latter became more likely to accept it. Of course, the last thing anyone wanted to do was turn this into Radio One Mk II. For 1Xtra to be sure of not losing the all-important core audience, it had to strike a balance. That, Ruby explains, brought its own set of problems:

'Once we got the right foundations in place, that generated so much because those people had connections with artists within their areas, some of whom were by then quite big artists. So there were people at our station who would know the Kanos and the Dizzees already, so when they're talking to them they're talking to them on a level, not with a kind of BBC-speak. The trouble with that, when we first started, was

The original 1Xtra staff: far more reflective of licence-fee payers across the board than had previously been the case at the Corporation.

some of those artists came to the station and treated it as if they were coming to a pirate station. You'd get artists coming late – *often* – or not turning up, whereas on something like Radio One that just wouldn't happen.

'For the first few years of 1Xtra you never knew *if* somebody was going to turn up, *when* they were going to turn up, or *who* they were going to turn up with, like how many people they were going to bring! But that kind of created the energy about the station, it made for loads of gossip, it made for loads of unions in terms of surprise artists – like Wiley would turn up with somebody who you didn't think he would turn up with, and they'd go on air together.

'It created great radio, really exciting, so it kept that kind of pirate vibe, but we realised we had to put some measures in to make sure that things were a bit more formalised. Funnily enough, the time we started thinking about that was the time when some of these artists were becoming much more known, and they were actually working with record labels who were saying to them "You have to be here at this time … you have to hold yourself in a certain kind of way", so they kind of worked hand in hand. A few issues did remain with the younger artists, but that wasn't difficult. Where it would have been difficult would have been in audience perception, because that was always like "How much of a cutting edge station are you going to remain?"'

A SIGNIFICANT PART OF 1XTRA'S CONTRIBUTION to contemporary black music lay in how it walked that line between underground cool and mainstream acceptability. Immediately, it provided a conduit between the two, as its staff were immersed in the underground, digesting it all to create a more accessible version. They went to the raves, surfed the internet and tuned into pirate radio, so you didn't have to – which benefitted the major labels as much as the station's listeners. 1Xtra also served as a short cut to the more mainstream Radios One and Two. All were in very close proximity at the BBC, and One and 1Xtra shared their own building. It was not unusual for acts enjoying daytime exposure on 1Xtra to make the jump to Radio One, with its considerably larger national audience. Marc is entirely enthusiastic about this function:

'1Xtra definitely helped us, and the really cool thing about it is it gave Lab a core bed quite quickly, and then he jumped through the transient layers quickly. It is possible to get stuck on 1Xtra, and a lot of artists do, but if you've got the material then it'll give you the chance to be heard and transcend genre-based radio.'

The truly liberating aspect of all this was that 1Xtra gave a platform to the full breadth of the new black music that was bubbling through, as it absorbed a spectrum of British influences. Almost as a by-product of how the station had set itself up, it was allowing black music that might have sprung from a strictly urban environment, but had pop/rock aspirations, the opportunity to move forward. Music that might have been too black for Radio One, and not black enough for the pirates, could now reach a sizeable audience, many of whom wouldn't be locked into preconceived ideas of what grime ought to sound like. This motivated artists to display the sort of ideas that helped to establish UK black music as the new pop music – Jammer's *Jahmanji* album, Dave Jones' *Biasonic Hotsauce* (as Zed Bias), and virtually any later stuff by Tinie Tempah, Wretch 32 or Tinchy Stryder being cases in point.

As far as audiences were concerned, the new station played an even more important role. By pitching itself between the anarchic world of pirate radio and the more, er, grown-up approach associated with the BBC, it defined an audience that had fallen between everybody's cracks, so to speak. This is what enabled contemporary black music to fulfil its pop potential, by opening up two influential demographics: those who thought they ought to be into the style but didn't think it was speaking to them – much as lovers' rock fans had approached roots reggae – and pop fans who liked a bit of grime but weren't sufficiently committed to go hardcore. Reaching these swing voters had been a deliberate part of 1Xtra's brief:

'We realised there was a big potential audience out there that loves urban music but they may not like – or even have patience for – some of the more underground-y bits. If we had remained completely underground all the time, tried to be like the pirates, then we were going to really alienate a lot of people, when the potential for this music was to spread a lot further. In the daytime we were much more mainstream, yet still *urban* enough to keep fans happy.

'Also you have to remember that something that's seen as underground one minute, in a year or two will be completely mainstream, and people understand it. Nothing remains like it first was, as far as being accepted is concerned, it just takes time to get used to the sound of a new music. 1Xtra gave so much of the music that time. And with some of the grime artists, I'd question whether it was actually authentic grime in the first place, because it was essentially pop music they were creating. But it's all part of the same thing, so we needed to make sure we did the more mainstream stuff as well as we do the more hardcore stuff.

'Whenever we got a story like Tinie Tempah or somebody going to number one in the album charts, it kind of justified our position and the work we were doing. Tinie came on 1Xtra when he was fifteen, and it was the first legal station that he'd done anything on; now he's 23 and a pop star, so you could say we launched his career.'

It's interesting that in the same way as Dizzee Rascal and Wiley continue to make mixtapes to keep in touch with their original fanbases, so those who kicked off on 1Xtra don't move far away. Even if they have to put some effort in doing so. Marc laughs at the apparent irony of Labrinth's double life:

'Because "Earthquake" was such a massive track, and it affected people so much, it allowed us to be accepted by Radio One straight away. Then the challenge that we had with our album, *Electronic Earth*, was it had such a breadth of sound, only a small percentage of it are 1Xtra records. "Last Time" is a little bit 1Xtra, but because 1Xtra wants it a bit harder than we're inclined to do, we've been having to come up with 1Xtra mixes for songs that are essentially not 1Xtra tracks!'

IT WAS THE COMBINATION of a nationally accessible conduit, and the self-sufficiency discussed in the previous chapter, which allowed London's black music, in the form of grime, to reach critical mass in the mid-noughties. Around long enough to be able to draw on its own heritage, it has become established enough to be a genuine movement rather than a trend or a fad. Marc explains the difference, and why it means so much for the future:

'Now, you've got new kids coming up and they don't allow it to sleep, one falls away or is away working on music and another comes through, it's like a constant scramble to the top of this mound they've got. And they've got this mound because there's been so much of it for so long. That's the difference now, that's what makes it a very strong movement and what encourages me.

'We've done this before, and every time we've done it the back-up hasn't been there. With jungle or drum'n'bass, Goldie forged ahead getting a beautiful album done which went all the way [*"Timeless", a top ten hit in 1995*], but there was nothing that came with it. So what had been underground with jungle, when it matured into drum'n'bass it matured to chart status but there was no back-up, no follow-up. There was no group mentality, and nothing coming through to take it further. What's happened with these guys is they done the same thing, started very young, very raw, very gritty and it's matured, then the likes of somebody like Labrinth comes along, who is away from grime and takes it further.

FRISKY BUSINESS
A peep inside the boutique sex party scene

STEPHEN MERCHANT
Why the £22 million funny man isn't laughing

TINIE HITS THE BIG TIME

He's sold a million records and is conquering America with Chris Martin as his mentor – meet the hardest-working man in rap

'We'd sit down and discuss how could you make a grime tune or a grime vibe, but something that's musically expansive and clever and has a turn on it. We'd concentrate on the musicality of it – how can we apply music theory to these sounds, so you're not just hitting up a beat, you're doing a chord because you know it's going to lift the spirit or bring it down. Then I'd add my old-school influences of jungle, drum'n'bass and all of that, and all of the stuff he'd learned hanging around.

'I believe that's what resonated in his head when he did "Pass Out" [*Labrinth produced and co-wrote Tinie Tempah's hit*] and stuff like that. It's my belief you sit down and think about these things, you theorise and you let go. You let it go, and then it comes back and it spools into your head when you're not thinking about it. You can't just sit down and say "I'm going to do this today", and I think that's how the likes of "Pass Out" and these really cool grooves started coming out. As the music matured, people started coming into it who were working in different ways.

'Then when you come up with something as clever as "Pass Out" it then exalts Tinie to become head of this *movement*.

But it's not just one record, it's not like it was with Goldie, it's one record but these kids understand the importance of maintaining market share in the same way as hip hop does in America and they kept it coming and kept it coming. Tinie was backed up by Wretch 32 ... then you've got Professor Green. You've got Caucasian kids coming through with the same vibe and the same energy ... you've got Devlin and you've got Plan B who adds a different element, another angle to that kind of sound. Because they're coming through like a movement, the radio can't just play it off like a one-off or a novelty track. That rave thing seemed too much like a novelty to the radio, but I think this generation have managed to transcend that.'

Marc makes an important point about the people coming into the music lately as not arriving via the traditional nursery slopes of pirate radio and raves. Ben Drew, aka Plan B, started off playing Brit pop soundalike guitar before graduating to hip hop. Labrinth's entry was even further removed; he came from a north London gospel-singing background. He and his eight siblings had a group called Mac-9, their family name being McKenzie. Hoping to learn what it would take to manage Timothy's career herself, his mother attended a music business course Marc was running at the Chocolate Factory. After two sessions, she had enough confidence in Marc to sign her son with him instead. The soon-to-be-Labrinth's influences ran from the Beatles to Bowie and Jimi Hendrix, then Marc 'crammed him full of George Benson and T. Rex ,plus my background from reggae, jungle and drum'n'bass'. At the moment, Plan B uses an actual band, while Labrinth deconstructs prospective samples and plays the various parts on real instruments.

Add to all this the point that Jammer made about grime being around for so long. Although these days many of the people coming into it don't know anything else as a format, that doesn't make them immune to London's myriad influences. They're creating music that completely reflects their lives in the capital, happily disregarding the tyranny of street credibility to make what's intrinsically black

Bringing extreme street fashion to a mainstream audience at the V Festival, 2012, Wiley demonstrates British black music has come as far sartorially as it has stylistically since the suits and hats on the *Windrush* sixty years ago.

music while still proudly acknowledging that there's more to it than that. That formula worked for Berry Gordy and Motown – a black style that wasn't afraid to adjust itself for a wider audience, scrub up and made a fortune – and the potential rewards are particularly attractive. Kids see Dizzee or Wretch on television, clearly doing well yet just as blatantly still of the 'ends'. Suddenly – and again just like Motown or, closer to home, lovers' rock – black kids aspiring to the music have role models to whom they can relate, which makes the whole process a bit more attainable. This time, however, unlike those two examples, they can see how they can control it.

Also, on the social side, for the current wave of black kids in the capital, making music has become far more viable a proposition for their parents to cope with than it was for the generation before. Quite apart from being able to practise and pretty much launch yourself from your bedroom, as a side-line to GCSEs, their 'born here' parents are part of the nation, rather than having come from somewhere else specifically

to work. That meant there was far less need to rebel against the factory or the clerical job – not that there were too many factories or clerical jobs by the 1990s. In addition, for mums and dads who have grown up around lovers' rock or Soul ɪɪ Soul sound systems, it's easier to understand the growing relationship between their kids and their music.

A mere two-and-a-bit generations on from Kitchener sing-ing "London Is The Place For Me" on the quayside, London's black music – grime – has achieved the same sort of cultural status as hip hop in the US. While hip hop is obviously a pop music, and informs other styles to such an extent that it's not really thought of as a left field music any more, whatever it absorbs, and whatever form it takes on, it's still hip hop. Jay-Z and Beyonce are true pop stars, yet they will always be hip hop. Over here, Tinie Tempah and Wiley are pop stars, yet everybody knows they're grime. That's total integration, not some kind of minstrel-style assimilation – hence the rush of prospective, largely self-sufficient and self-controlling black pop stars.

THE FUTURE FOR LONDON'S BLACK MUSIC, at the time of writing, looks even more exciting than its past. While the conventional music business has been falling apart, these guys – from Lloydie Coxsone and Dennis Bovell onwards – have developed the skills to progress without any big-money safety net. Now, more than ever, that unique black community experience, the sound system, will really come into its own. Thanks not merely to its self-sufficiency alone, but to the fearlessness that has seen it succeed in so many of the environments described in this book. Former soundman Marc sums it up precisely:

'These days [2013] people are a lot more scared. There's been a level of fear in the mainstream music business for a while, but with there being so little money about, everyone's a lot more scared to make moves. It's such a small cake now – with sales, *HMV*'s done now so forget it, it's all about online – there's a lot less optimism in the mainstream industry.

'Which actually leaves the door open to the sound system operators, or those who still think like that. Because what's the one thing every soundman's got in common? They're not scared of *nothing*! Which is why, at this very moment, you've got Wiley killing it – he's on every bloody track around ... you got Skepta at number one, they're banging them out left, right and centre because they ain't got no fear at all ... they're banging them out, when everybody else is scared to make a move. We're going back in to writing the second album, and everyone's on tenterhooks about what Lab's going to do on it, and I'm just like "Shut up, let him crack on".

'We'll get in, we'll write some music and we'll get it done... people are like "Should we do this?" ... "Are we going to make that kind of sound?" ... "Could he just chose one sound and go down that road?" I'm telling them "No!" and they should let him just do the same thing again. It may be a risk, but ...'

Thanks, Photo Credits, Index

Without Whom ...

||||||||||||||||||||||||||||||||||||||||||||||||||||||||||||||||||||||||||||||||||||||||||||||||

Sounds Like London: 100 Years of Black Music in the Capital wasn't, for me, the greatest leap of the imagination: I love London and I love black music, so why not put the two together? Far less immediately obvious, though, was what London's black music involved. It wasn't so much a case of what I knew about it, rather than a definition of what I didn't. London-conceived and London-created black music had been going on around me for my entire life, yet when I started looking at it properly, it seemed as if me, my friends, my days as a raver, my decades as a working music journalist and a record collection that couldn't quite be seen from space had simply been scratching the surface.

Beyond, around and behind my own limited experience, there was a series of stories that had either never been told or had simply never been told by the people who were actually responsible for them. It seemed as if a sizeable and very important collective social memory was in danger of being corrupted almost out of recognition, or simply being allowed to disappear. Had the latter become the case it would have left a gaping cultural and sociological hole in Great Britain's twentieth-century history. Some serious digging would be required, and I was going to need a guide.

What I ended up with were several guides. Seasoned individuals who not only led me down various stylistic and chronological rabbit holes, introduced me around and filled in as many blanks as they joined dots, but also made some of the best cups of tea I've ever enjoyed. Indeed, researching Sounds Like London may not have had the sheer bonkers adventure quotient that became part of writing my previous book on reggae, Bass Culture, but the Jamaicans have got a great deal to learn about Earl Grey. While I may not have had to leave the capital to put the vast majority of this story together, many of my journeys went far beyond an Oyster card's limit in terms of the discoveries and situations I arrived at. I owe safe and enlightening passage to the following formidable collection of pilots: Sterling Betancourt, Stephanie Calman, Lloydie Coxsone, Wala Danga, Dizzee Rascal, Graeme Ewens, Debbie Golt, Eddy Grant and Maria Kellman, Diana Hancox, Russ Henderson, Camelle Hinds, Jammer (and his mum and dad for their hospitality and genuine interest in the project), Norman Jay, General Levy, Hazel Miller, Louis Moholo-Moholo, Ruby Mulraine, Trevor Nelson, Nostalgia Steel Band, Teddy Osei, Dez Parkes, Maxine Stowe, Kenny Wellington, Mike Westbrook, Marc Williams and Kate, and Wookie. And not forgetting the PRs who put me in touch with a few of the above: James Heather, Rosie James and Chris Carr. If I've forgotten anybody, I'm truly sorry and please take it up with me next time you see me.

There were also those who went above and beyond what might have been expected. The reigning King and Queen of Lovers' Rock, Victor Romero Evans and Janet Kay were as funny and charming as they were helpful – find them at victorromeroevans.com and janetkay.com. Dennis Bovell, from whom any piece of help or advice would come with at least half a dozen hilarious and usually pointless anecdotes. Steve Salvari, the perpetually cheerful conduit to all things BritFunk and the best company a man could want for an evening in the alehouse. Root Jackson, whose live funk nights and participation in Sunday Sessions at the *Prince of Wales* in Willesden remain an inspiration. Dr Lionel McCalman, the dreadlock sage of the steel pan for whom nothing was too much trouble. Dave Jones aka Zed Bias (zedbias.co.uk), a man who appreciates a good caff as much as he does a good tune, and actually hoovered his studio in preparation for my arrival, and Derek Yates – top artist, top company, top Gooner.

The most heartwarming aspect of the whole process was how many of those mentioned had no idea who I was, but were happy to make time to talk to me in order to help preserve this vital musical history, or simply because they kind of liked the sound of it. Thank you, everybody.

Then there's those who supplied the fabulous visuals we amassed to illustrate 100 Years of Black Music in the Capital. Derek Yates once again merits special mention for opening up his archive of Soul II Soul artwork – see more of that at Derek-yates.co.uk – as do the photographers who did so for little more than good vibes: Ashes57, Adrian Boot, David Corio and Simon Wheatley. Not forgetting Melissa C Sinclair, editor/publisher of the rather wonderful online reggae culture magazine *G Mag* (www.gmag.org.uk) and their photographer Kenny V Passley – yes, they like a middle initial at G Mag – who generously let us use one of the standout images of the whole book. Also dubwise historian and keeper of all things Trojan, Laurence Cane-Honeysett, who made available a lovers' rock treasure trove; and *Mojo*'s Matt Turner for invaluable help and hysterically funny conversation about Sperz. Meanwhile huge props go to our terrier-like picture researcher Elissa Bradley, who tracked down some superbly appropriate shots, and her brother George who trusted us with his collection of Ayia Napa club flyers.

And those whose contributions were less straightforward but certainly no less crucial. Kes, Nicks, Eddie Webb and the rest of the JBs; Crackers, *Upstairs at Ronnie's*, *Columbo's*, *Hunters*, Paddington, West Hampstead & Waterloo *Birds Nests*, *Lacey's*, *Parnells* and *Whisky's*; Mick Eve, Tim Cansfield, Richard Bailey and all the players at the *Prince of Wales* in Willesden Lane; *The Map Café*; *Blacks*; *Contempo, One Stop, Sterns, Muzic City, Desmond's Hip City, Paul's, Groove, Black Market* and Keith at *Daddy Kool*; Bob Kilbourne, Chris May & Neil Spencer of *Blues & Soul, Black Music & Jazz Review* and the *NME*, respectively; Kevin LeGendre & Chris Wells – find them at echoesmagazine.co.uk; Ron Shillingford; Mike Connolly; Guy Crossman and Simon Hills; Simon Kanter; my agent Matthew Hamilton at Aitken Alexander Associates, who immediately got what this book should be about; and, of course, Arsenal FC.

Another important part of this whole process was the original idea for *Sounds Like London* – thanks, Peter Ayrton, formerly of Serpent's Tail – and the characters who kindly gave up their time to talk to me for that first manifestation: Keith Cullen, Spider Stacy, Terry Woods, Vince Power, Tony Murray, Andy

Wood, Gerry Lyseight, Talvin Singh, Kuljit Bhamra and the guys
from the Nasha sound system. I'm sorry it didn't go as far as
it might, and that's all down to me and certain aspects taking
on a life of their own, nothing to do with your high standard
of contribution, but one day a couple of prospective chapters
might make books of their own. In the meantime, I hope you
agree that what it became was worth it.

Of course none of this could have happened without
Serpent's Tail/Profile Books, and chiefly Greg Ward, exactly
the editor somebody as intrinsically cavalier as I need, yet
who turned the whole process into a bit of a laugh rather
than some sort of superannuated grammar lesson; Hannah
Westland, a most entertaining Capo di tutti capi and her
ludicrously good-natured consiglieri Big Mark Ellingham: a
publishing double act that got things done in spite of rather
than because of this particular author; Anna-Marie Fitzgerald,
a publicist who relies on charm rather than blag, and rather
sensibly too as she's got it in spades; Henry Iles, who made the
pages look as attractive and dynamic as they do; Peter Dyer,
who so deftly captured the spirit of the story on the cover;
and the fine proofreader Samantha Cook who caught all my
speeling mistoks. Thank you one and all.

The deserved celebrations and the backslapping over London reaching (very nearly!) 100 Years of Black Music, are for the
players of instruments, the producers and the singers – I'll sit in
a corner with the mistakes. While I'm over there I'll give props
to Linton Kwesi Johnson, Sade, Billy Ocean, JLS, Courtney Pine,
Loose Ends, Mica Paris, Black Slate, Mexicano, the legend that
is Carl Douglas and very likely a few more I've forgotten. All
made important and unique contributions to London's singular
black music catalogue, but for one reason or another couldn't
be made to fit the broad-brush approach necessary to tell a
story this big in so few pages. Thanks, guys, for all the joy and
stimulation you've brought me, London and the British black
music scene.

Which leaves just the most important, er, big ups. Jazzie
B, who not only helped out at every opportunity, but wrote a
killer foreword and is one of the funniest, most upful geezers

you could shake a staff at – if I ever hinted to Jazzie that this book might be getting the better of me, he'd give me half a dozen reasons why it shouldn't. And none of those would be the fine cigars and chilled tins of Guinness he produces every time I fetch up round his yard; visit him at Soul2Soul.co.uk. Then there's the late, great John Bauldie of *Q* magazine, who, with the patience of a saint, taught me how to write. And finally Diana, George and Elissa, who, for reasons best known to themselves, put up with me and the years of nonsense involved in writing a book. "Thanks" probably isn't a big enough word, but you know what I mean.

Lloyd Bradley, London, July 2013

Photo credits

Thanks to all those who have made photographs available for this book. We have attempted to contact copyright holders of all the images used, though some are lost in the depths of time. We apologise to anyone who has not been properly credited and ask that they contact the publishers so that we can amend this in any future edition of this book.

P17/18, 76, Ron Emrit/bestoftrinidad.com; 21, Douglas Miller/ Hulton Archive/Getty Images; 24, Bettmann/Corbis; 33, Popperfoto/Getty Images; 49, Gjon Mill/Time & Life Pictures/ Getty Images; 62, George Konig/Hulton Archive/Getty Images; 67, Gamma-Keystone via Getty Images; 70, 74 courtesy of Nostalgia Steel Band; 81, 108, 114, 123, 147, 150, 198, 202 Jak Kilby; 88, Shutterstock; 92, rantanddawdle.ca/Barbara Pukwana; 104, Jurgen Schadeberg/Premium Archive/Getty Images; 135, Merlyn Severn/Getty Images; 141, Courtesy of Prince Buster; 207/208, 216 Kenny V Passley/G MaG Online; 233, Adrian Boot; 241, David Corio; 247, Roy Sweetland; 263, Davina Misrock; 299, 319, 321 Derek Yates; 308, J Quinto/Wireimage/Getty Images; 334, Catherine McGann/Archive Photos/Getty Images; 341, Tabatha Fireman/Redferns; 347, 362, 380, 382, Simon Wheatley; 350, Lois Amore; 357, Ben Donaghue; 371, 372, 375 Ashes; 401, Mr Pics/Shutterstock.

Index

H

K